C000065795

Arabic–English Thematic Lexicon

The *Arabic–English Thematic Lexicon* is an invaluable resource for all learners of Arabic.

It contains some 8,000 entries, arranged into themes, including flora and fauna, food and drink, the human body, health care, the family, housing, clothing, education, IT, sports, politics, economics and commerce, the law, media, language, geography, travel, religion, arts, science and natural resources. Three appendices cover the names of Arab and selected non-Arab regions, countries and capitals, and international organisations.

The entries in the Lexicon have been drawn from an extensive corpus of contemporary Standard Arabic vocabulary, based on authentic sources. In addition to verbs, nouns and adjectives, the Lexicon includes phrases and commonly used collocations, providing users with the necessary vocabulary in order to communicate effectively and confidently in both written and spoken Standard Arabic.

The Lexicon is an indispensable vocabulary-building tool, as well as a useful reference guide.

Daniel Newman is Reader in Arabic and Course Director of the MA in Arabic/English Translation at the University of Durham.

Arabic–English Thematic Lexicon

Daniel Newman

Routledge
Taylor & Francis Group

LONDON AND NEW YORK

First published 2007
by Routledge
2 Park Square, Milton Park, Abingdon, Oxon OX14 4RN, UK

Simultaneously published in the USA and Canada
by Routledge
270 Madison Ave, New York, NY 10016

Routledge is an imprint of the Taylor & Francis Group, an informa business

Typeset in Helvetica Neue by RefineCatch Limited, Bungay, Suffolk
Printed and bound in Great Britain by MPG Books Ltd, Bodmin

British Library Cataloguing in Publication Data
A catalogue record for this book is available from the British Library

Library of Congress Cataloging-in-Publication Data
Newman, Daniel, 1963–
    [Arabic–English lexicon]
    The Arabic/English thematic lexicon / Daniel Newman. – 1st ed.
        p.   cm.
    1. Arabic language – Dictionaries – English.   I. Title.
    PJ6640.N46   2007
    492.7'321 — dc22   2006037980

ISBN10: 0–415–42093–8 (hbk)
ISBN10: 0–415–4094–6 (pbk)
ISBN10: 0–203–96087–4 (ebk)

ISBN13: 978–0–415–42093–8 (hbk)
ISBN13: 978–0–415–42094–5 (pbk)
ISBN13: 978–0–203–96087–5 (ebk)

Contents

Introduction

The task of the 'harmless drudge', as Dr Johnson called the lexicographer, is always challenging, and, it must be said, often thankless. Such is the ever-changing nature of language that no sooner has a dictionary appeared than it is already to some extent out of step with the living language. Consider, for instance, the developments in computing and the Internet and the concomitant surge in new terminology in the space of just one decade.

In the case of Arabic, the lexicographer's task is further complicated by the phenomenon of *diglossia* – i.e. the coexistence of several varieties along an acro-basilectal continuum – and the fact that many of the regional dialects are mutually unintelligible.

The normative variety of the language, which is commonly referred to as Modern Standard Arabic (MSA) – the so-called *fuṣḥā* (فُصْحى) – is the closest to the Classical Arabic of the Qur'ān in terms of grammar. This variety, which, of course, has been subject to many changes, not least in the area of lexis, is a language that is used exclusively for official and literary purposes. It diverges greatly, as it always has done, from the everyday language spoken by people in the street. Indeed, it is worth remembering that this variety has no mother-tongue speakers – it is the dialect which is the native language of the Arabic speaker. The normative variety is also the link language which allows educated Arabic speakers from Morocco to Iraq to communicate with one another.

In this Lexicon the emphasis is squarely on the standard language, rather than a given colloquial variety.

Unfortunately, things do not stop here for the Arabic lexicographer as within the normative variety there are often a number of competing geographical variants. This matter is not unrelated to the fact that there are a number of Arabic Language Academies (Egypt, Iraq, Jordan and Syria). For instance, 'mobile telephone' can be rendered by the following: مُتَنَقِّل, نَقَّال, جوّال, (جِهاز/هاتِف) خَلَوِيّ, مَحْمُول, سَيَّار and هاتِف مُتَحَرِّك, all of which are *fuṣḥā* terms. The only difference between them is where they were originally coined and their place (and frequency) of usage: the first three tend to be used more in North Africa, the fourth in Egypt, the fifth in the Levant and the sixth in some areas of the Gulf. Naturally, the Arabic speaker *understands* all coinings, but in the standard variety of his/her native area, one of them will probably be used to the exclusion of the others. What is more, it is very likely that in informal contexts the same speaker will use none of the above, choosing instead the borrowing موبايل ('mobile') or جي أس أم ('GSM')!

It is in the area of terminology, or specialized language, that this problem is sometimes the most acute. It is particularly problematic, of course, in the sciences where the prevailing orthodoxy is that of one-to-one correspondence, i.e. one meaning, one term. In reality, this principle is consistently overridden in Arabic where a plethora of terms may render one English scientific term. For instance, in research the present author conducted some time ago, no fewer than thirteen terms were found for the English linguistic term 'phoneme', all of which are used interchangeably by specialists in the field.

The large number of (near-)synonyms and/or competing coinings make it very difficult for the lexicographer to make a choice, particularly as consulting native speakers may sometimes obfuscate, rather than clarify, the issue. For instance, an educated speaker from, say, Iraq will state that a given term is the one in use in Standard Arabic (or at least that used in Iraq), whereas an educated Moroccan speaker will comment that s/he has never encountered that very same word. In most cases the informant will recognize that it is Standard Arabic, but in others they will condemn the term for being a colloquial variant.

At the same time, one should not exaggerate the problem either. The above remark applies to certain fields more than others, whereas in most cases the same word is used across the Arabic-speaking world.

In a work of this kind, one solution would be to list all 'standard' terms, irrespective of where they are used. Instead, it has been decided to select the one that is most frequently encountered in the corpus for a number of reasons, the principal one being userfriendliness, since it was never intended to produce a Thesaurus. In the event of several competing forms occurring with similar frequency, each was retained, with the reader being referred to the definition given elsewhere: e.g.

بَيْت : house

دار : see بيت

On the whole, geographically determined MSA terms were excluded. For instance, it is well documented that in former French colonies such as Tunisia, Algeria, or Lebanon, a number of MSA terms in use are calques from French, whereas in many countries in the Middle East there is often a noticeable influence from English. To put it differently, the author attempted to include only those terms whose use transcends a single country or area. In any event, it is impossible to remain entirely immune from accusations that such and such a term is less 'accurate' or 'widespread' than another.

Rather than a collection of entries culled from various dictionaries, the Lexicon is based on a corpus compiled over a period of many years, with the author relying on authentic data drawn from both written and audiovisual sources from a wide variety of countries. Only words whose usage was attested in a number of sources were included in the Lexicon.

The first question any dictionary compiler needs to address is whether the work deserves to be done, i.e. whether it fills a gap of some sort. The second one involves the target audience: who will be using the book, and perhaps equally important, why?

The origins of the Lexicon grew out of a desire and need to provide students with core vocabulary conveniently grouped together in thematic categories. Indeed, none of the basic vocabulary lists met this goal, whereas textbooks often frustratingly, albeit understandably, only give limited vocabulary relating to the same semantic field: for instance, students will be given only five colours, say, and will be expected to start compiling their own lists or, if they are lucky, rely on those provided by the teacher. Furthermore, it is much easier to assimilate lexis if it is presented in a logical and coherent format.

Like so many lexicographical endeavours, this Lexicon started out as a series of lists, which were handed to students when a particular area of vocabulary was tackled, i.e. for general vocabulary building, lexical extension, as well as translation exercises.

It is important to point out that, while the Lexicon was initially drawn up for learners of Arabic, it is equally suitable for Arabic-speaking learners of English, for whom the book will also be a very useful vocabulary-building tool.

Arguably, one of the the first thematic vocabulary lists was that compiled by the great French Arabist, Charles Pellat (*L'Arabe Vivant : mots arabes groupés d'après le sens et vocabulaire fondamental de l'arabe moderne*, 1961). Based on a study of a number of newspapers, the lexicon contains 6,000 words which are ordered according to themes, but not alphabetically (though the book came with, unfortunately all too often unreliable, French and Arabic alphabetical indices)! Other endeavours followed, both in the West and in the Middle East, yet none fully met students' needs for a number of reasons, ranging from layout and presentation (e.g. either only transliteration or only Arabic script without vowelling), to the number and types of categories included, or the absence of collocations and of basic grammatical metatext.

The present Lexicon is intended to meet the needs of students at all levels who wish to expand their vocabulary in a large number of everyday fields. The Lexicon contains about 8,000 entries, and also includes phrases and collocations. It can be used for both passive and active vocabulary use. Students who have mastered the vocabulary contained in the Lexicon will be able to communicate effectively and confidently in most daily contexts, both orally and in writing.

The thematic ordering makes the Lexicon eminently practical and suitable for both home and classroom use. At the same time, the layout encourages browsing. Although the Lexicon is designed for use by Arabic learners at all levels, both in formal and informal settings, the user must have a basic knowledge of Arabic grammar in order to be able to interpret and use the information effectively.

Throughout, the primary aim has been to provide all but the most technical vocabulary relating to a large number of fields which language users are likely to encounter. Naturally, choices again had to be made, in terms of the field in which certain words would have to be put, or the number of words in each field. Both questions were addressed pragmatically, and within practical constraints of length. Furthermore, the size of each category also depended on the nature and scope of the semantic field, and it is hardly surprising therefore that the section on 'Politics' contains significantly more terms than that on 'Fruit'. In theory, there was no fixed maximum (or minimum) number of words for each category.

As for the classification, there are, of course, cases in which the ultimate choice may be debatable, and to some degree subjective. However, one would hope that the inclusion of the term is considered more important than the category in which it is placed. Similarly, some users will undoubtedly lament the absence of this or that term, which they deem absolutely imperative for the student. All that can be said in defence is that there was undoubtedly good reason to do so, either because it was too technical, colloquial, or synonymous with a term that was attested more often in the author's corpus.

Consistently, the basic premise has been to class entries together as much as possible in meaningful categories and subcategories.

If (near-)synonyms are provided in English, they are separated by a comma.

The next question is a very practical one, i.e. how to use the dictionary. The entries are arranged according to themes and appear in straight Arabic alphabetical order within each category. In cases where the lemma includes the article 'اﻟ', it is listed according to the first character of the base word: e.g. الدّاما ('draughts') appears under 'د', not 'ا'.

Unlike in many Western dictionaries of Arabic, words patterned on the same root are not listed together, but in strictly alphabetical order. So, for instance, فَتَح ('to open') and مِفْتاح ('key') are not listed together. The main reason behind this was, once again, ease of use.

In line with common usage, Arabic verbs are listed in the third person singular preterite (الماضي) form. The appropriate conjugation vowel of the first-form (base-stem) imperfect (المُضارِع) is added in brackets next to the entry: e.g.

دَرَس (u)   to study

If there is more than one possible vowel, both variants are given: e.g.

خَمَش (i, u)   to scratch

In the case of so-called 'weak' verbs (those in which one of the root letters is و, ي or ا), the full imperfect third person singular form is given: e.g.

وَصَلَ (يَصِلُ) إلى   to arrive in

The plurals of Arabic words are only given if they are in some way irregular, i.e. if it involves a so-called 'broken' plural, or in cases of deviating pluralization (e.g. a sound feminine plural for words without the feminine marker ة, i.e. *tā' marbūṭa*): e.g.

باب   door
pl. أبْواب

مُصَخِّم   amplifier
pl. ـات

In cases where the plural is only rarely used, as is the case for a number of fruits, it is given but enclosed in round brackets: e.g.

كُمَّثْرَى   (*coll.*) pear

(pl. كُمَّثْرَيات)

Specific phrases which are often found on signs are capitalized: e.g.

مَمْنُوع الخُرُوج   NO EXIT

All Arabic words are fully vowelled; the absence of transcriptions has been a conscious choice inasmuch as it has a number of disadvantages, not least the fact that the learner will attempt to store two 'forms' in the mental lexicon, rather than one, i.e. the Arabic graphemic form. It is also hoped that beginners, in particular, will benefit from the additional reading practice.

Arabic nouns appear in pausal form, without the so-called 'nunnation' (تَنْوِين), i.e. case endings, except for some accusative and genitive indefinite inflections: e.g.

مَجاناً   free (of charge)
قاضٍ   judge

'Diptote' forms, i.e. those with reduced inflections, are indicated by means of a superscript *ḍamma* (ٌ) over the final consonant: e.g. مَدارسُ. The diptote marking is omitted, however, in recent borrowings and proper nouns as the inflected endings in those cases are never pronounced: e.g. بِرلين (not *بِرلينُ), 'Berlin'.

Relevant grammatical information is provided when necessary for both Arabic and English entries: e.g. English infinitives appear with 'to', whereas in cases of ambiguity, the appropriate grammatical category (e.g. adjective, noun) is indicated. Useful collocations are also listed, as are prepositions:

e.g.

رَسْمِيّ	official (*adj.*)
وافَقَ عَلَى	to approve
حَرْب (*f.*)	war
ضَرَبَ حَقْنًا	to give an injection

In cases of polysemy or homonymy (sc. multiple meanings) of Arabic words, the various meanings are included in the relevant categories: e.g. فَتَحَ in the sense of 'to open' will be found under 'Housing and Construction', whereas it reappears under 'The Military' in the meaning of 'to conquer'. If the different meanings are part of the same field, then they appear numbered next to the entry: e.g.

غُراب	1. raven
	2. crow

The following abbreviations are used in the Lexicon:

adj.	adjective
adv.	adverb
coll.	collective (noun)
el.	electricity
f.	feminine
fig.	figurative
gen.	generic (noun)
intrans.	intransitive (verb)
math.	mathematics
n.	noun
n. un.	unit noun
o. self	oneself
pass.	passive (voice)
perf.	perfect tense
pl.	plural
prep.	preposition
Qur.	Qur'an
s.o.	someone
s.thing	something
trans.	transitive (verb)
v.	verb
ـات	regular feminine plural
ـون	regular masculine plural
< >	the opposite of

Fruit

أَثْمَرَ	to bear fruit (tree, plant)	طازَج	fresh
أَناناس	pineapple	عِنَب (coll.) (أعْناب .pl)	grapes
بُرْتْقال (coll.)	oranges		
بَطيخ (coll.)	(water)melons	عُنْقود عَناقيدُ .pl	bunch (of grapes)
بَلَح (coll.)	dates		
بُنْدُق (coll.) (بَنادِق .pl)	hazelnuts	فاكِهة فَواكِهُ .pl	fruit
تُفّاح (coll.) (تَفافيحُ .pl)	apples	فِجّ	unripe
		فَراوْلة	strawberry
تَمْر (coll.)	(dried) dates	فُسْتُق (coll.)	pistachio nuts
تَمر هِنْد	tamarind	فول سوداني (coll.)	peanuts
توت	mulberry	كَرَز (coll.)	cherries
توت شَوْكيّ	raspberry	كُسْتَناء	chestnut
تين (coll.)	figs	كُمَثْرَى (coll.) (كُمَثْرَيات .pl)	pears
ثَمَر ثِمار .pl	fruit (produce)		
جَوافة	guava	لارِنج	grapefruit
جَوْز (coll.)	walnuts	لُبّ لُبُوب .p	core (e.g. apple)
جَوْز الهِنْد (coll.)	coconuts	لَوْز (coll.)	almonds
حَبّ الصَّنَوْبَر (coll.)	pine nuts	ليمُون (coll.)	lemons
خَوخ (coll.)	plums	ليمون حامِض	lime
زَبيب (coll.)	raisins	مانْجُو	mango
سُباط	cluster (fruit)	مِشْمِش (coll.)	apricots
سَفَرْجَل (coll.) (سَفارِجُ .pl)	quinces	مَوالِح	citrus fruits
		مَوْز (coll.)	bananas
شَريحة شَرائِحُ .pl	slice	ناضِج	ripe (fruit)
شَمّام (coll.)	musk melon	يَقْطين	squash
طابَ (i)	to ripen	يُوسُفِيّ	tangerine

Flora

أَبْنُوس	ebony		جُمَيْز (coll.)	sycamore
أَثْل (coll.) (أَثْول .pl)	tamarisk		حَبَّة حُلْوة	aniseed
أَرْز (coll.)	cedars		حِنَّاء	henna
أَزْهَرَ	to blossom (plant, flower)		حِنْطة	see قمح
أَصيص (أُصُص .pl)	flowerpot		خُزامَى	lavender
أُقْحُوان (أَقاحي ,أَقاح .pl)	1. camomile 2. daisy		خَشْب المُغْنة	mahogany
			خَشْخاش (coll.) (خَشاخيش .pl)	poppies
باقة	bunch of flowers, bouquet		خُنْشار	fern
بائِع الزُّهُور	florist		خُوص (coll.)	palm leaves
بَتُولا	birch tree		دُخْن	millet
بَخُور	incense		دَرْدار	elm
بخور مَرْيَم	cyclamen		ذَبَلَ (u)	to wilt, wither
بَذْرة (بُذُور .pl)	1. seed 2. pip, stone (fruit)		رُمّان (coll.)	pomegranates
بَرْدي	papyrus (plant)		زَنْبَق (coll.) (زَنابِق .pl)	iris
بَرْدية	papyrus (sheet)		زَهْر (coll.)	flowers
بَرْعَم	to burgeon		(أَزاهيرُ ,أَزْهار ,أَزْهُر ,زُهُور .pl)	
بُرْعُم (بَراعِم .pl)	bud		زَهْر اللُّؤْلُؤ	daisy
بَنَفْسَج	1. violet 2. lilac		سَرْو (coll.)	evergreen cypress
			ساق (سُوق .pl)	stem (plant)
تُرْمُس	lupin		سُمّاق	sumac
جِذْر (جُذُور .pl)	root		سُنْبُل (coll.) (سَنابِلُ ,-ات .pl)	ear, spike (grain)
جِذْع (جُذُور .pl)	trunk		سِنْديان (coll.)	oak
جَفَّ (i)	to dry out		سُوس	licorice
جَفَّفَ	to dry		سَوْسَن	lily of the valley

شَجَر (coll.)	trees	قَصَب هِنْدِيّ	bamboo
أَشْجار .pl		قَمْح	wheat
شَعِير	barley	قَنَب	hemp, flax
شُوَفان	oats	كَأْس	calyx
صُبّار	1. cactus	كِئاس ,كُؤُوس .pl	
	2. Indian fig	كافُور	camphor
صَفْصاف (coll.)	willow	كاكاو	cocoa
طَلَح	acacia	كَرْم	vine
عَبّاد الشَّمْس	sunflower	كُروم .pl	
عِرْق	1. see ساق (2)	كَسْتَناء	chestnut tree
عُرُوق .pl	2. vein (plant)	لَبْلاب	ivy
عُشْب (coll.)	grass	مَرْسِين	see آس
أَعْشاب .pl		مَزْهَرِية	vase
عُنّاب	jujube	نَبات (coll.)	plants, flora
غابة	reed	ـات .pl	
غار (coll.)	laurel trees	نَبات مُتَسَلِّق (coll.)	climbing plants, creepers
غَرَسَ (i)	to plant	نَبَتَ (i)	to grow (plants)
غَرْس	seedling	نَخْل (coll.)	palm trees
أَغْراس .pl		نَخِيل	see نخل
غُصْن	branch	نَرْجِس	narcissus
غُصُون ,أَغْصان .pl		وَرْد (coll.)	roses
فُلّ	Arabian jasmine	وُرُود .pl	
قُرُنْفُل	1. clove	وَرَق (coll.)	leaves
	2. carnation	أَوْراق .pl	
قِشْر	1. bark	وَرَق عِنَب (coll.)	vine leaves
قُشُور .pl	2. peel	ياسَمِين	jasmine
قَصَب (coll.)	reed, cane	ياسِنْت	hyacinth
قَصَب سُكَّر	sugar cane		

Herbs and spices

بِرْسِيم	clover	عَطِر	fragrant, aromatic
بِسْباسة	mace	عَبِير	aroma, fragrance
بَقْدُونس	parsley	غار	laurel
بَهار	herb	فِلْفِل ، فُلْفُل	pepper
تابِل	1. spice, condiment	فِلْفِل أَحْمَر	paprika
pl. تَوابِلُ	2. see كزبرة	فِلْفِل أَخْضَر	green pepper
ثُوم	garlic	فِلْفِل حارّ	chilli
جَوْز الطِيب	nutmeg	قُرْطُم	safflower
حَبَق	basil	قِرْفة	cinnamon
حَبَهان	cardamom	كُرْكُم	turmeric
حَصالُبان	rosemary	كَرَوْيا	caraway
خَرْدَل (coll.)	mustard seed	كاري	curry
دَرِس	dried clover	كُزْبَرة	coriander
رَيْحان	sweet basil	كَمُّون	cumin
زَعْتَر	wild thyme	مُعَطَّر	scented, perfumed
زَعْفِران	saffron	مِلْح	salt
زَنْجَبِيل	ginger	pl. أَمْلاح	
شِبِت	dill	نَباتات عطْرِيّة	aromatic plants
سِمْسِم	sesame	نَعْناع	mint
شَمَار	fennel	يَنْسُون	aniseed

Vegetables

أَرُزّ	rice	بِسِلّة	pea
باذِنْجان	aubergine	بَصَل (coll.)	onions
بامية	okra, ladies' fingers	بَطاطا	sweet potato, yam

بَطاطِس (coll.)	potatoes	طَماطِم (coll.)	tomatoes
بَنْجَر	beetroot	عَدَس (coll.)	lentils
جَزَر (coll.)	carrots	غَلّة	grain, cereals
حُمُّص، حِمّص (coll.)	chick-peas	غِلال, ‫ـات‬ .pl	
		فاصولِياء	European bean
خُرْشُوف (coll.) خَراشِيفُ .pl	artichokes	فِجْل (coll.)	radishes
		فُطْر (coll.)	mushrooms
خَسّ (coll.)	lettuce	فول (coll.)	beans, broad beans
خَضْرَوات	vegetables	قَرْع (coll.)	pumpkins, gourds
خِيار (coll.)	cucumbers, gherkins	قَرْنَبِيط (coll.)	cauliflower
ذُرَّة	maize	كُرّاث	leek
راوَنْد	rhubarb	كَرَفْس (coll.)	celery
زَيْتُون (coll.)	olives	كُرُنْب (coll.)	cabbage
سَبانِخ	spinach	كوسَى	courgette
شَوَنْدَر	white beet, chard	لِفْت	turnip
طازِج	fresh	لوبِياء	bean

Animals

Mammals

ابْن آوَى بَنات آوى .pl	jackal	إسْطَبْل ‫ـات‬ .pl	stable
ابْن عِرْس بَنات عِرْس .pl	weasel	آكِل النَّمْل	ant-eater
أرْنَب أرانِبُ .pl	1. rabbit 2. hare	أَلِيف	tame
		أَيِّل أيائِلُ .pl	stag
أسَد أُسود, أُسُد .pl	lion	بُرْثُن بَراثِنُ .pl	claw, paw

بَغْل	mule	حَذوة الحِصان	horse shoe	
pl. بِغال				
بَقَر (.coll)	1. cows	حِصان	stallion	
pl. أبْقار	2. see ماشية	pl. أحْصِنة, حُصُن		
بَهيمة	1. large domestic animal	حِمار	donkey	
pl. بَهائِمُ	2. quadruped	pl. حَمير		
	3. livestock (plural)	حِمار الوَحش	zebra	
ثَعْلَب	fox	حَمَل	lamb	
pl. ثَعالِبُ		pl. أحْمال, حُمْلان		
ثُنّة	fetlock	حَيَوان	animal	
pl. ثُنَن		pl. ـات		
ثَوْر	bull	حَيَوان ثَدْييّ	mammal	
pl. ثيران		حَيَوان مُفْتَرِس	predatory animal	
جاموس	buffalo	خاصِرة	flank (horse)	
pl. جَواميسُ		pl. خَواصِرُ		
جَحْش	young donkey	خَرْطُوم	trunk (elephant)	
pl. جِحاش		pl. خَراطيمُ		
جَدْي	kid (small goat)	خَرُوف	see حمل	
pl. جِدْيان		pl. أخْرِفة, خِراف, خِرْفان		
جُرَذ	rat	خُفّاش	bat	
pl. جِرْذان		pl. خَفافيشُ		
جَرْو	1. puppy	خَمَشَ (i, u)	to scratch	
pl. أجْرٍ, جِراء, أجْراء	2. cub	خِنْزير	pig	
		pl. خَنازيرُ		
جَمَل	camel	خِنْزير بَرّيّ	boar	
pl. جِمال		pl. خَنازيرُ بَرّيّة		
جَواد	race horse, charger	دُبّ	bear	
pl. جِياد		pl. دِبَبة, أدْبابُ		
حافِر	hoof	دُبّ كَسْلان	sloth	
pl. حَوافِرُ				
حِجْر	mare	دَواجِنُ	poultry	
pl. حُجُورة, حُجُور, أحْجار		ذَنَب	see ذيل	
حَديقة الحَيَوان	zoo	pl. أذْناب		

ذِئْب	wolf	عَنْز	see معز
pl. ذُؤْبان, ذِئَاب		pl. عِناز, عُنُوز, أَعْنُز	
ذَيْل	tail	غَزال	gazelle
pl. أَذْيال, ذُيُول		pl. غِزْلان	
رُباعي الأرْجُل	quadruped	غَنَم	see شاء (1)
رِدْف	croup	غُورِيلا	gorilla
pl. أرْداف		فَأْر (coll.)	1. mice
رَوْث	dung, droppings	pl. فيران, فِئْران	2. rats
pl. أرْواث		فَرَس	horse
زَرافة	giraffe	pl. أفْراسُ	
pl. زَرافَى, زرائفُ		فَرَس البَحْر	hippopotamus
سَبُع	1. beast of prey	فَرَس مَخْصِي	gelding
pl. سِباع	2. see أسد	فَرْو	fur
سَمُّور	sable	pl. فِراء	
pl. سَماميرُ		فَهْد	leopard, cheetah
سَنام	hump (camel)	pl. أفْهُدُ, فُهُود	
pl. أسْنِمة		فيل	elephant
سِنْجاب	(grey) squirrel	pl. أفْيال, فُيُول, فِيَلَة	
شاء (coll.)	1. sheep	قِرْد	monkey
pl. شِواه, شِياه	2. ewes	pl. قُرود	
شِمْبانْزِي	chimpanzee	قَرْن	horn
صَهْوة	back (horse)	pl. قُرُون	
pl. صِهاءُ, صِهاء ـات		قُضاعة	otter
ضَبْع	hyena	قِطّ	cat
pl. ضِباع		pl. قِطَط	
عِجْل	calf	قِطّ الزَّباد	civet cat
pl. عُجول		قُطَيْطة	kitten
عُرْف	mane (horse)	قَطِيع	flock, herd
pl. أعْراف		pl. أقْطاع, قِطاع, قُطْعان	
عُرْف الدِّيك	coxcomb	قُنْدُس	beaver
عَرين	lion's den, lair	قُنْفُذ	hedgehog
pl. عُرُن		pl. قَنافِذُ	

قارِض pl. قَوارِضُ	rodent	مَعْز، مَعَز (coll.) pl. أَمْعُز	goats
كَبْش pl. أَكْباش, كِباش	ram	مَهاة pl. مَهَوات	wild cow
كَرْكَدَنّ	rhinoceros	مُهْر pl. أَمْهار, مِهارة	foal
كَفّ (f.) pl. أَكُفّ, كُفُوف	paw, foot	مُهْرة	filly
كَلْب pl. كِلاب	dog	ناب pl. أَنْياب	tusk
كَمامة	muzzle	ناقة pl. نُوق	she-camel
كَمَّم	to muzzle	نَمِر pl. نُمُور	1. leopard 2. tiger
كَنْغَر	kangaroo	نِمْس pl. نُمُوس	1. mongoose 2. ferret, weasel
لامة	llama	نِيص	porcupine
لَبْوة	lioness	هَجِين pl. هُجْن	dromedary, racing camel
ماشِية	cattle	وَبَر pl. أَوْبار	hair, coat (camel, goat, cat)
ماعِز pl. مَواعِزُ	see معز	وَحْش pl. وُحُوش	wild animal
مُتَوَحِّش	wild	وَشَق	lynx
مُجْتَرّ	ruminant	وَطْواط pl. وَطاوِيط, وَطاوِط	see خفاش
مِخْلَب pl. مَخالِبُ	see برثن		
مَرْموط	marmot		
مَعّاز	goatherd		

Birds

باز pl. بِيزان	falcon	بَشَرُوش	flamingo
باضَ (i)	to lay eggs	بَطّ (coll.)	ducks
بَبْغاء	parrot	بِطْرِيق pl. بَطارِيق	penguin
بَجَع (coll.)	pelicans	بَلَشُون	heron

بُوم pl. أَبْوام	owl	طَيْرة	flight
تَدْرُج pl. تَدْرُجة	pheasant	طَيْر مُهاجِر	migratory bird
تَمّ (.coll)	swans	طَيْر جارِح pl. طُيُور جارِحة	bird of prey
جَناح pl. أَجْنِحة	wing	عَشَّش	to build a nest
حُبارَى pl. حُبارَيات	bustard	عُشّ pl. عِشَشة, أَعْشاش, عِشاش	nest
حِدْأة pl. حِدْان, حِداء, حِدْأ	kite	عُصْفُور pl. عَصافِيرُ	sparrow
حَمام (.coll)	pigeons, doves	عُقاب pl. عِقْبان, أَعْقُب	eagle
دَجاج (.coll)	chickens, hens	عَقْعَق	magpie
دِيك pl. أَدْياك, دُيُوك, دِيكة	cock	عَنْدَلِيب pl. عَنادِلُ	nightingale
دِيك رُومي	turkey (cock)	غُراب pl. غِرْبان	1. raven 2. crow
رِيش (.coll) pl. أَرْياش, رِياش	feathers, plumage	غُرْنُوق pl. غَرانِيقُ	crane
سُمّان (.coll)	quails	فَرَّخَ	to hatch (eggs)
سُمُنّ pl. سَمامِن	سمان see	قاق الماء	cormorant
سُنُونُو	swallow	قَفَص pl. أَقْفاص	cage
شَوْحة	vulture	قُنْبُر (.coll) pl. قَنابِر	larks
صَقْر pl. أَصْقُر, صُقُور	1. باز see 2. hawk	كَتْكُوت pl. كَتاكِيت	chick
طارَ (i)	to fly	كُرْكِي pl. كَراكِي	crane
طَنّان	hummingbird	كَناري	canary
طاوُوس pl. طَواوِيسُ	peacock	لَقْلاق pl. لَقالِقُ	stork
طَيْر (coll/n.un.) pl. طُيُور	bird		

مِنْقار	beak, bill	نَوْرَس (coll.)	sea gulls
pl. مَناقيرُ		pl. نَوارِسُ	
نَعام (coll.)	ostriches	هُدْهُد	hoopoe
(نَعائِم .pl)		pl. هَداهِدُ	
نَقّار الخَشْب	woodpecker	وَزّ (coll.)	geese
نَقَر (a)	to peck	وَقْواق	cuckoo

Marine animals

أَبو سَيْف	swordfish	رَعّاد (coll.)	electric ray
أُخْطُبُوط	octopus	زَعْنَفة	fin, flipper
أُمّ الحِبْر	squid	pl. زَعانِفُ	
بَرْمائِيّ	amphibian	سالْمُون	salmon
pl. ـات		سِرْب	shoal (fish)
بَلَح البَحْر	mussel	pl. أَسْراب	
بوري	(striped/red) mullet	سَرْدين (coll.)	sardines
تُنّ (coll.)	tuna	سَرَطان	1. crab
جَرّاد البَحْر	crayfish	pl. ـات	2. see جراد البحر
جَرِّيث	eel	سَرَطان بَحْرِي	lobster
حَبّار	see أم الحبر	سُقُمْرِي	mackerel
حَرْشَف	fish scale	سَمَك (coll.)	fish
pl. حَراشِفُ		pl. أَسْماك	
حَسَك (coll.)	fishbones	سَمَك التُّرْس	turbot
حُوت	whale	سَمَك مُوسَى	sole
pl. أَحْوات, حِيتان		شَبُّوط	carp
حَيَوان بَحْرِيّ	marine animal	صَدَف (coll.)	pearl oysters
pl. حَيَوانات بَحْرِيّة		pl. أَصْداف	
خَيْشُوم	gill	عِجْل البَحْر	seal
pl. خَياشِيمُ		قارُوس	seabass
دَلْفِين	dolphin	قُدّ	cod
pl. دَلافِينث		قِرْش	shark

قَرْمُوط	catfish	قِشْرِيَّة	crustacean
pl. قَرامِيطُ		قُنْفُذ البَحْر	sea urchin
قُرَيْدِس (coll.)	shrimp	كافيار	caviar
قِشْر (coll.)	fish scales		
pl. قُشور			

Reptiles and insects

أَفْعَى	adder, viper	دَبُّور	hornet
pl. أَفاعٍ		pl. دَبابِيرُ	
أَمِيبة	amoeba	دُود (coll.)	worms, maggots
بُرْص	gecko	pl. دِيدان	
بُرْغُوث	flea	دُودة الشَّرِيط	tapeworm
pl. بَراغِيثُ		دودة القَزّ	silkworm
بَقّ (coll.)	bedbugs	دُودِي	worm-like
بِنْت وِرْدان	earthworm	ذُباب (coll.)	flies
بَيْت العنكَبُوت	spider's web	(pl. ذِبّان، أَذِبّة)	
تَلّ النَّمْل	ant hill	ذُباب قارِض	horsefly
تِمْساح	crocodile	زاحِف	reptile
pl. تَماسِيحُ		pl. زَواحِفُ	
ثُعْبان	snake	زَحَفَ (a)	to creep, crawl
pl. ثَعابِينُ		زِيز (coll.)	cicada
جَراد (coll.)	locusts	سَحْلِية	lizard
حِرْباء	chameleon	pl. سَحالٍ	
pl. حَرابِيُّ		سِرْب	1. swarm (e.g. bees)
حَشَرة	insect	pl. أَسْراب	2. colony (ants)
حَلَزون	snail	سُلَحْفاة	tortoise
pl. حَلازِينُ		pl. سَلاحِفُ	
خَلِية النَّحْل	beehive	سَمَنْدَر	salamander
خُنْفُساء	dung beetle	سُوس (coll.)	mites, woodworms
pl. خَنافِسُ		(pl. سِيسان)	

شَرْنَقة	chrysalis
شَرانِق .pl	
صُرْصُور	1. cricket
صَراصِيرُ .pl	2. cockroach
ضِفْدِع	frog
ضَفادِع .pl	
طُفَيْلي	parasite
طُفَيْلِيَات .pl	
عُثّة	moth
عُثَث .pl	
عَنْكَبُوت	spider
فَرَس النَّبِي	praying mantis
فَراشة	butterfly
قُرادة	tick
قِرْدان .pl	
قَرْن الاسْتِشْعار	antenna

قَمْل (coll.)	lice
لَدَغَ (u)	to bite (snake), to sting
لَدْغة	snakebite, sting
مَصّاص الدِّماء	bloodsucker
مَنْحَل	apiary, beehive
مَناحِلُ .pl	
ناموس (coll.)	mosquitoes
نَوامِيسُ .pl	
نَحْل (coll.)	bees
نَسِيج العَنْكَبُوت	see بيت العنكبوت
نَمْل (coll.)	ants
(نمال .pl)	
يَرَقان (coll.)	larvae
يَرْقانة الضّفادِع	tadpole
يَسْعُوب	drone, male bee
يَعاسِيبُ .pl	

Animal sounds

بَطْبَطَ	to quack (duck)
ثَغا (u)	to bleat (sheep)
خار (u)	to moo, to low (cattle)
دَنَ (u)	to buzz, hum (insect)
زَأَر (a, i)	see زمجر, عجعج
زَقْزَقَ	to chirp (bird)
زَمْجَرَ	to roar (lion)
شَقْشَقَ	to twitter
صاح (i)	to cry (bird)
صَرَّ (i)	to chirp (cricket)
صَفَرَ (i)	1. to whistle (bird)
	2. see فح

صرّ see .3	
صَهَلَ (i)	to neigh
صَهِيل	neighing
صَوَى (i)	to peep, squeak
صِياح	cry (bird)
عَجْعَجَ	to bellow (e.g. bull)
عَنْدَلة	song of the nightingale
عَوَى (i)	1. to howl (wolf, jackal)
	2. to yelp
غَرِدَ، غَرَّدَ (a)	to sing, warble (bird)
فَحَّ (u, i)	to hiss (snake)
قاقَ (u)	to cackle, cluck (hen)

قَبَعَ (a)	1. to grunt (pig) 2. to trumpet (elephant)	نَعَبَ (a, i)	to croak (raven)
		نَعَرَ (a, i)	to snort
لَقْلَقَ	to clatter (stork)	نَقَّ (i)	1. see قاق 2. to croak (frog)
ماءَ (u)	to miaow		
مُواءِ	miaow	نَهَقَ (a)	to bray (donkey)
نَبَحَ (a)	1. to bark 2. to bay	هَبْهَبَ	see (2) نبح
		هَدَلَ (i)	to coo (pigeon)

Food and drink

إِبْريق pl. أَباريق	1. pitcher, jug 2. coffee pot	بُقْسُمات	rusk
أَدَوات المائِدة	cutlery	بَلَعَ (a)	to swallow
اسْتَنْشَقَ	to snuff	بيرة	beer
أَغْذِية	foodstuffs	بَيْض (coll.)	eggs
أَكَلَ (u)	to eat	بَيْضة بَرِشْت	soft-boiled egg
أَكْل	food	بَيْضة مَسْلُوقة جِدّاً	hard-boiled egg
أَلْبان	dairy products	تَجَمَّدَ	to freeze (intrans.)
انْتِشاء	intoxication	تَجْميل	embellishment, icing
انْتَشَى	to become intoxicated	تَعَشَّى	to have dinner (evening meal)
بَرَدَ (u)	to cool off	تَغَدَّى	to have lunch
بَرَّدَ	to chill, refrigerate	تَغَذَّى بـ/على	to live on
بُرْمة pl. بُرَم, بِرام	earthenware pot	تَغْذِية	nutrition
		تَنْشيقة	pinch of snuff
بَرّيمة	corkscrew	تُورْتة	pie, tart
بِسْكويت	biscuit	توسْت	toast
بَشَرَ (u)	to grate	ثَلّاجة	refrigerator
بَقّال pl. بَقّالة, ون-	grocer	جافّ	dry
		جامِد pl. جَوامِدُ	hard, solid

جَبَّان	cheese seller	خَلِيط	mixture
جِبْنة	cheese	خَمْر (m/f)	wine
		pl. خُمُور	
جِبْنة مَبْشُورة	grated cheese		
جَرَّة	jar	خَمِيرة	yeast, ferment
pl. جِرار		pl. خَمائِرُ	
جَزَّار	butcher	داعٍ	host, inviter
		pl. دُعاة	
جَزَرَ (u)	to slaughter (animals)	دَخَّنَ	to smoke (food)
جَمَّدَ	to freeze (trans.)	دَرَجة الجَمْد	freezing point
جِهاز القَهْوة	coffee machine	دَسْتة	dozen
حارّ	hot	دَعا (إلى) (u)	to invite s.o. (to)
حَساء	soup, broth	دَعْوة	invitation
حَشا (u)	to stuff	دَغْدَغَ	to crunch (with the teeth)
حَشْوة	stuffing	دَقِيق	flour
حَفِظَ (a)	to preserve, keep	دَلَقَ (u)	to spill (liquid)
حُلْو	sweet (adj.)	ذابَ (u)	to melt, dissolve
حَلْوائِيّ	confectioner	ذاقَ (u)	to taste
حَلْوَيات	sweets, confectionery	ذَوْق	taste
حَلِيب	milk	ذَوّاق	gourmet, foodie
حَمُضَ (u)	to be/become sour	ذَبَحَ (a)	to slaughter (by slitting the throat)
خَبَّاز	baker		
خُبْز	bread	راسِب	sediment, dregs
		pl. رَواسِبُ	
خَرْدَل	mustard	رَشَفَ (u, i)	to sip
خُشارة	leftover (of meal)	رَشْفة	gulp, sip (drink)
خُضَرِيّ	greengrocer	رَغْوة	foam, froth
خَفَقَ (i, u)	to beat (eggs), whip (cream)	رَغِيف	flat loaf of bread, roll
خَلّ	vinegar	pl. رُغُف, رُغْفان, راغِفة	
خَلَّلَ	to pickle, marinate	رُقاقة حَلْوى	waffle
خَلَطَ (i)	to mix	رَقَّقَ	to roll out

رُوح	essence	سُكَّر	sugar
زَبَدَ (u)	to churn	pl. سَكاكيرُ	
زَبَّدَ	to froth (milk)	سُكَّر الثِّمار	fructose
زُبْدة	butter	سُكَّر خام	raw sugar
زُبْدة مُصَفّاة	clarified butter	سُكَّر الشَّعير	maltose
زَبْدِية	bowl	سُكَّر العنب	dextrose
pl. زَبادي		سُكَّر القَصَب	cane sugar
زُجاجة	bottle	سُكَّر اللَبَن	lactose
زِقّ	skin (as receptacle for liquids)	سُكَّر مُكرَّر	refined sugar
pl. أزْقّة		سُكَّر ناعِم	powdered sugar
زَيَّتَ	to add oil to (food)	سُكَّر النَّبات	rock candy
زَيْت	oil	سَكْران	drunk (adj.)
pl. زُيوت			
زَيْت الزَيْتون	olive oil	f. سَكْرى; pl. سَكارى	
زَيْت نَباتي	vegetable oil	سَكْرة	drunkenness
زير	large conical (clay) waterjar	سُكَّرِيّة	sugar bowl
pl. زِيار, أزْيار		سَكَّرين	saccharin
سادة	unsweetened (tea, coffee)	سِكّير	drunkard
ساطور	chopper, cleaver	سِكّين	knife
سائل	liquid	pl. سَكاكينُ	
سَبَكَ (الطَّبْخ)	1. to braise	سُلْطانِيّة	tureen
	2. to stew	pl. سَلاطينُ	
سُجُقّ	sausage	سَمّاك	fishmonger
سَحَقَ (a)	to grind, crush	سَمْن	clarified butter
سُخْن	hot	pl. سُمون	
سَخَّنَ	to heat up	سَنْدويش	sandwich
سُفْرة	dining table	pl. ـات	
pl. سُفَر		شاي	tea
سَقّاء	water carrier	شاي بِالنَّعْنَع	mint tea
سَكِرَ (a)	to get drunk	شاي بِاللوز	almond tea

شَبِعَ (a)	to satisfy one's appetite	صَبَّ (u)	to pour
شَبْعان	sated, satisfied (eating)	صَحْن	plate
f. شَبْعى, pl. شَباعى, شِباع		pl. صُحُون	
شَحْم	fat (n.)	صَفار البَيْضة	egg yolk
شَراب	drink	صَفّا	1. to pour off (water)
pl. أَشْرِبة			2. to strain
شَرِبَ (a)	to drink	صُلْب	see جامد
شَرِبَ نَخْبَه	to drink to someone's health	صَلْصة	sauce
شُرْبة	1. soup	صِناعيّ	artificial
pl. شُرُبات	2. draught, swallow	صَوْم	fast(ing)
شَرَّحَ	to slice	صَيّاد	huntsman
شِرْش اللَبَن	whey	صَيّاد سَمَك	fisherman
شَرِه	glutton		
شَريحة	slice, sliver	صينية	serving tray
pl. شَرائِحُ		pl. صَوانٍ	
شَطيرة	see سندويش	ضَيْف	guest
pl. شَطائِرُ		pl. ضُيُوف	
شَعيريَّة	vermicelli	طاجِن	frying pan
		pl. طَواجِنُ	
شَفّاطة	siphon		
شَفّاطة كَهْرَبائيَّة	extractor hood	طَبّاخ	cook
شَمْبانيا	champagne	طَبَخَ (u, a)	to cook
شَوّاية	grill	طَبَخَ بِالبُخار	to steam
شَوْبَك	rolling pin	طَبَق	1. see صحن
pl. شَوابِكُ		pl. أَطْباق	2. dish (course)
شَوْكة	fork	طبق الفِنْجان	saucer
pl. شُوَك		طَبيعيّ	natural, organic
شَوَى (i)	1. to roast	طحّان	miller
	2. to grill	طَحَنَ (a)	1. see سحق
صادَ (i)	to hunt		2. to grind (coffee)
صامَ (u)	to fast	طَحين	flour

طَحين الذُّرَّة	cornflour	غَداء pl. أَغْدِية	lunch
طُرْشي	pickles	غِذائيّ	nutritional
طَريقة اسْتِعْمال	directions for use	غِرْبال pl. غَرابيلُ	sieve, colander
طَعام	see أَكْل		
طَعْم pl. طُعُوم	flavour	غَرْغَرَ	to simmer, bubble (food in pot)
طَهَى (u)	to cook, stew	غَضّ	tender, succulent
طَيَّبَ	to season	غَلّاية	kettle
ظَرْف البَيْضة pl. ظُرُوف -	egg cup	غَلَى	to boil
عَبَّأَ	to bottle	غَلَى (i) 	1. see غَلَى 2. to ferment
عِجّة	omelette	فاتِح الشَّهِيَّة	appetizing
عَجَنَ (i, u)	to knead	فارِغ	empty
عَجين pl. عُجُن	dough, batter, paste	فاسِد	see مُتَعَفِّن
		فاضٍ	see فارِغ
عَزَمَ (i)	see دعا	فاكهاني pl. فَكْهانِيّة	fruit seller
عَسَل pl. عُسُول, أَعْسال	honey	فُتات الخُبْز	breadcrumbs
عَسَل السُّكَّر	treacle	فَتّاحة (الزُّجاجات)	bottle opener
عَشاء pl. أَعْشِية	dinner, supper	فَتّاحة (العُلَب)	tin opener
عَصّارة	(fruit) press	فَخّ pl. فُخُوخ, فِخاخ	trap (animals)
عَصَرَ (i)	to squeeze, press (fruit)	فَخْذ	leg of lamb
عَصير	juice	فَرّامة	mincer
عصير الفَواكه	fruit juice	فَرَمَ (i)	to chop, mince
عَضّ (a)	to bite	فُرْن pl. أَفْران	oven
عُلْبة pl. عُلَب	packet, pack	فِشار	popcorn
عَلَكَ (i,u)	to chew	فَصّ pl. فُصُوص	1. clove (garlic) 2. segment (orange)
عِلْك	mastic, chewing gum		

فَطَرَ (u)	to have breakfast	قَلا (u)	to fry
فُطُور	breakfast	قُمْع	funnel
فِنْجان	cup	pl. أَقْماع	
pl. فَناجينُ		قِنّينة	1. flask
فَوَّال	beanseller	pl. قَنانٍ	2. see زجاجة
فوطة (سُفْرة)	napkin	قَهْوة	coffee
pl. فُوَط		قَهْوة عَرَبيَّة	Turkish coffee
فوطة الوَرَق	paper napkin	كَأْس	glass
قارُورة	long-necked bottle	pl. كِئاس, كَؤُوس, ـات	
pl. قَواريرُ		كَبَّ (u)	to pour out/away (liquid)
قائمة الطَّعام	menu	كَبَسَ (i)	to preserve (e.g. in vinegar)
قالِب	mould	كَبْشة	1. scoop
pl. قَوالِبُ			2. spatula
قَدِيَ(u)/قَدا (i)	to be savoury (food)	كَرار	pantry
قَدَح	cup, beaker	pl. ـات	
قِدْر	pot	كَسّارة الجَوْز	nutcracker
pl. قُدُور		كُسْتْليته	cutlet
قَديد	jerked meat	كَعْك	cake
قَرَمَ (i)	to nibble	كُوب	cup
قُرْمة	chopping block	pl. أَكْواب	
pl. قُرَم		لانَ (i)	to become soft
قَشَدَ (u)	to skim (cream)	لُبّ	core, kernel (fruit)
قِشْدة	cream	pl. لُبُوب	
قِشْدة مَخْفُوقة	whipped cream	لَبَّان	milkman
قَشَّرَ	to peel	لَبَن	see حليب
قِشرة الخُبْز	bread crust	لَبَن الخَضّ	butter milk
قَصَبَ (i)	to cut up (slaughtered animals)	لَبَن غَيْر دَسِم	skimmed milk
		لَبَن نُصف دَسِم	semi-skimmed milk
قَصَب السُّكَّر	sugar cane	لَحِسَ (a)	to lick
قَصْعة	bowl	لَحْم	meat
pl. قِصاع, قِصَع, قَصَعات		pl. لُحُوم	

لَحْم مَفْرُوم	minced meat	مُرّ	bitter
لَذيذ	tasty	مُرَبّى	jam
لَفَّ (u)	to roll up	مُرَطِّبات	soft drinks
لَهَب	flame	مَرَق	gravy
لَوْح الجَليد	block of ice	مَرْقُوق	thin (e.g. pastry)
pl. ألْواح, ـات		مَرْمَطُون	kitchen boy, scullery boy
ماءالزَهْر	orange-blossom water	pl. ـات	
ماءالوَرْد	rose water	مَزّة	mezze (appetizers)
مَأْدُبة	banquet	pl. مازة, ـ, ـات	
pl. مَآدِبُ		مَزَجَ (u)	to whip, mix (cream, eggs)
مالِح	salty	مَزيج	see خليط
ماوى	juicy	مَسْحُوق	ground, crushed
مايونيز	mayonnaise	مَشْرُوب	beverage
مِبْشَرة	grater	pl. ـات	
مُبَطَّن ب	lined with	مَشْرُوبات رُوحِيَّة	spirits, alcoholic beverages
مُتَبَّل	spicy	مَشْوي	1. grilled
مُتَعَفِّن	rotten, mouldy		2. roasted
مَجْزَرة	slaughterhouse	مَصَّ (a, u)	to suck
مُجَفَّف	dried	مِصْفاة	1. colander
مُجَفَّفات	dried foodstuffs	pl. مَصافٍ	2. percolator
مَحْشِى	stuffed	مَصَلَ (u)	to curdle
محْمَصة الخُبْز	toaster	مَصْل	whey
مَحْفُوظات	tinned goods	مَضْبُوط	medium sweet (coffee, tea)
مُحَلّى	sweetened	مِضْرَب	see مخفقة
مِخْفَقة	eggbeater, whisk	pl. مَضارِبُ	
مُخَلَّفات	leftovers, scraps	مَضْروب	scrambled (eggs)
مُخَلَّل	pickled	مَضَغَ (a, u)	see علك
مَدْعُو	guest, invitee	مُضْغة	chewing gum
مِدَقّ	pestle	pl. مُضَغ	
		مَطْبَخ	kitchen
		pl. مَطابِخُ	

مَطْبَخ pl. مَطابِخُ	cooker		2. to cure
		مِلْعَقة pl. مَلاعِقُ	spoon
مَطْبُوخ	cooked	مُمَلَّح	salted, cured
مِطْحَنة البُنّ	coffee mill	مِنْديل pl. مَناديلُ	see فوطة
مِطْحَنة قَهْوة	see مِطْحَنة البُنّ		
مَطْحُون	see مسحوق	مَنْهُوم	1. see شره 2. greedy
مَطْعَم pl. مَطاعِم	restaurant	مُوَقِّت بيض	egg-timer
مِطْهاة	pan	مَوْقِد pl. مَواقِدُ	stove (gas)
مَعْمَل اللَبَن	dairy (plant)		
مِغْرَفة	ladle	نادِل pl. نُدُل	waiter
مَفْرَش pl. مَفارِشُ	tablecloth	ناضِج	cooked (< > raw)
مِفْرَمة	meat grinder	نَخَلَ (u)	to strain, sift
مُفَلْفَل	peppered	نَشاء	corn starch
مُقَبِّلات	hors d'oeuvres	نَشَوِيّات	starchy foodstuffs
مِقْدار pl. مَقاديرُ	measure (quantity)	نُصْف ناضِج	half-cooked
مُقَرْمَش	crisp, dry	نَضِجَ (a)	to be(come) well cooked
مِقْلاة pl. مَقالٍ	see طاجن	نَمْلِية	food safe, meat safe
مَقْلِيّ	fried	نَهَم	gluttony
مَكَرُونة	macaroni	نَواة pl. نَوَيات	kernel, stone
مُكَرَّر	purified, refined	نِيّ	raw
مُكَعَّبة سُكَّر	sugar cube	هاوُون pl. هَواوِينُ	mortar (vessel)
مَلّاحة	salt cellar	هَشّ	see غَضّ
مَلّاحة فُلْفُل	pepper cellar	هُلام	jelly
مَلآن	filled	وَجْبة pl. وَجَبات	1. meal 2. see طبق (2)
مَلَّح	1. to season with salt		

وَجبة ناشفة	dry rations
وَصْفة طَبْخ	recipe

يابِس	1. firm
جافّ	2. see

The human body

أُبْض pl. آباض	hollow of the knee
إبْط pl. آباط	armpit
إبْهام pl. أباهيمُ	1. thumb 2. big toe
إجْهاض	1. miscarriage 2. abortion
أجْهَضَ	1. to miscarry 2. to abort
أخْمَص القَدَم	arch of the foot
أدْرَد f. دَرْداء, pl. دُرْد	to be toothless
أُذْن pl. آذان	ear
اسْتَمْنا	to masturbate
اسْتِمْناء	masturbation
إصْبَع pl. أصابِعُ	finger
إصبع الأوْسَط	middle finger
إصبع الرِّجْل الكَبِير	big toe
إصْبَع القَدَم	toe
أصْل اللِسان	tongue root
أطْلَقَ لِحْيَته	to let one's beard grow
أعْضاء التَّناسُل	genitals

إفْراز	secretion, discharge
إفرازات أُذْنِيّة	earwax
إفرازات مِهْبَلِيّة	vaginal discharge
أنْجَبَ	to give birth
إنْسان العَيْن	pupil (eye)
انْقَصَّ الوَزْن	to lose weight
أُنْمُلة pl. أناملُ	fingertip
أنْف pl. آناف, أنُوف	nose
أوْتار صَوتِيّة	vocal folds
أيْر pl. أيور	penis
باطِن القَدَم	sole of the foot
باطِن الكَفّ	palm of the hand
بالَ (u)	to urinate
بِراز	faeces
بُرْجُمة pl. بَراجِمُ	knuckle
بروستات	prostate
بَشِع	see قبيح
بُصاق	saliva, phlegm
بَصَر	sight

بَصَرِيّ	visual	تَوْليد	child delivery
بَصُرَ (u)	to look	ثانِية	front incisor
بَصَقَ (u)	to spit	ثَدْي	breast, bosom
بَصْمة الأصابِع	fingerprint	pl. أثْداء	
بَطّة السّاق	calf	ثَنِيّة	middle incisor
بَطْر	clitoris	pl. ثَنايا	
pl. بُطور		ثُؤْباء	yawn
بَطْن	belly	ثُؤْلُول (ة)	wart
pl. أبْطُن, بُطون		pl. ثآليلُ	
بَكَى (i)	to cry, weep	جاذِبِيّة الجِنْس	sex appeal
بُلْعوم	pharynx	جاعَ (u)	to be hungry
pl. بلاعيمُ		جائِع	starved, famished
بِنْصِر	ring finger	pl. جِياع	
pl. بَناصِرُ		جَبْهة	forehead
بُنْيان	physique, stature	pl. جِباه, جَبَهات	
بُؤْبُؤ العَيْن	see انسان العين	جُثّة	corpse
بَوَّزَ	to pout	pl. أجْثاث, جُثَث	
بَوْل	urine	جَحَظَ (a)	to protrude (eye)
pl. أبْوال		جَسَد	see جسم
بُوَيْضة	ovum	pl. أجْساد	
تَبَرَّزَ	to defecate	جِسْم	body
تَثاءَب	to yawn	pl. أجْسام	
تَجاعيد	wrinkles (face)	جَعْدة	curl, lock
تَجَشَّأَ	to burp	جَعْدِيّ	curly
تَخَلَّصَ من الوَزْن	see انقص الوزن	جَفْن	eyelid
تَدْليك	massage	pl. أجْفان, جُفون	
تَصْريحة	hairdo (women)	جِلْد	skin
تَنَفَّسَ	to breathe	pl. جُلود	
تَنَفُّس	breathing, respiration	جَمال	beauty
تَوَشْوَشَ	see همس (1)	جُمْجُمة	skull
		جَميل	beautiful

جَنِين	foetus	حَمْل	pregnancy
pl. أَجْنُن, أَجِنَّة		pl. حِمال, أَحْمال	
جِهاز عَصَبيّ	nervous system	حَنْجَرة	larynx
جِهاز هَضَميّ	digestive system	pl. حَناجِرُ	
جُوع	hunger	حَنَّطَ	to embalm (corpse)
جَوْعان	hungry	حَنَك	palate
جَيْب أَنْفيّ	sinus	pl. أَحْناك	
حاجِب	eyebrow	حَوْصلة مَرارِيّة	gall bladder
pl. حَواجِبُ		حَوْض	pelvis
حاف	barefooted	pl. أَحْواض	
pl. حُفاة		خَدّ	cheek
حافة اللِسان	tongue edge	pl. خُدود	
حالِب	urether	خِصْب	fertility
pl. حَوالِبُ		خَصِب	fertile
حامِل	pregnant	خَصْر	waist, haunch
حَبَل	conception	pl. خُصُور	
حَبْل الوَرِيد	jugular vein	خُصوبة	see خِصْب
الحِجاب الحاجِز	diaphragm	خُصْية	testicle
pl. أَحْجِبة, حُجُب		pl. خُصىً	
حِجْر	lap	خَطّ شَعْريّ	hairline
حَسَّ (u)	to feel, sense	خِلالة	toothpick
حِسّ	sense	pl. أَخِلَّة	
pl. أَحْواس		خَنَّ (i)	to speak with a nasal twang
حِسِّيات	sensations	خُنَّة	nasal twang
حَشَفة	glans	خِنْصِر	little finger
حَلَّاق	hairdresser, barber	pl. خَناصِرُ	
حَلْق	throat	خَيْشوم	see أنف
pl. احْلاق, حُلوق		pl. خَياشِيمُ	
حَلَقَ (i)	to shave (head, beard)	دار التَّوْلِيد	maternity home
حَلَمة	nipple	دَبُّوس للشَعْر	hairpin
pl. حَلَم		دَرَق	thyroid gland

دَغْدَغَ	to tickle	رَضَعَ	to suck (baby)
دَلَّكَ	to massage	رضِع ثَدْيَ أُمّه	to suckle at the mother's breast
دَم pl. دِماء	blood	رَضَّع	to breast-feed
دِماغ pl. أَدْمِغَة	see مَخّ	رَضِيع pl. رِضائِعُ, رُضَعاء	suckling
دَمَعَ (a)	to water (eyes)	رَضْفة	kneecap
دَمْع (coll.) pl. دُموع	tears	رَقَبة pl. رِقاب, ـات	neck
دُموع	watery, tearful (eyes)	رَقَدَ (i)	to lie down
دَوْرة دَمَوِيّة	blood circulation	رُكْبة pl. رُكَب, رُكْبات	knee
دورة شَهْرِيّة	period (menstruation)	رَيَّلَ	to drool, slaver
ذِراع pl. أَذْرُع, ذُرْعان	arm	زائِدة pl. زَوائِدُ	appendix
ذَقْن pl. ذُقون, أَذْقان	chin	زائِدة أَنْفِيّة	adenoids
ذَكَر pl. ذُكور	see أَير	زادَ الوَزْن (i)	to put on weight
ذَيْل الحِصان	ponytail	زائِدة الوَزْن	weight gain
رَأى (u)	to see	ساعِد pl. سَواعِدُ	forearm
رائِحة pl. رَوائِحُ	smell	ساق pl. سيقان	1. leg 2. shank
رِجْل pl. أَرْجُل	leg	سَبّابة	index finger
راحة pl. راح, ـات	palm	سَبَلة خَدِّيّة	sideburns
رَأْس pl. رُؤوس	head	سَحاءة pl. سَحايا	cortex
رُباعِيّة	lateral incisor	سُرّة	navel
رَحِم pl. أَرْحام	womb	سَرَّحَ (شَعْرَه)	to comb, do one's hair
		سَقْف الفَم	roof of the mouth
		سَمانة الرِّجْل	calf
		سَمِعَ (i)	to hear, listen

سَمْع	hearing	شَعْرِيّ	hairy, hirsute
سمعيّ	auditory, aural	شَفة	lip
سَمِنَ (a)	to become fat	pl. شفاه	
سِمْنة	obesity	الشَّفة السُّفْلَى	lower lip
سَمِين	fat	الشَّفة العُلْيا	upper lip
pl. سِمان		شَفْرة	razor blade
سِنّ	tooth	pl. شِفار, شَفَرات	
pl. أسْنان		شَمَّ (u, a)	to smell, sniff
سِنّ الرُّشْد	the age of reason	شَمّ	smelling, sense of smell
سِنّ قاطعة	incisor	شَهِقَ (a, i)	to inhale
سِنْخ	teeth-ridge, alveolum	شُوشة	tuft of hair
pl. أسْناخ		صالُون الحلاقة	barber's shop
شارب	moustache	صَحَّ (u)	to wake up
pl. شَوارِبُ		صَحَّى	to wake (trans.)
شامة	mole, birthmark	صَدْر	chest
pl. شام, -ات		pl. صُدور	
شائِب	white-haired, old	صَدْغ	temple
شَباب	youth	صَغير	short
شَبَكيَّة العَيْن	retina	pl. صِغار	
شَحْمة الأُذُن	ear lobe	الصَّفْراء	bile
شَخَرَ (i)	to snore	صَقَّف	to arrange one's hair
شَرْج	anus, rectum	صَفَن	scrotum
pl. أشْراجُ		pl. أصْفان	
شِرْيان	artery	صَوْت	1. sound
pl. شَرايين		pl. أصْوات	2. voice
شُعْبة	bronchus	ضاحك	premolar
pl. شُعَب		pl. ضَواحكُ	
شَعَرَ (u)	see حسّ	ضَجَّ	to be noisy, to clamour
شَعْر	hair	ضِرْس	molar tooth
pl. شُعُور		pl. أضْراس	
شَعْر مُسْتَعار	wig	ضِرْس العَقْل	wisdom tooth

ضَرَطَ (i)	to break wind	عَرَق	sweat
ضَرْط (coll.)	fart	عُرْقوب pl. عَراقيبُ	Achilles' tendon
ضِلَع, ضِلْع pl. أضْلاع, ضُلوع	rib	عُرْيان pl. عَرايا	1. see عار 2. nakedness
طاحِن pl. طَواحِنُ	see ضرس	عُرْيانِيّة	naturism
طَأْطَأَ (رَأْسَه)	to bow one's head	عَصَب pl. أعْصاب	1. nerve 2. sinew
طِحال pl. طُحُل, ـات	spleen	عَصِي النُّطْق	incapable of speech
طَرَفَ (i)	to wink	عَضِل	muscular, brawny
طَرْف	blink of an eye	عَضَلة	muscle
طَرَف اللِسان	tip of the tongue	عَضَلِيّ	muscular (compounds)
طُول pl. أطْوال	height, length	عُضْو pl. أعْضاء	limb, organ
طَوِيل pl. طِوال	tall	عَطّار	perfume vendor
ظُفُر pl. أظافِرُ	nail	عِطْر pl. أعْطار	scent, perfume
ظُنْبوب pl. ظَنابيبُ	shinbone	عَطَسَ (i, u)	to sneeze
ظَهْر pl. أظْهُر, ظُهور	back	عَطَّسَ	to cause to sneeze
		عَطْسة	sneeze
عارٍ	naked	عَطِشَ (a)	to be thirsty
عازِل جِنْسِيّ	condom	عَطَش	thirst
عاشَ (i)	to live, be alive	عَطْشان	thirsty
عانة	groin, pubis	عَظْم pl. عِظام, أعْظُم	bone
عَبْرة	see دمْع	عَظْم كَتِفِيّ	shoulder blade
pl. عَبَرات, عِبَر		عَظْم وَجْهِيّ	cheekbone
عَجوز pl. عَجائِزُ	old, elderly	عُقْدة pl. عُقَد	joint
عَرِقَ (a)	to sweat	عُقْم	infertility

عَقيم	infertile	فُرْشة الأسْنان	toothbrush
عَمُود فَقْريّ	spine, spinal column	فُرْشة الشَّعْر	hairbrush
عُنْفُوان الشَّباب	the prime of youth	فَرْق	parting (hair)
عُنُق	see رقبة	فَرْوة الرَّأْس	scalp
pl. أَعْناق		فَصّ	lobe
عَوْرة	pudendum	pl. فُصُوص	
عَوَّلَ	to wail, howl	فَصيلة دَمَويّة	blood group
عَويل	wailing	فَقارة	vertebra
عَيْن	eye	فَكّ	jaw
pl. عُيُون		pl. فُكُوك	
غُدَّة	gland	فَم	mouth
pl. غُدَد		pl. أَفْواه	
الغُدَّة الحُلْوة	pancreas	قام (يَقُومُ) (u)	to stand up
الغُدَة الدَّرَقيَّة	see درق	قامة	build, stature
غَرْغَرَ	to gargle	قَباحة	ugliness
غُرْلة	prepuce, foreskin	قَبْضة اليَد	fist
pl. غُرَل		قَبيح	ugly
غَسَلَ (i)	to wash	pl. قَبْحَى، قِباحِي، قِباح	
غِشاء البكار	hymen	قَدَم	foot
غَفا (u)	to take a nap, doze off	pl. أَقْدام	
غَفْوة	nap	قَذَفَ (المنَى) (i)	to ejaculate
غَمّارة	dimple (cheek)	قَذْف المنَى	ejaculation
فَتْحة الأَنْف	nostril	قُزَحِيَة	iris
فَخْد	thigh	قِشْرة	dandruff
pl. أَفْخاد		قَصَبة الرِّئة	windpipe, trachea
فَرْج	vagina	قَصَبة المَرىء	gullet
pl. فُرُوج		قَطَبَ جَبينه (i)	to frown
فَرَّشَ	to brush	قَفاء	nape
فُرْشة	brush	قَفَص صَدْريّ	thorax
pl. فُرَش		pl. أَقْفاص صَدْريّة	

قَلْب	heart
pl. قُلوب	
قَهْقَهَ	to guffaw
قَوْس	arch (foot)
pl. أَقْواس	
كاحِل	ankle
pl. كَواحِلُ	
كالُو	corn (toes)
pl. كالوهات	
كاهِل	upper part of the back
pl. كَواهِلُ	
كَبْد	liver
pl. كُبود	
كَبَرَ (u)	to grow up
كَتِف	shoulder
pl. أَكْتاف	
الكُرَيّات البَيْضاء	the white corpuscles
الكُرَيّات الحَمْراء	the red corpuscles
كُشّة	lock of hair
كَعْب	heel
pl. كِعاب, كُعوب	
كَفّ	see راحة
pl. كَفوف	
عَجْز	1. backside
pl. أَعْجازُ	2. buttocks
كِرْش	paunch
pl. أَكْراشِ	
كُلْية	kidney
pl. كُلْيَتان, كُلًى	
لِثة	gums
لَحْم	flesh

لِحْية	beard
pl. لُحًى	
لِسان	tongue
pl. أَلْسُن, أَلْسِنة	
لِسان المِزْمار	epiglottis
لُعاب	drool, dribble
لَقاح	sperm
لَقَّحَ	to impregnate
لَمْس	touch
لَهاة	uvula
pl. لَهَوات	
لَوْزَتان	tonsils
لَوَّنَ	to dye (hair)
مَأْقة	sob
ما وَراءَ الوَعْى	the subconscious
مِبْرَد الأظافِر	nail file
pl. مَبارِد-	
مَبيض	ovary
مُخّ	brain
pl. مِخَخَة, مِخاخ	
مُخاظ	nasal mucus, snot
مُدَلَّك	masseur
مُرْتَفِع	loud (voice)
مِرْفَق	elbow
pl. مَرافِقُ	
مَريء	gullet
مُزَيِّن	hairdresser (women)
مَسامّ	pore
pl. ـات	

مَسَحَ (i)	to wipe, rub off	نَبَتَ (u)	to grow (e.g. teeth)
مَشَطَ (شَعْره) (u, i)	to comb (one's hair)	نَبَضَ (i)	to throb, to beat (heart, pulse)
مُشْط pl. مِشاط, أَمْشاط	comb	نَبْض pl. أَنْباض	pulse
مُشْط الرِّجْل	instep	نَحَلَ (u, a)	to grow thin
مَشيمة pl. مَشايِمُ, مَشيم	placenta	نَحيف pl. نُحَفاء, نِحاف	see ناحل
مَعْجُون الأَسْنان	toothpaste	نَحيل pl. نُحَل, نَحْلَى	see ناحل
مِعْدة pl. مِعَد	stomach	نُخاع pl. نُخُع	bone marrow
مِعْصَم pl. مَعاصِمُ	wrist	نَشَجَ (i)	to sob
مِعًى pl. أَمْعاء	bowels	نَعْسان	sleepy
المِعَى الدَّقيق	the small intestine	نَهَضَ (a)	to get up (from bed)
المِعَى الأَعْوَر	caecum, blind gut	نَهْنَهَ	see نشج
المِعَى الغَليظ	the large intestine	نَوْم	sleep
مَفْصِل pl. مَفاصِلُ	joint	نونة	chin dimple
مُقْلة العَيْن pl. مُقَل	eyeball	هُدُب (coll.) pl. أَهْداب	eyelashes
مُكَرِّش	having a paunch	هَزَّ رأسَه	to shake one's head
مَوْلُود pl. مَواليدُ	infant	هَزَلَ (i)	to be(come) emaciated
ناب pl. أَنايِيبُ, نُيُوب, أَنْياب	canine tooth	هَضْم	digestion
ناحل pl. نُحَل, نَحْلَى	slim, thin	هَضَمَ (i)	to digest (food)
ناصية pl. نَواصٍ	forelock	هَمَسَ (i)	1. to whisper 2. to mumble, mutter
نامَ (a)	to sleep	هَمْس	whisper
		هَيْئة	appearance, shape
		هَيْكَل عَظْمِيّ	skeleton
		واطِىء	soft (voice)

وَتِين pl. أوْتِنة, وُتُن	aorta
وِجْدان	emotional life
وَجْه pl. وُجوه	face
وَرِك pl. أوْراك	hip
وَرِيد pl. أورِدة	vein
وَسَخَ (يَوْسَخُ)	to be(come) dirty
وَسِخ	dirty
وُسْطَى	middle finger

وَسِيم	handsome
وَشْوَشَ	see هَمَس (1)
وِعاءدَمَوِيّ pl. دَمَوِيّة أوْعِية	blood vessel
وِلادة	birth
وِلادة مُعَجَّلة	premature birth
وَلِيد	newborn baby
يافوخ pl. يوافيخ	crown (head)
يَد pl. أياد, أيْد	hand

Diseases and health care

أبَحّ	hoarse
إحْباط	see اكتِئاب
احْتِقان	congestion
احتِقان الدَّم	vascular congestion
اخْتَصّ ب	to specialize in
اخْتِصاصِيّ	specialist
اخْتِصاصِيّ الجِهاز الهَضْمِيّ	gastroenterologist (doctor)
أخْرَس	dumb
أداة تَشْخِيصِيّة	diagnostic tool
إدْمان المُخَدِّرات	drug addiction
أدْمَنَ على	to be addicted to
ارْتِجاج المُخّ	concussion

ارْتَعَشَ	to shiver, tremble
ارْتِفاع ضَغْط الدَّم	hypertension
أرَق	insomnia, sleeplessness
إرْهاق	stress, fatigue
إزالة الرَّحِم	hysterectomy
اسْتِئْصال	removal (of an organ) by surgery
اسْتَأْصَلَ	to remove (an organ) by surgery
اسْتَحَمَّ	to take a bath
اسْتِحْمام	bathing
اسْتِراحَ	to take a rest
اسْتَخْرَجَ الوَعْى	to regain consciousness
اسْتِسْقاء	dropsy

اِسْتِعادة	recuperation	أُغْمِيَ عَلَيْهِ	to faint, lose consciousness
اِسْتِنْساخ الكائنات	cloning	أَقْلَعَ	to extract, pull out
اِسْعاف	medical assistance	اِكْتِئاب	depression
الإسْعاف الأوَّليّ / الفَوْريّ	First Aid	إِكْزيما	eczema
		آلام المَعْدة	stomach ache
إِسْفَنْج	sponge	اِلْتِهاب	inflammation
إِسْهال	diarrhoea	التهاب الجيُوب الأنفيَّة	sinusitis
أَشعَّة فَوْق البَنَفْسَجيَّة	ultraviolet rays	التهاب الحَلَق	throat infection
أَشَلّ	paralysed, paralytic (adj.)	التهاب الحَنْجَرة	laryngitis
شلُّوء .pl ; شَلّاء .f		التهاب رئويّ	lung infection
إِصابة	injury	التهاب الزَّائدة الدُوديَّة	appendicitis
أُصيبُ بـ (pass.)	to be afflicted by (a disease)	التهاب السِّحائيّ	meningitis
أَصْلَع	bald	التهاب الشُّعَب	bronchitis
صلُع ;صَلْعاء .pl. f		التهاب عِرْق النَّسا	sciatica
أَطْرَش	deaf	التهاب الغُدَّة النَّكافيَّة	mumps
طُرُش .pl ;طَرْشاء .f		التهاب كِبْديّ	hepatitis
إعادة التَّأهيل	rehabilitation	التهاب كلُويّ	nephritis
أَعْرَج	lame	التهاب اللِّثة	gingivitis
عُرُج .pl ;عَرْجاء .f		التهاب المَفاصل	arthritis
أَعْشاء	night-blind	التهاب اللَّوْزَتَيْن	tonsilitis
عَشْواء .f		التهاب معَويّ	gastritis
أَعْمَى	blind	اِلْتَوَى	to twist (e.g. ankle)
عُمْيان ,عُمْى .pl ;عَمْياء .f		التواء	sprain
أَعْوَر	one-eyed	ألِمَ (a)	to be in pain
عُور .pl ;عَوْراء .f		ألَم	pain, ache
إعْياء	exhaustion, fatigue	آلام .pl	
إغْماء	unconsciousness		

أَلَم الأَسْنان	toothache	بَنْج	chloroform
أَلَم الحَيْض	menstrual pain	بَنَّجَ	to chloroform
أَلَم العَضَلات	muscle ache	بَواسِيرُ	haemorrhoids
إمْساك	constipation	بُودرة	powder
انْبَطَحَ	to be prostrated	بيلهارْسِيا	schistosomiasis, bilharziasis
أُنْبوبة	tube (e.g. toothpaste)	تاج	crown (teeth)
أَنابِيبُ .pl		تِيجان .pl	
انْتَحَرَ	to commit suicide	تَأمين صِحّيّ	health insurance
انْتَعَشَ	to recover (from illness)	تَبَلُّل لَيْلِيّ	bedwetting
انْتِكاس	relapse	تَتَنوس	tetanus
انْتَكَسَ	to suffer a relapse	تَجْوِيف	cavity (tooth)
انْسِداد عَضَلَة القَلْب	infarctus	تَحْتَ إشْراف طِبّيّ	under doctor's supervision
		تَحْلِيل	analysis
انعاش	resuscitation	ـات .pl	
انْفِصام	schizophrenia	تَحْلِيل البُول	urine analysis
انْقِباض	contraction	تَحْلِيل الدَّم	blood analysis
انْهِيار عَصَبِيّ	nervous breakdown	تَحْمِيلة	suppository
أَوْجَعَ	to cause pain	تَحامِيلُ .pl	
أورطى	aorta	تَخْدِير	anaesthesia
بَتَرَ (u)	to amputate	(a) تَخِمَ	to suffer from indigestion
بَتْر	amputation	تُخْمة	indigestion
بَثْرة	pimple	تَدَرُّن	سلّ see
بُثُور .pl		تراخوما	trachoma
بَجَّ	to be hoarse	تِرْكِيبات أَسْنان	braces (teeth)
بُحَّة	hoarseness	تِرْياق	antidote
بَخّاخة	spray	تَسَمُّع	auscultation
بَرَداء	feverish chill	تَسَمُّم بُولِيّ	uraemia
بَكْتِيرِيّ	bacterial	تَسَمُّم دَمَوِيّ	blood poisoning
بَكْتِيرِيا	bacteria	تَسَمُّم الطَّعام	food poisoning

تَسَوُّس	dental caries	جُدَرِيّ	smallpox
تَشْخيص	diagnosis	جُدَرِيّ الماء	chickenpox
تَشْريح جُثّة	autopsy	جُذام	leprosy
تَشَنَّجَ	1. to have convulsions	جَرَّاح	surgeon
	2. to twitch	جِراحة	surgery
تَشَنُّج	convulsion, spasm	جِراحة التَّجْميل	cosmetic surgery
تَشَنُّجِيّ	spasmodic, convulsive	جَرَب	scabies
تَشْويه	deformity, mutilation	جُرْثُوم	1. microbe
تَصَلُّب الشَّرايين	arteriosclerosis	pl. جَراثيمُ	2. bacillus
تَضَخَّمَ	to swell, distend		3. bacteria
تَطْعيم	inoculation, vaccination	جَرْح	wound
تَعالَجَ	to undergo medical treatment	pl. جُروح	
تَعْبان	tired	جُرْعة	dose, potion
تَعَرَّضَ لِ	to be exposed to	pl. جُرَع, -ات	
تَقَلُّص	cramp	جِسْم مُضادّ	antibody
تَقْليل النَّسْل	birth control	جُلْطة	clot
تَقَيَّأَ	to vomit	جُلْطة دَمَوِيّة	blood clot
تَلْقيح	vaccination	جِهاز المَناعة	immune system
التَّلَيُّف الحَوْصَلِيّ	cystic fibrosis	حادِث	accident
تَمَزُّق	laceration, tear	pl. حَوادِث	
تَنَفُّس صِناعِيّ	artificial respiration	حَبّ الشَّباب	acne
تَهيُّج	irritation	حَبّة	pill
تَوَحُّد	autism	pl. حُبوب	
تُوُفِّيَ	see مات	حَبْل سُرَّيّ	umbilical cord
تيتانوس	tetanus	حُجْرة الطَّوارِئ	Accidents and Emergency Room
تيفوس	typhus	حُجْرة العَمَلِيّات	operating theatre
جَبَرَ	to set (broken bones)	حَجْز صِحِّيّ	quarantine
جَبيرة	splint	حَدَقة	pupil
pl. جَبائِرُ		حَرارة	burning (of the skin)

حَرْق حُرُوق .pl	burn
حَسَّاسِيّ	allergic
حَسَّاسِيَّة (لِ)	allergy (to)
حَسَر البَصَر	short-sightedness
حَسِير	short-sighted
حَشا (u)	to fill (e.g. teeth)
حَشْو	filling (teeth)
حَصاة	calculus
حَصاة بُولِيَّة	bladder stone
حَصاة صَفْراوِيَّة	gallstone
حَصْبة	measles
حَفَّ (i)	1. to depilate 2. to trim (beard)
حِفاض ـات .pl	nappy
حِفاض الحَيْض	sanitary towel
حَقَنَ (i, u)	to give someone an injection
حَقْن	injection
حقن في الوَرِيد	intravenous injection
حُقْنة شَرْجِيَّة حُقَن .pl	enema
حَكَّ (u)	to itch
حِكَّة	itch
حَلَّلَ	to analyse
حُمُوضة المَعْدة	heartburn
حُمِّى (a)	to be feverish
حُمَّى	fever
حُمَّى قَرمَزِيَّة	scarlet fever
حُمَّى القَشّ	hay fever

الحُمَّى الصَّفْراء	yellow fever
حُمَّى مَعِدِيَّة	gastric fever
حُمَّى مَعَوِيّ	typhoid fever
حَمِيد	benign (e.g. tumour)
حُوَيْصلة	cyst
خَبِيث أَخْباث ,خُبَثاء ,خُبُث .pl	malignant (disease, tumour)
خَدَشَ (i)	to scratch
خُراج (coll.)	abscess
خُراقة	blister
خَرَف	senility
خِلْقِيّ	congenital
خَلِية خَلايا .pl	cell
خَوْف من الأماكن المُغْلَقة	claustrophobia
خَيْط الأَسْنان	dental floss
داء	see مرض
داء الكَلْب	rabies
دائخ	dizzy
دار النَّقاهة	convalescent home
دَجّال دَجاجلةُ ,-ون .pl	quack
دَقّة القَلْب	heartbeat
دَقِيق اللَّواقِح	pollen
دَم دِماء .pl	blood
دَمَلَ (u)	to scar
دُمْل دَمامِيلُ ,دَمامِلُ .pl	1. abscess 2. boil

دَمَوِيّ	bloody	رُوَيْصة	sleepwalking
دَمِيَ (a)	to bleed	رُوماتِزم	rheumatism
دَمَّى	to cause to bleed	زَرْع عَضْو	transplant
دهانة	unguent, cold cream	زُكام	cold
دَهينة	pomade	زُكِمَ (pass.)	to catch a cold
دَواء pl. أَدْوِية	drug, medicine	زُلاليات	proteins
دَوائيّ	medicinal	زُهَرِيّ	syphilis
دُوار البَحْر	seasickness	زَيْت خُروع	castor oil
دُوار الجَوّ	air sickness	زَيْت سمَك	cod-liver oil
دُوار السَفَر	travel sickness	ساعات العِيادة	consultation hours (doctor)
دَوْخة	vertigo	سُبات	lethargy
دُوسِنتاريا	dysentery	سجارة pl. سَجائِرُ	cigarette
ذِبْحة صَدْرِيّة	angina pectoris	سَحَجَ (a)	to graze (the skin)
رِباط	dressing (wound)	سَحْج	abrasion
رَبَطَ (i, u)	to dress (a wound)	سُدَّة شِرْيانِيّة	embolism
رَبْو	asthma	سَرَطان	cancer
رجال الإسْعاف	ambulance men	سُعال	cough
رَضّ	to bruise	سُعال دِيكيّ	whooping cough
رَضّ (u) pl. رُضوض	bruise	سَعَلَ (u)	to cough
رِضاعة	nursing bottle	سَقْطة	fall
رَضيض	bruised	سَكّاتة	dummy, pacifier
رُعاف	nosebleed	سَكْتة دِماغِيّة	skull fracture
رَعْشة	shiver	سَكْتة قَلْبِيّة	heart attack
رعشة الحُمّى	feverish shiver	سَكَّنَ	to soothe (pain)
رَعَفَ أنْفُهُ (u, a)	to have a nosebleed	سُلّ	tuberculosis
رَغْبة جِنْسِيّة	libido	سَليم البُنْية	of sound health
رَقَدَ (u)	to lie down	سَليم العَقْل	sane
		سُمّ	poison

سَمَّاعة	stethoscope	صَمَل	stiffness, rigidity
سِنّ اصْطِناعيّ أسْنان اِصْطِناعيّة .pl	false tooth	صَمَل جِيفِيّ	rigor mortis
سُوء التَغْذية	malnutrition	صُورة أشِعّة	X-ray
سيّارة الإسْعاف	ambulance (car)	صَيْدَليّ	pharmacist
شاش	gauze	صَيْدَلية	pharmacy
شَدّ عَضَليّ	muscle cramp	الصَيْدَلية الخافِرة	duty pharmacy
شَرَجيّ	anal	ضَرَبَ حَقْناً (i)	to give an injection
شَرَّحَ	to dissect (a corpse)	ضَرْبة الشَمْس	sunstroke
شِفاء	1. remedy	ضَعيف	weak
	2. cure	ضَعائِف .pl. f, ضِعاف, ضُعَفاء .pl. m	
شَفَى (i)	to cure, heal	ضَغْط الدَّم	blood pressure
شَلَّ (a)	to be paralysed	ضَمان اِجْتِماعيّ	social security
شَلَل	paralysis	ضيق النَّفَس	shortness of breath
شَلَل الأطْفال	polio	طارِئة طَوارِئُ .pl	emergency
شَلَل اِهْتِزازيّ	Parkinson's Disease	طاعون	plague
شَهادة طبِّيّة	medical certificate	طِبّ الأعْشاب	homeopathy
شَهية	appetite	الطِبّ البَديل	alternative medicine
صابون	soap	طِبّ وَقائيّ	preventive medicine
صابون الحِلاقة	shaving soap	طَبيب أطِبّاء .pl	doctor
صِبْغة اليُود	tincture of iodine	طبيب الأذْن و الأنْف والحَنْجَرة	ear, nose and throat specialist
صُداع	headache	طبيب الأسْنان	dentist
صَدْمة عَصَبيّة	mental shock	طبيب الأطْفال	paediatrician
صَرَع	epilepsy	طبيب أمْراض النِّساء	gynaecologist
صَفْراويّ	bilious	طبيب العُيون	opthalmologist
صَلَع	baldness	طبيب نَفْسانيّ	psychiatrist

طُحال	splenitis	عِلاج	1. remedy
طَفْح	rash		2. therapy, treatment
طَفْح الحفاضات	nappy rash	عِلاج كيميائِيّ	chemotherapy
طَرَش	deafness	عِلاجِيّ	therapeutic
طَهَّرَ	to disinfect	عِلْم التَّشْريح	anatomy
عالٍ	high (e.g. blood pressure)	عَلى الرِّيق	on an empty stomach
عالَجَ	to treat (disease)	عَمَل الوِلادة	labour (childbirth)
عَثَرَ (u, i)	to stumble	عَمَلِيَّة جِراحِيَّة	operation
عَثَرَ به	to trip s.o. up	عَمَلِيَّة قَيْصَرِيَّة	Caesarean section
عاجِز جِنْسِياً	impotent	عُمْيان	blindness
عَجْز	disability	عِناية طِبِّيَّة	medical care
عَجْز جِنْسِيّ	impotence	عِناية مُرَكَّزة	intensive care
عَدَسة لاصِقة	contact lens	عَنْبَر	ward
عَدْوى	infection, contagion	pl. عَنابِر	
عَرَض	symptom	عَياء	inability, feebleness
pl. أعْراض		عِيادة	doctor's surgery (office)
عرض جانِبِيّ	side-effect	عِيادة خارِجِيَّة	outpatient clinic
عِصابة	dressing, bandage	عَيْن زُجاجِيَّة	glass eye
pl. عَصائِب		عَيْن السَّمَكة	corn (toes)
عَضّة صَقِيع	frostbite	عَيْنة	sample
عُضال	incurable (disease)	عَيِّنة البول	urine sample
عَقّار	drug, remedy	عَيِّنة الدَّم	blood sample
pl. عَقاقِير		عَيْنِية	eye-piece
عَقّار وَهْمِيّ	placebo	غَثَيان	nausea
عَقَمَ (u)	to be sterile (woman)	غَرْغَرَ	to gurgle
عَقَّمَ	1. to sterilize	غُرْفة الإفاقة	recovery room
	2. to disinfect		

غُرْفة الانْتِظار	waiting room
غُمِيَ عَلَيْه	to faint, lose consciousness
غَنْغَرِينا	gangrene
فَأْر تَجارِب	guinea pig
فاسِد	rotten, festering
فتاق	hernia
فَحَصَ (a)	to examine
فَحْص	(medical) examination, check-up
فَحْص الدَّم	blood test
فِطْرِيّ	inborn
فَقَدَ صَوابَهُ	to lose one's mind (i)
فِقْدان الذَاكِرة	amnesia
فَقْر الدَّم	anaemia
فَنّ التَّوْليد	midwifery
فُواق	hiccup
قابِل للشِّفاء	curable
قالَب صابون	bar of soap
قُرْحة	1. sore (n.)
	2. tablet, lozenge
قَرْحة مِعَوِيّة / قُرَح .pl	ulcer
قِسْم العناية المُرَكَّزة	intensive care unit
قَصَرِية	chamberpot
قَطّارة	pipette, dropper
قَطَّرَ	to let fall in drops (medicine)
قَطْر أَنْف	nose drops
قَطْر العَيْن	eye drops
قَطْرة	drop
قَطَعَ (i)	to cut
قَطْع / قُطُوع .pl	cut
قُوّة	strength
قَوِيَ (a)	to be strong
قَوِى / أَقْوِياء .pl	strong
قَيْء	vomiting
قُياء	vomit
قَيَّحَ	to fester
قَيْح / قُيوح .pl	pus
كَأَب	depression
كابُوس / كَوابِيسُ .pl	nightmare
كَبْسُول	capsule
كَئِيب	depressive
كريم	cream
كَسَرَ (i)	to break, fracture
كَسْر / كُسور .pl	fracture
كِماد (ة)	compress
كُوليرا	cholera
كِينة	quinine
لَبْخة / لَبَخات .pl	poultice

لَصوُق	plaster	مَذَل	paraesthesia, pins and needles
لَفْحة الشَمْس	sunburn	مُرَبِّية	nanny
لَقَّحَ	to vaccinate	مَرِضَ (a)	to become ill
لَوىً pl. ألْواء	colic	مَرَّضَ	to nurse
لين العِظام	softening of the bones	مَرَض pl. أمْراض	disease
ماتَ (u)	to die	مرض باطِنيّ	internal disease
مِبْضَع pl. مَباضِعُ	scalpel	مَرَض تَناسُليّ	venereal disease
مُتَخَصِّص	specialist (n.)	مَرَض حَسّاسيّ	allergic disease
مُتّداع	frail (constitution)	مرض السُكَّر	diabetes
مُتَقَطِّع	intermittent	مرض صَدْريّ	pulmonary disease
مُتَقَيِّع	festering (e.g. wound)	مرض عَصَبيّ	nervous disease
مُتَواصِل	persistent	مرض عَقْليّ	mental disorder
مَثانة	bladder	مرض القَلْب	heart disease
مُثَبِّت الشَعْر	hairspray	مَرَض الكَبْد	liver disease
مُجَفِّف الشَعْر	hair dryer	مرض مُعْدٍ	contagious disease
مَجْنُون	crazy, insane	مرض مَعْديّ	gastric illness
مِحْقَنة pl. مَحاقِنُ	syringe	مرض نَفْسيّ	psychiatric illness
مُخاط	nasal mucus	مرض النَّوم	sleeping sickness
مُخَدِّر pl. ـات	1. anaesthetic 2. narcotic	مرض يَتَعَلَّقُ بالمِهْنة	occupational disease
مَخَطَ (u, a)	to blow one's nose	مَرْضِع (ة) pl. مَراضِعُ	wetnurse, foster mother
مَدَّ (u)	to stretch	مَريض	1. ill 2. patient (n.)
مُدْمِن المُخَدِّرات	drug addict	مَرْهَم pl. مَراهِمُ	ointment
مَديد البَصَر	long-sighted	مُزْمِن	chronic
		مُزيل الرائحة	deodorant

مُزيل العَرَق	anti-perspirant	مَعامِل .pl	
مُسَبِّب للسَّرَطان	carcinogenic (n.)	مَغْص	colic
مُسْتَحْضَر دَوائيّ ـات .pl	medical preparation	مَغْص كُلَويّ	renal colic
مُسْتَشْفىً مُسْتَشْفيات .pl	hospital	مَفْصُوم	schizophrenic
		مَفْعُول جانبيّ مَفاعيلُ جانبيّة .pl	side effect
مُسْتَشْفى الأمْراض العَقْليَّة	mental hospital	مِقَصّ الأظافِر	nail clippers
مُسْتَعِدّ لـ	prone to, predisposed to	مُقَوٍّ مُقَوِّيات .pl	tonic, restorative
مُسَكِّن ـات .pl	sedative, analgesic	مُقَيِّء مُقَيِّئَات .pl	emetic
مُسَمّ	poisonous, toxic	مَلاريا	malaria
مُسَهِّل ـات .pl	laxative, purgative	مَلْجأَ الشُّيُوخ	home for the elderly
مَشّاية	baby walker	مِلْح إنْكليزيّ	Epsom salts
مَشْرَحة	1. operating table 2. autopsy room	مِلْقَط	tweezers
		مُمَرِّضة	nurse
مَشْلُول	paralysed	مُميت	lethal
مُصاب بـ	afflicted by (a disease)	مَناعة	immunity
مَصْرَع مَصارِعُ .pl	fatal accident	مَنْع الحَمْل	contraception
مَصْل مُصُول .pl	serum	مُنَوِّم	anaesthetic, sedative
		مَوادّ التَّطْبيب	medicaments
مُضاعَفات	complications	مواد مُضاد للحَيَوان	antibiotics
مُطَهِّر	disinfectant	مَوْت أمْوات .pl	death
مُعاقٍ	disabled		
مَعْجُون الأسْنان	toothpaste	مَوْت أبْيَض	natural death
مَعْجُون الحِلاقة	shaving foam	مَوْت الغَفْلة	sudden death
مُعْدٍ	contagious	مُوسى (.f) أمْواس ,مَواسٍ .pl	straight razor
مَعْمَل	laboratory		

مُؤَقَّت	temporary	نَقْل الدَّم	blood transfusion
مُوَلِّدة	midwife	نَقَهَ (a)	to recover
مُؤْلِم	painful	نَكَفة	parotid gland
ناجِع	beneficial, healthful	نَوْبة	fit, attack
ناسُور	fistula	نوبة عَصَبِيَّة	nervous crisis
pl. نَواسِيرُ		نَوَّم	to anaesthetize
ناعور	haemophilia	هذاء	delirium, ravings
نُتُوء	growth, swelling	هَذَى (i)	to rave, be delirious
النَجْدة,النَجْدة	help! help!	هَرَّ (i)	to whimper, whine
نَجَعَ (a)	to have a salutary effect	هَوَس	paranoia
نَدَب	scar	واطِىء	low (blood pressure)
pl. نُدُب ,أَنْداب		واهِن	weakened, debilitated
نَزَفَ (i)	to draw off (blood)	pl. وُهُن	
النَزَف الدَمَوِيّ	haemophilia	وَخَزَ (يَخِزُ)	to sting
نَزِيف	bleeding, blood loss	وَخْز	stinging, twinges
نَظَّارات	spectacles	وخز بالإبَر الصِينِيَّة	acupuncture
نَظَّاراتِيّ	optician	وَخْزة بالخَصْر	stitch (in the side)
نَعْش	bier	وِراثِيّ	genetic, hereditary
نَعَى (a)	to announce s.o.'s death	وَرَم	tumour, swelling
نَعْية	death notice	وَصْفة	prescription
نُقَاض	ague, fit	وَفاة طِبِّيَّة	clinical death
نَقَاهة	convalescence, recovery	وِقاية مِن	prophylaxis
نِقْرِس	gout	يَرَقان	jaundice

The family, human relations and emotions

أب pl. آباء	father	إِخْلاص	sincerity
ابن pl. أَبْناء	son	اِخْتَلَطَ بِ	to mix with
اِبْن عَمّ	cousin (son of paternal uncle)	اِخْتَلَفَ	to be different
اِبْن خال	cousin (son of maternal uncle)	اِخْتِلاف pl. ـات	difference
اِتَّفَقَ	to agree	اِخْتَفَى	to hide
اِجْتَمَعَ	to assemble, gather	(u) أَخَذَ	to take
أَحَبَّ	to love	آخر	other
اِحْتاجَ إلى	to need	آخَرُونَ .pl, أُخْرَى .f	
اِحْتِرام	respect	أَخْرَجَ	to take out
اِحْتَرَمَ	to respect	أَخَوِيّ	brotherly
اِحْتَرَسَ	to be wary of	أُخُوَّة	brotherliness
اِخْتارَ	to choose	(a) آذَى	to harm, wrong
اِحْتِقار	contempt, disdain	أَذىً pl. أَذِيَّة, أَذاة	harm, offence
اِحْتَقَرَ	to despise	أَرادَ	to want
أَخ pl. إِخْوَة	brother	إِرادة	will, wish
إِخاء	fraternity, friendship	إِرادِي	intentional
أُخْت pl. أَخَوات	sister	اِرْتَزَقَ	to make a living
أُخْت الزَّوْجة	sister-in-law (sister of wife)	أَرْمَل pl. أَرامِل	widower
اِخْتِلاط	social intercourse	أَرْمَلة pl. أَرامِل, أَرامِلة	widow
اِخْتِيار	choice	اِزْدادَ	to increase
أَخْشَن pl. خُشْن, f. خَشْناء	rude, uncouth	اِسْتَخْدَمَ	to use
		اِسْتَطاعَ	to be able
		اِسْتَعْمَلَ	see استخدم

اِسْتَغْفَرَ لِ	to ask (s.o.) for forgiveness	أَطْلَقَ عَلَيْهِ اسِم	to name/call somebody (after s.o.) . . .
اِسْتَغَلَّ	to exploit, take advantage of	أَظْهَرَ	to show
اِسْتَمَرَّ	to continue	أَعالَ	to support (family members)
اِسْتِنْتاج	deduction	اعْتِبارِيّ	subjective
اِسْتَنْتَجَ	to deduce, infer	اعْتِباطِيّ	accidental, coincidental
اِسْتِياء	indignation, discontent	اعْتِدال	moderation
إِسْراف	extravagance, immoderateness	اعْتِذار	apology
أَسْرَعَ	to hurry	إِعْتَذَرَ لِ (مِن)	to apologize to s.o. (for s.thing)
(a) أَسِفَ عَلى	to regret, feel sorry for	اعْتَمَدَ عَلى	to depend on
أَسَف	regret	اعْتَنَقَ	to embrace, hug
أَسِف	sorry, regretful	أَعَدَّ	to prepare
أَسْفَرَ عن	to result in	أَعْطَى	to give
أَسْقَطَ	to throw down	أَغارَ	to make jealous
أَسْلاف	ancestors	أَغْرَى	to seduce
اسْم	given name	إِغْراء	temptation
pl. أَسْماء			
الاسِم الثَّانِي	middle name	افْتَخَرَ بِ	to be proud of
اسِم كامِل	full name	افْتَرَضَ	to assume
اِشْتِباه	suspicion	اِفْتَرَضَ عَلى	to impose s.thing on s.o.
اِشْتَبَهَ	to suspect	افْتَقَدَ	to miss (s.o., s.thing)
اِشْتِهار	notoriety	افْتَكَرَ	to think
أَشْفَقَ عَلى	to pity, feel sorry for	أَفْزَعَ	to frighten
أَصْبَحَ	to become	أَقامَ	to set up, raise
أَصَرَّ عَلى	to insist on	اقْتَرَحَ عَلى	to propose
أَضاعَ	to lose	أَقْلَقَ	to disturb, bother
اِضْمَأَنَّ	to come to rest	أَقْنَعَ بِ	to persuade s.o. to do s.thing
(على) أَطاق	to stand, tolerate (s.thing)	اكْتَشَفَ	to discover

اِكْتَفَى	to content, satisfy	اِنْدَهَشَ	to be astonished
أَكَّدَ	to assure, confirm	أَنْذَرَ (ب)	to warn s.o. (against s.thing)
أَكِيد	certain	اِنْضِباط	discipline
أَلَحَّ	to pester	اِنْطَبَعَ	to be impressed
إِلْحاح	insistence	اِنْطِواء (على) النَّفْس	introversion
أُمّ pl. أُمَّهات	mother	أَنْكَرَ	to deny
اِمْتَدَحَ	to praise	اِنْكِماش	absorption, preoccupation
إِمْرَأة (المَرْأة) pl. نِسْوان، نِسْوَة، نِساء	woman	أَنْهَى	to finish, end
		أُنُوثة	femininity, womanliness
أُمّ الزَّوْج (ة)	mother-in-law	آنَسَ	to keep someone company
أَمَلَ (i)	to hope	أَنِيس	pleasant, affable
أَمْل pl. آمال	hope	أُنَساءُ .pl	
		أَهانَ	to treat with contempt, humiliate
أَمِين pl. أُمَناء	loyal, honest		
		إِهانة	affront, insult
أَنانِيّ	selfish	اِهْتَمَّ بـ	to be interested in
أَنانِية	selfishness, egoism	اِهْتِمام بـ pl. ـات	concern, care
أَنَّبَ	to blame		
اِنْبَهَرَ	to be dazzled	إِهْمال	carelessness, negligence
اِنْتَظَرَ	to wait	أَهْمَلَ	to neglect, disregard
اِنْتِقام	revenge	أَوْقَعَ	to drop
اِنْتَقَدَ	to criticize	أَوْقَفَ	to stop, cease (trans.)
اِنْتَقَمَ مِن	to take revenge on s.o.	بادَلَ	to exchange
اِنْتَهَى	to be finished	بالبَداهة	spontaneously
أُنْثَى pl. أَناثى، إِناث	female, feminine	بالتَّناوُب	successively
		بالدَوْر	alternately, in turns
اِنْدِفاع	impetuosity, rashness	بالصُّدْفة	by chance
اِنْدَفَعَ	to be impetuous	باعْتِدال	moderately

باكِرة pl. بَواكِرُ	first-born	تَجاذُب	mutual attraction
باهِر	dazzling, splendid	تَجاهَلَ	to pretend not to know
بُخْل	avarice	تَجَنَّبَ	to avoid
بَخِلَ (a)	to be stingy	تَحامُل	prejudice
بَخيل pl. بُخَلاء	1. miser 2. stingy, mean	تَحَرُّش	interference, meddling
بَدَأَ (a)	to begin	تَحَقَّقَ	to make sure
بَدَى (يَبْدُو)	to seem	تَحِيّة	greeting
		مع تَحِيّات	best wishes (closing formula in letter)
بَرّاق	sparkling, glittering	تَحَيَّرَ	to become confused
بَسَطَ (u)	to spread out	تَحَيُّر	confusion, bewilderment
بَسيط pl. بُسَطاء	simple	تَخَيَّلَ	to imagine
بَشِع	offensive, repugnant (e.g. act)	تَذَكَّرَ	to remember
بِطانة pl. بَطائِنُ	entourage	تَرَدَّدَ	to hesitate, waver
		تَرَدُّد	hesitation, reluctance
بكارة	virginity	تَرَمَّلَ	to become a widow(er)
بِنْت pl. بِنات	1. girl 2. daughter	تَزَوَّجَ	to get married
		تَساءَلَ	to ask oneself
بِنْت الأخ	niece (brother's daughter)	تَسامُح	tolerance
بنت الأُخْت	niece (sister's daughter)	تَساهُل	leniency, indulgence
بِنْت العَمّ	cousin (paternal uncle's daughter)	تَشاؤُم	pessimism
		تَشاؤُمِيّ	pessimistic
بنت الخال	cousin (maternal uncle's daughter)	تَشابُه	similarity
بُؤْس	misery	تَشَوَّقَ الى	to long for
تاريخ الميلاد	date of birth	تَصَرَّفَ	to act, behave
تَبَنَّى	to adopt	تَصْميم	determination
تَبَنٍّ	adoption	تَصَوَّرَ	see تخيّل

تَظاهَرَ بِ	to pretend	تَهْديد	threat
تَظاهُر	dissimulation, pretending	تَهْنِئة	congratulation
تعاسة	see بؤس	تَهانٍ .pl	
تَعَجَّبَ	to be surprised, wonder	تَواضُع	humility, modesty
تَعَرَّفَ (بِ)	to become acquainted (with)	تَوْأَم	twin
تَعَرُّف (بِ)	acquaintance (with)	تَوائِمُ, تَوْأَمان .pl	
تَعْزِية	condolences	تَوَحُّد	1. loneliness
تَعازٍ .pl			2. seclusion
تَعْطيل	interruption	تَوَقَّعَ	to expect
تَعْقيد	complication, entanglement	ثابَرَ على	to persist, persevere in
ـات .pl		ثِقة	confidence, trust
تَعَهَّدَ بِ، لِ	to commit oneself to s.thing	جادّ	serious
تَعَهُّد	commitment, pledge	جافَزَ على	incentive, spur for
ـات .pl		جامِح	unruly, headstrong
تَعَوَّدَ على	to get used to	جَبان	coward
تَعيس	miserable, unhappy	جُبَناءُ .pl	
تُعَساءُ .pl		جَبانة	cowardice
تَغاضَى عن	to ignore	جِدّ	seriousness
تَفاؤُل	optimism	جَدّ	1. grandfather
تَفاؤُليّ	optimistic	أَجْداد, جُدُود .pl	2. ancestor
تَقْدير	appreciation	الجَدّ الأعْلى	1. great-grandfather
تَكَبُّر	arrogance		2. ancestor
تِلْقائي	spontaneous	جَدَّة	grandmother
تَمَكَّنَ من	to be able to	جَذّاب	attractive, enchanting
تَمَلَّقَ	to flatter s.o.	جَذَع	young man
تَمَلُّق	flattery	جُذْعان .pl	
تَمَنٍّ	wish	جُنّاز	funeral rites
تَمَنِّيات .pl		جَنانيزُ .pl	
تَناقُض	contradiction	جِنازة	funeral
		جَنائِزُ, ـات .pl	

جِنْس	sex, gender	حَسَّاسِيَّة	sensitivity
pl. أَجْناس		حَسَدَ (u)	to envy
مارَسَ الجِنْس	to have sex	حَسَد	envy
جِنْسِيَّة	sexuality	حاضِنة	nursemaid
جَهِلَ (a)	to not know, be ignorant	pl. حَواضِنُ	
جَيِّد	good	حَفْلة زَواج	wedding
pl. جِياد		حَفيد	grandson
حادّ الطَّبْع	hot-tempered, irascible	pl. حَفَدة	
حاسِد	envious	حَفيدة	granddaughter
pl. حَسَدة, حُسّاد		حُجّة	pretext
حاشِد	crowded	pl. حُجَج	
حاقِد	spiteful, rancorous	حَزْر	guess
حُبّ	love	حَقّ	right
		pl. حُقوق	
حَبيب (ة)	darling, sweetheart	حَقَدَ (على) (a)	to have feelings of hatred (against)
m.pl. أَحْباب, أَحِبّة, أَحِبّاءُ			
حَثَّ (u)	to urge, incite (to do s.thing)	حِقْد	hatred, rancour
حِداد (على)	mourning (for)	pl. حُقود, أَحْقاد	
حَدَقَ (i)	to glance, look at	حَقير	low, base, contemptible
حَذَّرَ بِ	see أنذر	pl. حُقَراءُ	
حَرَّشَ بَيْن	to sow discord between	حِكاية حُبّ	love affair
حَرَصَ على (i)	to strive towards	حَم	father-in-law
حِرْص	1. see طَمَع	pl. أَحْماء	
	2. aspiration, endeavour	حَماة	mother-in-law
		pl. حَمَوات	
حَزَرَ (i, u)	to guess	حَميم	close friend
حَزِنَ (a)	to be sad	pl. أَحِمّاء	
حُزْن	sadness, sorrow	حَنَق	fury, rage
حَزين	sad	حَنون	affectionate, kind
pl. حَزانى, حُزَناءُ		حَنين	1. yearning
حَسّاس	sensitive		2. nostalgia
			3. homesickness

حَيَّا	to greet	خَذَلَ (u)	to desert, leave in the lurch
حَياء	shyness	خُصُوصيّ	private, personal
حَياة pl. حَيَوات	life	خُصُوصيَّة	privacy
حَيْثِية	angle, viewpoint	خَطَبَ (u)	to ask for a girl's hand in marriage
حَيْران	confused, perplexed	خَطِيب pl. خُطَباء	1. suitor 2. fiancé
حِيلة pl. حِيَل	ruse, trick	خَطِيبة	fiancée
حَيَوِيّ	vital, lively	خُطُوبة	engagement
حَيِى	shy	خَلَق pl. أَخْلاق	character, morals
خابَ (i)	to be dashed, unsuccessful (hopes)	خَلُوق	upright, of firm character
خارِق العادة	extraordinary	خَلِيل pl. خُلان, أَخلاء	1. bosom friend 2. boyfriend
خاضَ (u)	to undergo	خِناق	quarrel, row
خافَ (a)	to be afraid	خَوْف	fear
خال pl. أَخْوال	maternal uncle	خِيانة	1. betrayal 2. adultery
خالة	maternal aunt		
خالِص	sincere	خَيَّبَ	to disappoint (s.o.)
خانَ (u)	to betray	خَيبة	disappointment, failure
خانَقَ	to quarrel, row	خَيَّلَ إلى أَن	to lead s.o. to believe that
خائِف pl. خُوَف	afraid, scared	دِبْلة الخُطُوبة	engagement ring
خائِن pl. خَوَنة, خُوَان	disloyal, treacherous	داعِر pl. دُعَار	immoral, lewd, obscene
خَتَن pl. أَخْتان	son-in-law	داهَنَ	to flatter, fawn on s.o.
خَجِلَ من (a)	to be ashamed of	دَبَّرَ	to arrange, work things out
خَجَل	shame	دَعارة	indecency, immorality
خَجْلان	ashamed, embarrassed	دَعِرَ (a)	to be immoral
		دَلَّعَ	to spoil (child)

دَناية	meanness, vileness	رَفيع	thin
دَنِي pl. أَدْنِياء	mean, despicable	رَقيق pl. رِقاق, أَرِقّاء	fine, delicate
دَهْش	astonishment	روَّقَ دمَه	to placate, cool s.o. off
ذاتِيّ	subjective	زَفّة	wedding procession
ذَريعة pl. ذَرائِعُ	pretext, excuse	زِناء	adultery, promiscuous behaviour
ذكَّرَ	to remind	زَنَى (i)	to commit adultery, be promiscuous
ذكَر pl. ذُكُور	male, masculine	زَواج	marriage, wedding
		زَواج المَصْلَحة	marriage of convenience
ذلَّلَ	to overcome (obstacle)	زَوْج pl. أَزْواج	husband
ذَمَّ (u)	to blame, criticize		
ذَميم	objectionable	زوَّجَ	to marry off (girl)
رابّ	stepfather	زَوْجة	wife
رابَة	stepmother	زَوْجان	married couple
راسِخ	deep-rooted	زَوْجِيّ	marital, conjugal
رَبيب pl. أَرِبّاء	stepson, foster son	ساذَج	naive, gullible
		ساقِط pl. سُقّاط	disreputable
رَبيبة	stepdaughter, foster daughter		
رَجُل pl. رِجال	man	ساقِطة	fallen woman, harlot
		سَئِمَ مِن (a)	to be fed up with
رَجُولة	manhood	سَخِرَ مِن (a)	to mock, ridicule s.o.
رَداءة	wickedness	سُخْط	annoyance, irritation
رَديء	bad, wicked, evil	سَذاجة	naivety
رَذيلة pl. رَذائِلُ	vice	سُرُور	joy
		سَطْحِيّ	superficial
رَزين	calm, composed	سَعيد pl. سُعَداء	happy
رِسالة غَرامِيّة	love letter		
رَغِبَ في (a)	to wish	سِلْف pl. أَسْلاف	brother-in-law (husband's brother)

سِلْفة	sister-in-law (sister of husband)	شَكَّ (u)	to doubt
سُلُوك	behaviour	شَكّ pl. شُكُوك	doubt
سَلِيم النِّية	well-intentioned	شَكَرَ (u)	to thank, be grateful
سِنّ الرُّشْد	age of reason	شُكْر	gratitude
سَهْل الخَلَق	easy-going, obliging	شُكْراً	thank you!
سُوء الحَظّ	bad luck, misfortune	لا شُكْرَ على الواجِب	you're welcome!
سُوء الخَلَق	ill nature	شَهْر العَسَل	honeymoon
سُوء السُّلُوك	misbehaviour	شَهْوة	lust
سُوء الفَهْم	misunderstanding	شُهْوانِيّ	sensuous, lascivious
سُوء المُعامَلة	mistreatment	شَيُوخة	old age
شابّ pl. شَبَاب, شُبَّان	youth, young man	صَبَرَ (i)	to be patient
شارِد الفِكْر	absent-minded	صَبْر	patience
الشَّبِيبة	youth, young people	صَبُور	patient
شَجَن	anxiety, distress	صَداقة	friendship
شَخْصية	personality	صَدَقَ (u)	to tell the truth
شَرْمُوطة	whore	صَدَّقَ	to believe, consider true
شَعَرَ (u)	1. to perceive, sense 2. to realize	صَديق pl. أَصْدِقاء	friend
شُعُور	awareness, perception	صَراحة	frankness, openness
الشُّعُور بالنَّفْس	self-consciousness	صَريح pl. صَرائِح, صُرَحاء	frank, open
شَفَقة	compassion, kindness, tenderness	صَمَّمَ على	to be determined to do s.thing
شَفُوق	kind, tender, compassionate	صَغير السِنّ	young
شَقاوة	mischief, naughtiness	صِهْر	1. brother-in law (sister's husband)
شَقِيّ pl. أَشْقِياء	naughty	pl. أَصْهار	2. son-in-law
شَقيق pl. أَشِقَّاء, أَشِقَّة	full brother (as opposed to half-brother)	صُورة نَمَطِيّة pl. صُوَر-	stereotypical image

ضايَقَ	to annoy, irritate	طَمُوح	ambitious
ضَرَّ	1. harm 2. disadvantage	طُمُوح	ambition
ضَرَاء	adversity	طيبة	goodness
ضَرُورة	necessity	طَيْش	frivolity, recklessness
ضَرُورِيّ	necessary	ظَرْف	elegance, grace
ضَرُورِيّات الحَياة	necessities of life	ظَريف pl. ظَرائفُ، ظُرَفاء	nice, charming
ضَغينة pl. ضَغائنُ	rancour, grudge	ظَنَّ (u)	to think, believe
ضيافة	hospitality	ظَهَرَ (u)	to appear, seem
ضَيْف pl. ضُيُوف	guest	عابِس	sullen, grim
طَبَعَ (a)	to impress	عادي	usual, normal
طَبْع pl. طِباع	nature, character	عاشِق (ة)	lover
طَرَأَ (a)	to happen to s.o.	عاطِف	affectionate, loving
طَرْحة العَرُوسة	bridal veil	عاطفة pl. عَواطِف	1. affection 2. emotion
طِفْل pl. أَطْفال	baby, infant	عاطفيّ	emotional, sentimental
طُفولة	childhood	عاقِل	intelligent
طَلاق	divorce	عاكَسَ	to tease
طَلَقَ (u)	to get a divorce (woman)	عانِس pl. عَوانِسُ	old spinster
طَلَّقَ	to divorce, repudiate (one's wife)	عائد لـ/إلى	belonging to
طَليقة	repudiated wife	عائلة	family
طَمَّاع	greedy	عِتاب	reprimand
طَمَع	1. greed 2. see طُموح	عَجَّبَ	to amaze, astonish
		عَجَزَ على (i)	to be incapable of
		عَجَل	haste
طَمَّنَ	to calm, appease	عَجُوز pl. عُجُز، عَجائزُ	1. old man 2. old

عَديل	brother-in-law (sister's husband)	عَطوف	compassionate
pl. عَدائِل		عِفّة	modesty, chastity
عَديم الشُّعُزر	insensitive	عَفْوِيّة	spontaneity
عَذَرَ (i)	to excuse s.o.	عَقَلَ (i)	to be reasonable
عُذْر	excuse	عَقْلِيّة	mindset, mentality
pl. أَعْذار		عَقْلانيّ	rational
عَذْراء	virgin	عَقْلانيّة	reason, rationality
pl. عَذارى		عَقْلَنَ	to rationalize
عَرَفَ إلى	to introduce s.o. to	عَقْلَنَة	rationalization
عِرْق	race, stock	عَمّ	paternal uncle
pl. عُروق		pl. أَعْمام, عُمومة	
عَروسة	bride	عَمّة	paternal aunt
pl. عَرائِس		عِناد	stubbornness
العَروسان	the bride and groom	عَنَّفَ	to reprimand
عَريس	groom	عَنيد	stubborn
pl. عُرُس		pl. عُنُد	
عَزاء	comfort, consolation	غارَ (a)	to be jealous
عَزَب	bachelor	غَرَض	see هدف
pl. أَعْزاب, عُزّاب		pl. أَغْراض	
عُزْبة	bachelorhood, celibacy	غازَلَ	to flirt
عَزَمَ على (i)	to be determined to do s.thing	غاوٍ	seducer
عَزّى	to offer one's condolences	غَرام	infatuation
عَشِقَ (a)	to love passionately	غَراميات	romances, adventures
عِشْق	passion	غُرور	vanity
عَصَبِيّ	nervous	غَريب	stranger
عَصَبِيّة	nervousness	pl. غُرَباء, أَغْراب	
عَصى (i)	to disobey	غَريزة	1. natural disposition
			2. instinct
عَضَدَ (u)	to support, assist	غُرور	vanity
عَطَلَ	to interrupt	غَضِبَ (a)	to be angry

غَضَب	anger	قاصِر	minor, legally under age
غَضْبان	angry	قَبَّلَ	to kiss
غَفَرَ (i)	to forgive, pardon	قُبْلة	kiss
غَفْر	forgiveness, pardon	قَدَحَ (a)	to reproach, rebuke
غَيْر اِنْضِباطِيّ	undisciplined	قَدَّرَ	to appreciate, value
غَيْر مَعْقُول	unreasonable	قَريب pl. أَقْرِباءُ	relative (n.)
غَيْر مُبالٍ	indifferent	قَساوة	cruelty
غَيْرة	jealousy	قَصْدِيّ	intentional
فَتاة pl. فَتَيات	young girl	قَلَق	anxiety, worry
فَتَّشَ عَن	to look for	قَلِقَ (a)	to be uneasy, anxious
فَرَّجَ عن	to comfort	كاذِب	liar
فَرِحَ (a)	to be happy	كَتُوم	secretive, discreet
فُسْتان الزَّفاف	wedding dress	كَذَّاب	inveterate liar
فَشَّار	braggart	كَذَبَ (i)	to lie, deceive
فَشَرَ (u)	to brag, boast	كِذْب	lie
فَضْل pl. أَفْضال	favour, service	كَرامة	1. dignity, self-respect 2. generosity
فُضُولِيّ	inquisitive, curious	كَريم pl. كُرَماءُ	generous
فَضيلة pl. فَضائِلُ	merit, virtue	كَرِهَ (a)	to hate, dislike
فَطِن	smart, clever	كُرْه	hatred, dislike
فَظيع	horrible	كَنَّة pl. كَنائِنُ	daughter-in-law
فُكاهِي	humorous	لاأَنانِيّ	altruistic
فِكْرة pl. فِكَر	thought	لاأَنانِّية	altruism
قابَلَ	to meet	لاإنْسانِيّ	inhuman(e)
قاسٍ pl. قُساة	cruel	اللاشُعُور	the subconscious
		لاشُعُورِيّ	unconscious, subconscious

لامَ (u)	to blame	مُتَسامِح	lenient, tolerant
لامُبالاة	indifference	مُتَشائم	pessimist
لايُغْفَرُ	unforgivable	مُتَعَوَّد على	accustomed to
لائمة pl. لَوائمُ	reproach, rebuke	مُتَفائل	1. optimistic 2. optimist
لَجَّ (a)	to persist, persevere	مُتَفَوَّق	outstanding
لَطيف pl. لِطاف, لُطَفاءُ	kind, gentle	مُتَكَبِّر	arrogant, haughty
		مُتَكَلَّف	affected, artificial
لَقَب	1. family name, surname 2. nickname	مُتَلَهِّف	impatient
		مُتَمَرِّد	rebellious, recalcitrant
لَقِيَ (a)	1. to find 2. see قابل	مُتَناقِض	contradictory
لَمَسَ (i, u)	to touch	مُتَواضِع	humble
لِواط (ة)	(male) homosexuality, sodomy	مُتَوَحِّد	lonely
		مُثابَرَة	tenacity
لُوطِيّ	(male) homosexual sodomite	مُثير	exciting
لياقة	propriety, decency	مُجازِف	reckless
لِيلة الزِّفاف	wedding night	مُجازَفة	recklessness
مَأْزِق pl. مَأزِقُ	predicament	مَحاسِنُ	good qualities
		مُخيف	frightening, fearful
مَأساة pl. مَآسٍ	tragedy	مُخْتَلَف	different
		مُداهَنة	flattery, sycophancy
مَأساويّ	tragic	مَدْح pl. أمْداح	praise
ماكِر	cunning, sly		
مَألُوف	familiar, accustomed	مَدَحَ (a)	to praise
مَتاعِب	troubles, difficulties	مُدْهِش	astonishing
مُتَأكِّد (من)	convinced (of)	مَدْهُوش	astonished
مُتَرَدِّد	hesitant	مُذْهِل	amazing, baffling
مُتَزَوِّج	married	مُراهِق	adolescent

مُراهَقَة	adolescence, puberty	مكان الميلاد	place of birth
مُرَبَّك	confused, bewildered	مَكَرَ (u)	to deceive
مُرْتاب	doubtful	مَكْر	cunning, slyness
مُرْتاح	comfortable	مَلَّ (a)	to be bored
مُرْضٍ	satisfactory	مَلال	boredom
مَسَكَ (u, i)	1. to hold 2. to grab, seize	مَلْجَأ الأيتام	orphanage
مُشابِه	similar	مُلْهِم	inspirational
مُشابَهة	resemblance	مَليح pl. أمْلاح, ملاح	pleasant, agreeable, nice
مَشاعِرُ	feelings	مُمْتاز	outstanding, excellent
مَشْبوه	suspicious	مُمْتِع	pleasant, enjoyable
مَشْكوك فيه	see مرتاب	مُمِلّ	boring
مُصادَفة	chance encounter	مَمْنون	indebted, grateful
مُصَمِّم على	determined (to do s.thing)	مُنافِق	hypocrite
مُضايَقَة	harassment, annoyance	مُناقِض	contradictory
مَضَض	agony	مَنْزِلة	status, standing
عَلَى مَضَض	reluctantly	مُنْضَبِط	disciplined
مُعانَقة	embrace, hug	مُنْطَوٍ (على النَّفْس)	introverted, self-absorbed
مَعْرِفة	acquaintance	مُنْعِش	refreshing, invigorating
مُعَقَّد	complicated, complex	مُهانة	contempt, humiliation
مَعْقول	reasonable	مُهين	humiliating, degrading
مَعْقوليَّة	rationality	مَوْثوق	trustworthy
مُعيل	breadwinner	مُوجِب pl. ـات	motive, reason
مَغْرور	vain	مُؤْذٍ	hurtful, offensive
مُغْرٍ	tempting	مَوْضوعيّ	objective
مُغازَلة	flirtation	مَوْضوعيّة	objectivity
مَقْصِد pl. مقاصِدُ	intention, goal	مَوْعِد pl. مواعيدُ	appointment, rendezvous

مِيزة	peculiarity, distinguishing feature	هَدَف pl. أَهْداف	aim, objective
مِيعاد pl. مَواعِيد	see مَوعد	هَنَّأَ على	to congratulate s.o. for (s.thing)
نادِم pl. نُدَّام	regretful, remorseful	هَوْن	disgrace, shame
نَباهة	intelligence	واجِب pl. وَجائِب	duty, obligation
نُبْه	insight, acumen	وارِث pl. وُرَّاث, وَرَثة	heir
نَبِيه pl. نُبَهاء	intelligent, perspicacious	واقِعِيّ	realistic
نَجابة	nobility, noble descent	والِد (dual) والِدان .pl	parent
نَجَب	noble		
نَدامة	remorse, regret	وَثِقَ (يَثِقُ) بـ	to trust (in)
نَدَبَ (u)	to mourn	وَجَدَ (يَجِد)	to find
نَدَّدَ بـ	see انتقد	وَجِيه pl. وُجَهاء	1. eminent, distinguished 2. notable
نَدِمَ على (a)	to regret	وَدَّعَ	to say goodbye
نَسِيَ (i)	to forget	وَدُود	affectionate
نَسِيب pl. أَنْساب	1. kinship 2. lineage, descent	وَدِّيّ	friendly, amicable
نَسْل pl. أَنْسال	offspring, descendant	وِراثة	inheritance
نَشاط	liveliness, energy	وَرِثَ (يَرِث) (a)	to inherit
نَشِيد لَيْلِيّ	serenade	وَرَّثَ	to bequeath
نَشِيط	lively, energetic	وَسامة	gracefulness, charm
نَفاد الصَّبْر	impatience	وَسِيم pl. وُسَماء, وِسام	handsome
نِفاق	hypocrisy	وَعَدَ (يَعِد)	to promise
نَمَّ (u)	to gossip	وَعْد	promise
نِية pl. نَوايا	see مَقصد	وَغْد pl. وُغْدان, أَوْغاد	scoundrel
هَدَّدَ	to threaten	وَقاحة	impudence, insolence

وَقِح	impudent, insolent	وَهْم pl. أوْهام	delusion
وَلَد pl. أوْلاد	1. boy 2. child	يَأس	despair
وَلَد الأخ	nephew	يَئِسَ (i, a)	to give up hope
وَلَد الأُخْت		يَتيم pl. يَتامَى, أيْتام	orphan
وَلَد الزِّناء	illegitimate child	يَوْم الزِّفاف	wedding day

Housing and construction

أبادَ	to exterminate (e.g. rats)	اسْتأْجَرَ	to rent
إبادة	extermination (e.g. rats)	أسْفَلْت	asphalt
إبْقاء	maintenance	أسْمَنْت	cement
أثاث	furniture	إضاء	lighting
أثَّثَ	to furnish (house, etc.)	أطْفأ	1. to switch off (e.g. appliance) 2. to extinguish (fire)
أجَّرَ	to rent out		
آجَرّ (coll.)	baked bricks	أطَلَّ على	to look out on
إحْتَرِس من الدّهان	CAREFUL – FRESH PAINT	أطْلال	ruins, remains
احْتَرَقَ	to burn	أعْمال مَنْزِليّة	household chores
أداة المَطْبَخ pl. أدَوات -	kitchen utensil	إفْريز الحائط	moulding
		أغْلَقَ	to close, shut
أداة مَنْزِليّة pl. أدَوات -	household effect	أقْفَلَ	to lock
		أنْبُوبة pl. أنابيبُ	pipe
أدارَ	to switch on (appliance, etc.)		
أرْض	floor, ground	انْتِقال	removal
أرْض بالبِناء	building land	انْتَقَلَ إلى	to move (house)
		انْجِراف	erosion
أساس pl. أسُس	foundation	إيجار	rent (money)

باب	door
pl. أبْواب	
باب دَوّار	revolving door
بَرّاد	fitter (machinery)
بِرْكة	1. pond
pl. بِرَك	2. pool
بِرْواز	frame (picture)
pl. بَراوِيزُ	
بَرْوَزَ	to frame
بِساط	carpet
pl. أبْسِطة	
بُسْتانيّ	gardener
بَطّانية	blanket, duvet
pl. ـات, بَطاطينُ	
بَلَّ (u)	to wet
بَلاطة	1. floor tile
	2. flagstone
بَلَّطَ	to pave
بِناء	building (construction)
pl. أبْنِية	
بَنّاء	bricklayer, mason
بِناية	building (structure)
بَنَى (i)	to build
بَنْيو	bath-tub
pl. ـات	
بَهْو	hall
pl. أبْهاء	
بَوّاب	doorman
بَيْت	house
pl. بُيوت	
تَأْثيث	furnishing

تَأْجير	renting out
تَأَكَّلَ	to be eaten away, corroded
تَبَلَّلَ	to be(come) wet
تَدْفِئة	heating
تَدْفِئة مَرْكَزِيّة	central heating
تُراب	dust, earth
pl. أتْرِبة	
تِرْباس	bolt (door, window)
pl. تَرابيسُ	
تَرْبَسَ	to bolt (door)
تَرْميم	renovation, restoration
تَسَرُّب	leakage
تَصْميم	design
pl. تَصاميم, ـات	
تَكَدَّسَ	to pile, heap up
تَكْسِية	wainscoting, panelling
تَمْليك	conveyance of property
ثُقْب	hole (drilled)
pl. ثُقوب	
جار	neighbour
pl. جيران	
جاوَرَ	to adjoin
جَبَّسَ	to plaster
جِبْس	gypsum, plaster of Paris
جِدار	wall
pl. جُدْران, جُدُر	
جَديد	new
pl. جُدُد	
جَرَس	bell
pl. أجْراس	

جَرَسَ (i)	to ring (the bell)	حَديقة pl. حَدائِق	garden
جَسيم pl. جِسام	large, significant	حَشْو pl. ـات	1. stuffing (e.g. cushions) 2. panel
جَلَسَ (i)	to sit	حَريق pl. حَرائِق	fire
جُمْر	live coal, embers	حِصْن pl. حُصُون	fortress
جِناح pl. أَجْنِحة	wing (house)	حَطَب pl. أَحْطاب	firewood
جِهاز إِطْفاء الحَريق pl. ـ أَجْهِزة	fire extinguisher	حَفّار القُبُور	gravedigger
جِهاز مَنْزِلِيّ pl. أَجْهِزة مَنْزِلِيَّة	household appliance	حَمّام	1. bathroom 2. bath
جَهْد	tension, voltage	حَمام السِّباحة	swimming pool
جهد عالٍ	high tension	حَنَفِيّة	tap (water)
جَهَّزَ	to fit out	حَوْش pl. حيشان, أَحْواش	enclosure
جِوار	neighbourhood	حَوْض pl. أَحْواض	1. basin 2. reservoir
حاجِز	partition	خابِئة pl. خَوابِىءُ	vat
حادّ	sharp	خادِم pl. خُدّام	servant
حاوية	container	خَرّاط	lathe-turner
حائط pl. حيطان	see جدار	خَرَسانة	concrete
حائط عَزْل الحَريق	fire wall	خَرَطَ (i, u)	to turn (lathe)
حائِل pl. حَوائِلُ	folding screen	خُرْطُوم pl. خَراطيمُ	hose
حَبْل pl. حِبال	rope	خَزّان pl. ـات, خَزازينُ	storage tank, reservoir
حَجّار	stonemason	خزان الوَقُود	fuel tank
حَجَر الخَفاف	pumice stone	خَزَف	pottery
حَجَر رَمْلِيّ	sandstone		
حجر الزّاوية	cornerstone		
حَدّاد	blacksmith		

خَزْنة	safe (storage)
خَشَبة pl. أَخْشاب، ـات	plank, board
خَفير pl. خُفَراء	watchman
خَيْشة pl. خيَش، ـات	straw mattress
دَبْش	rubblestone
دَرابَزين	railing, bannister
دُرْج pl. أَدْراج	drawer
دَرَج pl. أَدْراج	staircase
دَرَجة	step (stairs)
دعامة pl. دَعائمُ	prop, support
دَفَعَ (a)	to push
دَقَّ (u)	to knock (on the door)
دكّة pl. دِكَك	bench
دَلْو pl. دلاء	bucket
دَهّان	house painter
دَهَنَ (u)	to paint
دَوْر pl. أَدْوار	see طبقة
دَوْرة المياه	lavatory
دُوش pl. ـات	shower
دُولاب pl. دَوَليبُ	cupboard

رَتَّبَ	to tidy
رجال المطافئ	fire brigade
رَجُل المَطافئ	fireman
رَدَمَ (i, u)	to fill up with earth
رَدَّمَ	to repair
رَدْهة	entrance hall
ردهة الاسْتِقْبال	reception hall
رَسْم تَخْطيطيّ	rough draft, design
رَشَّ (u)	to spray
رَشَحَ (a)	to leak
رَشْح	leak
رَفّ pl. رُفُوف	shelf
رُكْن pl. رُكُون، أَرْكان	1. support, buttress 2. corner, nook
رَمَّ (u, i)	to repair, overhaul
رَمَّمَ	to restore, to renovate
رَمى (i)	to throw away
زاوية pl. زَوايا	corner, nook
زَبالة	see قمامة
زَفَّتَ	to asphalt
زِفْت	pitch
زُلَيْج	ornamental tile
زَيَّقَ	to creak (hinge)
ستارة pl. سَتائرُ	curtain
ستائر مَعْدَنيَّة	Venetian blinds
سَحَبَ (a)	to pull

سَداد التَّوْصيل	plug (el.)	شبّاك	window
		شبابيكُ .pl	
سَجّادة	carpet	شَرْشَف	bedsheet
سَجاجيدُ .pl		شَراشفُ .pl	
سُخّان	boiler	شَركة إيجار	rental company
سرْداب	cellar, basement	شَركة البناء	construction company
سَرَديب .pl		شَقّ	fissure, crack
سَرير	bed	شُقُوق .pl	
سَراير, سُرُر, أَسرَة .pl		شَقَّة	flat
سرير مزْدَوج	double bed	شُقَق .pl	
سرير فَرْديّ	single bed	شَمْعة	candle
سَطْح	(flat) roof	شُموع .pl	
أَسْطُح, أَسْطحة, سُطُوح .pl		شَمْعَدان	candlestick
سَعْدانة الباب	door knob	شَماعدُ .pl	
سَقالة	scaffolding	صاج مُضَلَّع	corrugated iron
سَقْف	1. roof	صَبَّنَ	to soap
سُقُوفٌ .pl	2. ceiling	صَحْن	courtyard
أَسْقُف, سُقُف		صُحُون .pl	
سَكَنَ (u)	to reside, dwell	صُفَّة	moulding, ledge
سلك التَّوْصيل	lead (el.)	صُفَف .pl	
سَلّة	basket	صَقَلَ (u)	to polish, burnish
سلال .pl		صُنْدُوق	box, chest
سلة المُحْمَلات	wastepaper basket	صَناديقُ .pl	
سُلَّم	stairs	صندوق القُمامة	dustbin
سَلالمُ, سَلاليمُ .pl		صُورة	1. picture
سلم مُتَحَرِّك	escalator	صُوَر .pl	2. photograph
سُور	enclosing wall	ضَجيج	noise, din
أَسْوار .pl		ضَريح	mausoleum
سياج	fence	أَضْرحة, ضَرائحُ .pl	
أَسْياج, أَسْوجة, ـات .pl		طابق	see طبقة
شاليه	chalet	طَوابقُ .pl	
شاهَرَ	to rent by the month		

طابِق أرْضِيّ	ground floor	غرفة الأكل	dining room
طاوِلة	table	غرفة الجُلُوس	lounge
طَبَّة	stopper, plug	غرفة النَّوْم	bedroom
طَبَقة pl. طِباق	floor, storey	غطاء pl. أغْطِية	lid, cover
طَريقة البِناء	building style	غطاء المِخَدَّة	pillow case
طَقْم pl. طُقُوم	service (e.g. china)	فانُوس pl. فَوانيسُ	lantern
طَلَى (i)	to coat, overlay	(i) فَتَحَ	1. to open 2. to switch on (e.g. tv)
طَلَى بالذَّهَب	to gild	فُتْحة الخُرْطُوم pl. ـات, فُتَح	hose nozzle
طَلَى بالكَهْرِباء	to galvanize		
طِلاء	coat (e.g. paint)	فَخْم	stately
طَنْطَنَ	to ring, tinkle (bell)	فِراش pl. فُرُش	mattress
طَوَّاب	brickmaker	فُرْشاة	brush
طُوب (coll.)	bricks	فَسِيح pl. فِساح	spacious
طوب أحْمَر	baked bricks		
عارضة pl. عَوارِضُ	doorpost	فَضْلة pl. فَضَلات	waste
عازِل	insulator (el.)	فيلا	villa
عَتَبة	threshold	قابِل للإحْتِراق	flammable
عَدَّاد pl. ـات	counter, meter	قاعدة pl. قَواعِدُ	1. groundwork 2. pedestal, base
عَرَقة	transom	قالَب pl. قَوالِبُ	shoe tree
عَقار pl. ـات	real estate, property	قائمة pl. قَوائِمُ	main support
عمارة pl. عَمائِرُ ات	see بِناء	(i, u) قَبَرَ	to bury
عَمُود pl. أعْمِدة	column	قَبْر pl. قُبُور	tomb, grave
غُرْفة pl. غُرَف	room	قَديم pl. قُدام	old

لَبِنة	brick
للإيجار	FOR RENT
للبَيْع	FOR SALE
لوح النّافذة	window pane
لوحة الاسْم	door plate
مأخَذ pl. مآخِذُ	socket (el.)
مادّة البناء pl. مَواد -	building material
مالك pl. مُلّاك	owner
مأوىً pl. ماوٍ	shelter (e.g. for the homeless)
مائدة pl. مَوائدُ	see طاولة
مُباع	SOLD
مُبلّط	paved
مَجْوة pl. مِجاء, مَجَوات	(horizontal) tombstone
مُجاور	neighbouring
مخَدّة pl. مَخادُّ	pillow, cushion
مخْدَع pl. مَخادِعُ	small room, cabinet
مُخَرْبَشات	graffiti
مُخطّط	layout, design
مَدْخُل pl. مَداخِلُ	entrance
مَدْخَنة pl. مَداخِنُ	chimney
مُدرّج pl. -ات	open-air staircase, fliers

قَذارة	dirt
قَرْمَدَ	1. to plaster / 2. to cover with tiles
قِرْميد (coll.) pl. قَراميدُ	tiles
قَزّاز	glass merchant
قَصْر pl. قُصُور	palace
قَطْرَنَ	to tar
قُفْل pl. أقْفال	1. lock / 2. padlock
قَلْعة pl. قُلُوع, قِلاع	castle
قُمامة	refuse, garbage
قواعد السُّلُوك	etiquette
قَوْس pl. أقْواس	arch
كارتون	cardboard
كُرْسِيّ pl. كَراسٍ	chair
كُرْسِي هَزّاز	rocking chair
كَسا (ب) (u)	to cover, line, drape (with)
كَمَرة	beam
كَنَسَ (u)	to sweep
كَنَفَ (u)	to hedge in
كَهْرُبائيّ	electrician
كَوالِيني pl. كَوَلِينِيّة	locksmith
كُوخ pl. أكْواخ	hut
كِيس القُمامة	bin liner

مِدْفَأَة pl. مَدَافِىءُ	heater, stove	مِطْفَأَة ٢. see جهاز إطفاء الحريق	1. fire engine 2. see
مَدْفَن pl. مَدَافِنُ	burial ground	مَطْلُوب لاسْتِئْجار	WANTED TO RENT
مِرْآة pl. مَرايا, مَرَاءٍ	mirror	مَطْلُوب لشراء	WANTED FOR PURCHASE
مَرانة	pliability, elasticity	مَعْجُون pl. مَعاجينُ	putty
مُرَتَّب	tidy	معمل النِّجارة	timbermill
مِرْحاض pl. مَراحيضُ	urinal	مَغْسَلة	sink
مُريح	comfortable	مِفْتاح pl. مَفاتِيحُ	1. key 2. switch (el.)
مَسَّاح	land surveyor	مَفْرُوش	furnished
مِساحة	surveying	مَفْرُوشات	see أثاث
مِساحة أرْضِيَّة	acreage	مُفَصَّلة	hinge
مُسْتَأْجِر	tenant	مُقاوِل	building contractor
مُسْتَقيم	straight	مُقاوَمة	resistance (el.)
مَسَحَ (a)	to polish	مَقْبَرة pl. مَقابِرُ	cemetery
مَسْقُوف	roofed	مَقْعَد pl. مَقاعِدُ	1. settee 2. armchair
مَسْكَن pl. مَساكِنُ	residence	مقعد طَويل	chaise longue
مِصْباح pl. مَصابيحُ	lamp	مَكَثَ (u)	to stay, remain
مِصْعَد pl. مَصاعِدُ	lift	مِكْنَسة pl. مَكانِيسُ	broom
مِصْهَر pl. ـات	fuse (el.)	مكنسة كَهْرَبائِيَّة	vacuum cleaner
مَصيف	summer home	مِلاط	mortar (material)
مَضْجَع pl. مَضاجِعُ	couch	مَلِض	smooth, slippery
مَطْبَخ pl. مَطابِخُ	kitchen	مَمَرّ pl. ـات	corridor, hallway
		مِمْسَح pl. مَماسِحُ	1. dust cloth 2. scraper

مِمْسَح الأَرْجُل	doormat	نَجَّاد	upholsterer
مُنَبِّه	alarm clock	نَجَّار	carpenter
pl. ‑ات		نِجارة	carpentry
مَحْنًى	curve, bow	نَجَفة	chandelier
pl. مَحانٍ		نَحَّات	1. stonemason
مُنْحَنٍ	bent, crooked		2. sculptor
مِنْفَضَة	ashtray	نَحَّاس	coppersmith
pl. مَنافِضُ		نَحَتَ (a)	to carve (wood)
مُهَنْدِس	engineer	نُشارة	sawdust
مهندس كَهْرَبائيّ	electrical engineer	نَسَّاج	weaver
مهندس مِعْماريّ	architect	نَشَرَ (u)	to saw apart
مُوارَب	ajar (door)	نَظافة	cleanliness
مُؤَجِّر	landlord	نَظَّفَ	to clean
مُؤَسَّسة ذات مَنْفعة عامّة	public utility company	نَظيف pl. نِظاف, نُظَفاءُ	clean
مُوكيت	fitted carpet	هَدَمَ (i)	to demolish, pull down (building)
ناشِف	dry	هَدَم	demolition
ناصِية	street corner	وَزَرة	skirting
pl. نَواصٍ			
نافِذة	see شباك	وسادة	see مخدة
pl. نَوافِذُ		وَسائدُ, ‑ات .pl	
ناقِل أَثاث	removal man	وَضَعَ (يَضعُ)	to put, place

Clothing

إِبْرة	needle	إِسْكاف	shoemaker
أَحْمَر الشِّفاه	lipstick	pl. أَساكِفة	
اِرْتَدى	to put on (shoes, clothes)	إِعْتَمَّ	to put on/wear a turban

أَلْبِسة جاهِزة	ready-made clothes	تَقْويرى	neckline
اَلة الخِياطة	sewing machine	تَكْسِية	lining, draping, covering
أمالَ	to tip, tilt (e.g. hat)	تَنْظيف كِيمِيائيّ	dry cleaning
أناقة	elegance	ثَنْية	crease
أنِقَ (a)	to be elegant (dress)	pl. ثَنَيات	
أنيق	elegant, chic	تُوكة الشَّعْر	hairclip
بابُوج	slipper	تُول	tulle
pl. بَوابيج		ثَوْب	see ملبس
بَدْلة	suit	pl. ثِياب	
pl. بِدَل		ثَوْب الحِداد	mourning clothes
بَدْلة تَشْريفاتِيّة	gala dress	ثِياب السَّهْرة	evening clothes
بَدْلة الحَمّام	bathing suit	جاكيت	jacket
بدلة الغَوْص	diving suit	جِلْد	1. leather
بدلة مُلْكِيّة	civilian clothes	pl. أجْلاد, جُلُود	2. animal skin
بُرْنيْطة	European hat	جِلْد طَبيعيّ	genuine leather
pl. بَرانيطُ		جلد لَمّاع	patent leather
بَطانة	lining	جَوْرَب	stocking
بَنْطَلون	European-style trousers	pl. جَوارِبُ	
بَنْطَلون قَصير	shorts	جَوْهَرة	jewel
بِجامة	pyjamas	pl. جَواهِرُ	
بلوزة	blouse	جَيْب	pocket
بَياض	linen	pl. جُيُوب	
بَياضات	linen goods	جينْز	jeans
بَيْت الزّينة	beauty parlour	حاكَ (i)	to weave, knit
تَسْريحة	hairdo	حائِك	weaver
تَطْريز	embroidery	pl. حاكة	
تَقَلَّدَ	to adorn o.self with a necklace	حَبَكَ (i, u)	to braid, knit
		حِجاب	headscarf, hijab
		pl. أحْجِبة, حُجُب	

حِذاء pl. أَحْذِيَة	shoe
حِذاء بالرَّقْبَة	boot
حَرير	silk
حِزام pl. حُزُم, أَحْزِمة, ـات	belt
حِلْية pl. حِلىً	decoration, embellishment
حَمَّالة صَدْر	bra
حِياكة	weaving
خاتِم pl. خَواتِم	ring
خَرْز (coll.)	beads (strung)
خُرْم الإبْرة	eye of the needle
خَشِن pl. خِشان	coarse, rough (<> fine)
خُوان الزِّينة	dressing table
خَلْخَل pl. خَلاخِلُ	anklet
خَلَعَ (مَلابِسَه) (a)	to take off (clothes)
خَلَق (m./f.) pl. أَخْلاق, خُلْقان	threadbare
خَيَّاط	tailor
خَيْط pl. خِيطان, أَخْياط, خُيُوط	thread
خَيَّطَ	to sew
دَبَّاغ	tanner
دَبَغَ (a, i, u)	to tan (leather)
دَبُّوس pl. دَبابيسُ	pin
دَبُّوس صَدْر	brooch

دَبُّوس انْكليزِي	safety pin
دَعَكَ (a)	to scrub (laundry)
دُمْلُج pl. دَمالِجُ	bracelet
ديباج	brocade
رِباط الحِذاء	shoelace
رِباط العُنُق	necktie
رَبَطَ (i)	to tie
رَبْطة السَّاق	garter
رَسَقَ (i)	to fasten, insert
رَشاشة	atomizer
رَصَّعَ	to inlay (e.g. with precious stones)
رَفَأَ (a)	1. to darn (socks) 2. to mend (clothes)
رَفْرَف pl. رَفارِفُ	visor (hat)
رَقَعَ (a)	to patch (a garment)
رُقْعة pl. رِقاع, رُقُع	piece of cloth
رَوْنَق	splendour, beauty
زِرّ pl. أَزْرار	button
زِرّ كُمّ القَميص pl. أَزْرار-	cufflink
زَوْج	one of a pair
زَوْجان	couple
زِينة	toilette
سادِج	plain, not coloured (fabric)
ساعة	watch

ساعة الجَيْب	pocket watch	صِبْغ	dye
سُتْرة pl. سُتَر	see جاكيت	صُدْرة	waistcoat
سَحّاب	zipper	صَقَلَ (u)	to polish
سَدَّدَ	to thread (yarn through needle)	صَلَّحَ	to repair
سَرَّحَ شَعْره	to do one's hair	صَمَّمَ (لـ)	to design (clothing) (for)
سِرْوال	trousers	صُوف	wool
سِكَّافة	shoemaking	ضَعْف pl. أَضْعاف	fold (of a garment)
سِلْسِلة pl. سَلاسِلُ	chain	طاقِية pl. طُواقِي	skull-cap
سِمْط pl. سُمُوط	string (necklace)	طَرَزَ	to embroider
سَمَلَ (u)	to be worn, in tatters (clothes)	طَقْم pl. طُقُوم	1. set (of cufflinks, pens, etc.) 2. see بدلة
سَمَل pl. أَسْمال	worn clothes, rags	طِلاء الأظافِر	nail polish
سُنْدُس	silk brocade	طَوْق	1. see ياقة 2. frame (spectacles)
شال pl. شِيلان	shawl	طَيّة	1. pleat 2. lapel
شِبْشِب pl. شَباشِبُ	slipper	ظِلّ العَين	eyeshadow
شَدَّ (i)	to tighten	عَباء pl. أَعْبِئة	all-body woollen wrap
شُرَاب pl. ـات	see جورب	عُرْوة pl. عُرى	buttonhole
شَرِيط pl. شَرائِط	ribbon	عِطْر pl. عُطُورات, عُطُور	scent, perfume
شَمْسِيّة	parasol	عِقْد pl. عُقُود	necklace
صائِغ	goldsmith	عَلَّاقة (الثِّياب)	coathanger
صَبّاغ	dyer	عَلامة	label (in item of clothing)
صَبَغَ (u, i, a)	to dye	عَلَّقَ	to hang up (clothes)

عمامة	turban	قَصَب الذَّهَب	gold brocade
عَمائِمُ .pl			
غُرْزة	stitch	قُفّاز	gloves
غُرَز .pl		قَفافيزُ ,-ات .pl	
غَزّال	spinner	قُفْطان	caftan
		قَفاطينُ .pl	
غَزَلَ (i)	to spin	قلادة	see عقد
غَزْل	yarn	قَلائِدُ .pl	
غُزُول .pl		قُماش	fabric, cloth
غَسّال	laundryman	اقْمِشة .pl	
غَسّالة	washing machine	قَميص	shirt, blouse
		أقْمِصة ,قُمُص ,قُمْصات .pl	
غَسَلَ (i)	to wash, launder	قَميص النَّوْم	nightgown
غَسيل	laundry, washing	كَبْسُول(ة)	press stud
غَطا (u)	to cover (up)	كُبْشة	hook, clasp
غطاء	covering	كُبَش .pl	
أغْطِية .pl		كَتّان	linen
فاتِن	seductive, charming	كَسْم	cut, style (of a dress)
فَواتِن .pl			
فانِلّة	vest, undershirt	كُشْتُبان	thimble
		كَشاتينِ .pl	
فَرْو (coll.)	fur	كَشْكَش	seam, hem
فِراء .pl		كَشاكِشُ .pl	
فُسْتان	dress, gown	كُمّ	sleeve
فَساتينُ .pl		أكْمام .pl	
فُسْتان السَّهْرة	evening dress	كَنْزة	sweater
فَصّ	stone (of a ring)	كَوّاء	ironer
فُصوص .pl			
فَكَّ (u)	to untie, undo	كَوَى (i)	to iron
قَبْقاب	wooden clog	كَيّ	pressing (clothes)
قَباقيبُ .pl		لِباس الرَّأْس	headgear
قُطْن	cotton	لِباس السَّهْرة	party dress
قُرْط	earring, pendant	لِباس وطَنِيّة	national costume
قُرُوط ,قِراط ,أقْراط .pl		لَبِسَ (a)	to get dressed

لَبَّسَ	to dress someone	مُكَسَّم	well shaped
لَوْح الكَيّ pl. ألْواح -	ironing board	مكْوىً pl. مَكاوٍ	iron (device)
ماسِح	bootblack	مَلابِس خارِجِيَّة	outer clothes
ماكياج	make-up	مَلابِس داخِلِيَّة	underwear
مُجَوْهَرات	jewellery	مَلابِس عَسْكَرِيَّة	military uniform
مُخْمَل	velvet (n.)	مَلابِس رِسْمِيَّة	uniform
مَرْيَلة	apron, pinafore	مَلابِس الزِّفاف	wedding clothes
مَرْيُول	bib	مَلْبَس pl. مَلابِسُ	garment
مُزْدَوِج	double	مِلْفَع	headshawl
مَزَقَ (i)	to tear	مِنْديل pl. مَناديلُ	handkerchief
مَزْق	tear		
مَزَّقَ	to shred	مُهَنْدَم	well dressed, tidy
مُزَيَّنات	ornaments, jewellery	مُوضة	fashion
مِشْجَب pl. مَشاجِبُ	1. clothes hook 2. clothes rack	نَسَجَ (u)	to weave
مُشَجَّر	with plant designs (fabric)	نَسيج pl. أنْساج, أنْسِجة, نُسُج	woven fabric
مُصَمِّم الإزْياء	fashion designer	نِقاب	face veil
مِظَلَّة	umbrella, parasol	نَمُوذَج pl. نَمَاذِج, -ات	pattern
مِعْطَف pl. مَعاطِفُ	overcoat	وَرْشة غَسيل	laundry (place)
مِعْطَف فَرْو	fur coat	وِشاح pl. وَشائِحُ, أوْشِحة, وُشُح	cummerbund
مِغْزَل pl. مَغازِلُ	spindle	وَشَّحَ	to get dressed up
مُقَوَّر	low-necked (e.g. dress)	ياقة	collar

School and education

General

اِجْتِهاد	diligence	إلْهام	inspiration
أجَل	deadline	‑ات .pl	
آجال .pl		اِمْتِحان	examination
إحْصائيّ	statistician	‑ات .pl	
أحْمَق	stupid	اِمتحان تَحْرِيرِيّ	written exam
حُمُق ,حَمْقاء. f		اِمتحان شَفَهِيّ	oral exam, viva
إخْتِصاصِيّ	specialist	إمْلاء	dictation
أخْطَأ	to make mistakes	أمْلى على	to dictate
إذْن	permission	أُمِّيّ	illiterate
أساس	base, basis	أُمِّيَّة	illiteracy
‑ات .pl		أمين المَكْتَبة	librarian
أسْتاذ	professor, university lecturer	اِنْتِقاد	criticism
أساتِذة .pl		اِنْتَقَلَ إلى الصَّفّ العالِي	to go to a higher form/class
أُسْتاذ مُشارك	associate professor		
أُسْتاذ مُساعِد	assistant professor	إنْشاء	composition, writing class
اِسْتِراحة	break, recreation	أوْضَحَ	to explain, clarify
اِسْتِعارَ	to borrow (e.g. books)	إيضاح	explanation
اِسْتَقْضى عُطْلة	to spend holidays	‑ات .pl	
اِسْتَهْجى	to spell	باحِث	researcher
اِسْتَوْعَبَ	to comprehend, take in	الباقِي	remainder (math.)
أُطْرُوحة	dissertation	بَرَّاية (الأقْلام)	pencil sharpener
إعارة	borrowing period (e.g. library)	بِرْجَل	compasses, dividers
		بَراجِل .pl	
أعَدَّ	to prepare (one's lesson)	بَرْنامِج	1. programme
		بَرامِج .pl	2. curriculum
أُفُقِيّ	horizontal	بَساطة	simplicity
آلة الكِتابة	typewriter	بِطاقة الطُّلاب	student card

بَكالُورِيُوس	Bachelor's degree	تَغَيَّبَ عَن المَدْرَسة	to play truant
بِمَثابة	tantamount to	تَفاضُل	rivalry for precedence
بِمُناسِبة	on the occasion of	تَقْرير مَدْرَسِيّ	school report
بِواسِطة	by means of	تَكاسُل	laziness
بَيَّضَ	to make a fair copy (of a text)	تَكْرير	repetition
بَيْضاوِي	oval	تِلْميذ	pupil
		pl. تَلامِذة	
بَيْنَ	between, among	تَمْرين	exercise
تَأَخَّرَ عن الدَّرْس	to be late for class	pl. تَمارين	
تالٍ	next	تَمَكَّنَ من	to be capable of
تَبْسيط	simplification	تَهْجِية	spelling
تَبْسيطِيّ	simplified	تَوْطِئة	preface
تَبْييضة	fair copy	جامِعة	university
تَجْرِبة	test, trial	جاهِل	ignorant
pl. تَجارِب		pl. جَهّال, جُهَلاءُ, جَهَلة, جُهَّل	
تَحَذْلَقَ	to be pedantic	جاوَزَ	to exceed, go beyond
تَحْليل	analysis, parsing	جائِز	prize
تَخَرَّجَ (من)	to graduate (from)	pl. جَوائِزُ	
تَخْريج	graduation	جَدْوَل	1. roster
تَدْريب مِهْنِيّ	vocational training	pl. جَداوِلُ	2. schedule, timetable
تَدْريجِياً	gradually	جَرَّبَ	to test, try out
تَرْبِية	education, upbringing	جَرَس	bell
تَرْبِية بَدَنِيّة	physical education	pl. أَجْراس	
تَفاعُلِيّ	side effect	جَمَعَ (i)	to collect, gather
تَقْريباً	approximately	جَمْع	adding (math.)
تَرَكَّزَ عَلَى	to concentrate on	جَهْد	effort
تَعْليم عالٍ	higher education	pl. جُهُود	
تَعْليم مُخْتَلَط	coeducation	جَيْد	B (result)
تَعْليم مُسْتَمِرّ	continuing education	جَيْد جِدّاً	A (result)
		حاسِبة	calculator

حاسِبة الجَيْب	pocket calculator	دار الحَضانة	crèche, day nursery
حاصِل	result (multiplication, division)	دائِرة pl. دَوائِرُ	circle
حاوَلَ	to try	دَبّاسة	stapler (device)
حِبْر	ink	دُرْج pl. أَدْراج	drawer
حُجْرة الأَساتذة	teachers' room, common room	دَرَجة	1. mark, result 2. see صف
حُجْرة الدِّراسة	classroom	دَرَسَ (u)	to study, learn
حَجْز	detention	دَرَّسَ	to teach
حَدّ أَدْنَى	minimum	دَرْس pl. دُروس	lesson
حَدّ أَقْصَى	maximum		
حَذْلَقة	pedantry	دَفّة	cover (book)
حِصّة pl. حِصَص	class period	دُكْتوراة	doctorate
حَضانة	bringing up, nursing	دكتوراة فَخْرِيّة	honorary doctorate
حَفِظَ (a)	to learn by heart, to have in memory	دَواة pl. دُوِي, دَوَيات	inkwell
حَفِيف	rustling (e.g. papers)	ذاكَرَ	to study (one's lesson)
حَقِيبة المَدْرسة	satchel	ذُهُول	consternation, perplexity
حَياة طُلّابِيّة	student life	راجَعَ	to revise
خاطِىء	wrong	رَبَّى	to bring up (child)
خَتْم pl. أَخْتام, خُتُوم	stamp (imprint)	رَتَّبَ	to arrange, organize
خَتّامة	stamp (device)	رَجَعَ	1. to hand in (e.g. assignment) 2. to look up
خَرَّج	to train	رَدّ الفِعْل	reaction
خَطّ pl. خُطُوط	line	رُزْمة pl. رِزَم	ream
الخَطّ المائِل	oblique, slash	رَسْم pl. رُسُوم	drawing
خَطَأ	mistake, error		
خُلاصة	excerpt	رَفَضَ (i, u)	to refuse

رَسَبَ (u)	to fail (an exam)
رَسْم تَخْطِيطِيّ	rough sketch, draft
رُسُوب	failure (exam)
رَفِيق المَدْرَسة pl. رُفَقاءُ	classmate, school friend
رَكَّزَ في	see تركز
رَوْضة الأطْفال pl. رِياض الأطْفال	kindergarten, nursery school
رِياضِيّ	mathematician
رِيشة pl. رِيَش	nib
زاوية pl. زَوايا	angle
زاوية حادَّة	acute angle
زاوية قائمة	right angle
زاوية مُنْفَرِجة	obtuse angle
زَميل الدِّراسة pl. زُمَلاءُ	see رفيق المدرسة
سَبُّورة	1. blackboard 2. slate
سَجَّلَ في	to register, enrol in
سَقَّطَ	to fail somebody (exam)
سلّة المُهْمَّلات	wastepaper basket
سَمَّعَ	to recite, say one's lesson
سَهْل	easy
سُهُولة	easiness
سَوَّدَ	to make a draft of something
شارِد الفِكْر	absent-minded
شاطِر	clever
شَبَكَ (i)	to attach, staple
شَحْطة	dash (punctuation)
شائِع	widespread
شَديد pl. شِداد، أشِدّاء	strong, intense
شَرَحَ (a)	to explain, comment
شَرْح pl. شُرُوح	1. see إيضاح 2. commentary (e.g. text)
شَريط لاصِق	adhesive tape
شَطارة	cleverness
شَطَبَ (u)	1. to erase (e.g. a word) 2. to cross out
شَكْل pl. أشْكال	1. form, shape 2. illustration (book)
شَيْء pl. أشْياءُ	thing
صَحِيح	right (<> wrong)
صَعْب pl. صِعاب	difficult
صُعُوبة	difficulty
صَغِير pl. صُغَراء، صِغار	small
صَفّ pl. صُفُوف	class, form
صُلْب	hard, firm, rigid
ضَبَطَ (i, u)	to set, regulate
ضَجَّ (i)	to be noisy
ضَرْب	multiplication
ضَخْم pl. ضِخام	thick, big, voluminous

ضَلِيع	skilled, knowledgeable	عَلامة	mark, grade
طالِب pl. طُلّاب	student	عَلِمَ (a)	see عرف
طالَعَ	to study, peruse	عَلَّمَ	see درّس
طَباشِير	chalk (for blackboard)	عَمَلِيّ	practical
طَرْح	subtraction	عَمُود pl. عَوامِد	column (writing)
طَرَدَ (u)	to expel	عَمِيد pl. عَمَداء	dean
طَرَد	expulsion		
طَفْرة نَوْعِيّة	quantum leap	غامِض pl. غَوامِض	mysterious, abstruse
عاصٍ pl. عُصاة	disobedient	غَرا (u)	to glue
عاقِل pl. عُقَلاء	intelligent	غِراء	glue
عالِم pl. عُلَماء	scientist	غَشَّ (u)	to cheat
عِبارة	1. expression 2. phrase	غَلَط pl. أَغْلاط	see خطأ
عَبْقَرِيّ pl. عَباقِرة, -ون	genius	غَلْطة pl. غَلَطات	see خطأ
عَبْقَرِية	genius, ingenuity	غَيْر واضِح	unclear
عَدَد pl. أَعْداد	number	فَرَقَ (u)	to separate, divide
عَدَد صَحِيح pl. أَعْداد صَحِيحة	integer	فَصْل pl. فُصُول	1. see صفّ 2. chapter (book)
عَرَفَ (i)	to know	فَعَلَ (i)	to do, make
عُطْلة	holidays, vacation	فَلَكِيّ	astronomer
عُطْلة الصَّيْف	summer vacation	فِهْرِس pl. فَهارِس	index
عَقْل	reason, intelligence	فَهِمَ (a)	to understand
عَكْس	opposite	فَهَّمَ	to explain, instruct
بالعَكْس	on the contrary	فَيْلَسُوف pl. فَلاسِفة	philosopher

قَارَنَ	to compare	كُتَيِّب	booklet
قَاسِم	denominator (*math.*)	كَرَّرَ	to repeat
قَاعِدة pl. قَوَاعِدُ	rule	كُرَّاسة pl. كَرَارِيس	copybook, notebook
قاعة المَرَاجِع	reference section (library)	كَسْر pl. كُسُور	fraction
قاعة المُطَالَعة	reading room, study room		
قَاعِدة pl. قَوَاعِدُ	rule (e.g. grammar)	كَسْلان pl. كَسَالى f. كَسْلانة, كَسْلا	lazy
قَائِم	perpendicular	كَشَّفَ (i)	to reveal
قَبِلَ (a)	to admit (e.g. to a school)	كُلِّيّة	1. faculty 2. college
قَبُول	admission		
قَدَّرَ	to esteem highly	بالكُلِّيّة	entirely
قُدْرة	ability	كُلِّيّة التِّجارة	business school
قَرَأَ (u)	to read	كُلِّيّة الشُّرْطة	police academy
قَرَأَ عَلَى	to study under s.o.	كُلِّيّة الطِّبّ	medical school
قِراءة	reading	كِيمِيائِيّ	chemist
قِسْمة	division	لاحَظَ	to observe, remark
قُطْر pl. أَقْطار	diameter	لَقَب التَّعْلِيم	academic title
قَلَم pl. أَقْلام	pen	ماجِسْتِير	Master's degree
		مادَّة pl. مَوادُّ	school subject
قلم الألْوان	crayon	مائِل	slanting
قلم جافّ	ball-point pen	مُتَحَذْلِق	pedant
قلم الحِبْر	fountain pen	مُتَخَرِّج (من)	graduate (from)
قلم الرَّصاص	pencil	مُتَوازى السُّطُوح	parallelepiped
قَوْس pl. أَقْواس	arc, arch	مُتَوازى الأضْلاع	parallelogram
كتاب pl. كُتُبُ	book	مُثَلَّث pl. ـات	triangle
		مُجْتَهِد	zealous

مَجْدِيّ	praiseworthy	مُسْتَحِيل	impossible
مُجَلَّد	volume (book)	مُسَجِّل	registrar
pl. ـات		مِسْطَرة	ruler
مَجْمُوع	sum total	pl. مَساطِرُ	
مَحا (u)	to erase	مُسْتَطِيل	rectangle
مُحاضِر	lecturer	مُسَوَّدة	draft, rough copy
مُحاضَرة	lecture	مِشْبَك	staple
مِحْوَر	axis	pl. مَشابِكُ	
pl. مَحاوِر		مِشْبَك الوَرَق	paper clip
مُحِيط الدّائِرة	circumference	مُشْرِف	supervisor (e.g. PhD)
مَخْرُوط	cone (*math.*)	مُطافَأة	reward
مَدَّد	to extend (e.g. borrowing period)	مَطْرُوح	subtrahend (*math.*)
		المطروح مِنْهُ	minuend
مُدَرِّس	teacher	مُطِيع	obedient
مَدْرَسة	school	مَعارِف عامّة	general knowledge
pl. مَدارِس		مَعْهَد	institute
مدرسة ابْتِدائيّة	primary school	pl. مَعاهِدُ	
مدرسة ثانَوِيّة	secondary school	مُعَيَّن	rhombus
مدرسة مِهْنِيّة	vocational college	مُفَتِّش	inspector
مُذاكِرة	learning, study	مَفْهُوم	notion, concept
مُرَبَّع	square	pl. مَفاهِيمُ	
pl. ـات		مُقارَنة	comparison
مَرْتَبة	class (degree)	مَقْبُول	pass (mark)
pl. مَراتِبُ		مُقَدِّمة	introduction
مَرْجِع	reference work	مَقْسُوم	dividend (*math.*)
pl. مَراجِعُ		مَقْسُوم عَلَيْه	divisor (*math.*)
مُرَكَّب	compound	مِقْلَمة	pen case
مَرْئِي	visible	مَكْتَب	desk
مَسّاحة	wiper (blackboard)	pl. مَكاتِبُ	

مَكْتَبَة	1. library	مُوازَنة	balance, equilibrium
pl. ـات, مَكاتِب	2. bookstore	مُوجَز	summary
مُكَثَّف	intensive (course)	مُؤَرِّخ	historian
مُكَعَّب	cube	مَوْسُوعة	encyclopaedia
مُلاحَظة	remark	مَوْضُوع	topic, subject
مَلْجَأ الأطْفال	children's home	pl. مَواضيعُ	
مُلْحَق	appendix	ناظِر	principal, headteacher
pl. مَلاحِقُ		pl. نُظّار	
مُلْحَق صُورِيّ	legend (caption)	نالَ (u)	to grant, award
مُلَخَّص	abstract (n.)	نَباتِيّ	botanist
مُمْتاز	with distinction (grade)	نُبْذة	leaflet
مِمْحاة	eraser	pl. نُبَذ	
pl. مَماحٍ		نَتيجة الحائط	wall calendar
مُمْكِن	possible	pl. نَتائِجُ -	
مُنْتَبِه	alert	نَجاح	success
مِنْحة	grant, allowance	نَجَحَ في (a)	to pass (exam)
pl. مِنَح		نُزْهة مَدْرَسِيّة	school trip
مِنْحة جامِعِيّة	university grant, scholarship	نُسْخة	copy
مِنْحة دِراسِيّة	study grant	pl. نُسَخ	
مُنْحَرِف	trapezium	نَشّافة	blotting pad
مِنْقَلة	protractor	نَصّ	text
مَنْهَج التَّعْليم	teaching curriculum	pl. نُصُوص	
مَنْهَجِيّ	methodological	نِصْف قُطْر الدّائِرة	radius
مَنْهَجِيّة	methodology	نَظَرِيّ	theoretical
مُهِمّ	important	نَظَرِيّة	theory
مُهْمِل	sloppy, neglectful	نَفْس	same
مُوازاة	equal distance, parallelism	نِقابة الطُّلاب	student union
مُوازِل	parallel to	نَقَلَ (u)	to copy
		نِهائِيّ	infinite

هادِىء	calm, quiet	وَرَق (.coll)	paper
هامِش	margin	pl. أوْراق	
pl. هَوامِش		وَرق الرَّسْم (.coll)	drawing paper
هامِشِيّ	marginal	وَرق الشّاهِدة (.coll)	carbon paper
هائِل	formidable, extraordinary	وَرق شَفَّاف (.coll)	tracing paper
هِواية	hobby	وَرق عادِم (.coll)	wastepaper
هيئة تَعْليمِية/		وَرق الكِتابة (.coll)	writing paper
تَدْريسِيَّة	teaching staff, faculty	وَرق اللَّفّ (.coll)	wrapping paper
واجِب	homework, assignment	وَرق النَّشّاف (.coll)	blotting paper
pl. ـات		وَقْت فَضاء	leisure time

Sciences and academic subjects

إحْصائِيَّة	statistics	رياضِيات	mathematics
أدَب/آداب	literature	طِبّ	medicine (science)
أدب مُقارِن	comparative literature	طِبّ الأسْنان	dentistry
إدارة	management	طِبّ الأمْراض	
إدارة فُنْدُقِيَّة	hotel management	الجِلْدِيَّة	dermatology
بيُولوجيا	biology	طِبّ شَرعِيّ	forensic medicine
التّاريخ	history	طِبّ نَفْسانِيّ	psychiatry
الجَبْر	algebra	عِلْم	science
جيُولُوجيا	geology	pl. عُلُوم	
الحِساب	arithmetic	عِلم الآثار القَديمة	archaeology
حِساب التَّفاضُل	differential calculus	عِلم الآثار المِصْرِيَّة	egyptology
الحُقُوق	law	عِلم إدارة الأعْمال	business administration
الدّين	religious education	عِلم الإرْصاد الجَوِّيَّة	meteorology
الرَّسْم	drawing	عِلم التَّرْجَمة	translation science
		عِلم اجْتِماعِيّ	sociology
رِياضة	gymnastics, PE	عالِم الأحْياء	biologist

علم الأدْوِيَّة	therapeutics	علم الكائنات الدَّقيقة	microbiology
علم الاقْتِصاد	economics	علم الكمبيوتر	computer science
علم الأمْراض	nosology	علم الكِيمياء	chemistry
علم الإنْسان	anthropology	علم الكيمياء الحَيَوِيَّة	biochemistry
علم البَكْتيريا	bacteriology	علم المَعادِن	mineralogy
علم التَّرْبية	educational science	علم المَنْطِق	logic
علم التَّشْريح	anatomy	علم النَّبات	botany
علم الجُغْرافيا	geography	علم النَّفْس	psychology
علم الجَمال	aesthetics	علم الوِراثة	genetics
علم الحَشَرات	entomology	علم وَظائِف الأعْضاء	physiology
علم الحَيَوان	zoology	علْم الوِلادة	obstetrics
علم الزِراعة	agronomy	العُلُوم الاجْتِماعيَّة	social sciences
علم السُمُوم	toxicology	الفَلْسَفة	philosophy
علم السِيّاسة	political science	لِسانِيات	linguistics
علم الطَبيعة	physics	مَعْلُوماتِيّة	Information Technology (IT)
علم الطُّيُور	ornithology	هَنْدَسة	engineering
علم العُيُون	ophthalmology	هَنْدَسة مَدَنِيّة	civil engineering
علم الفَلَك	astronomy	هندسة ميكانيكيّة	mechanical engineering
علم الفيزيا	physics	الهَنْدَسِيّة	geometry

Computing

اتَّصَلَ	to connect	إدارة البَيانات	data management
أجْهِزة الكُمْبيوتِر	hardware	أدْمَجَ	to insert
اِخْتِصار	shortcut	أرْفَقَ	to attach (e.g. file)
أخْرَجَ	to exit	أزال	to delete
أداة	tool		
pl. أدَوات		اِسْتَبْدَلَ	to substitute, swap

اِسْتَرْجَعَ	1. to retrieve (e.g. data) 2. to restore	بَرِيد مُزْعِج	spam
اِسْتَعْرَضَ	to browse	بوابة	portal site
اِسْتَوْرَدَ مِن	to import (document) from	بورت	port
أُسْطُوانة	disk	تَجَوَّلَ	to surf
أسطوانة رَئِيسِيَّة	master disk	تَحَكُّم الطِّبَاعة	printer control
اِسْم المُسْتَخْدِم	user name	تَحَكُّم عَن بُعْد	remote control
أَصْدَرَ	to export (a document)	تَحْوِيل	conversion
إِعْدادات	settings	تَخْزِين	storage
أَلْغَى	1. to cancel 2. to delete	تَرْتِيب أَبْجَدِيّ	alphabetization
		تَرْتِيب رَقْمِيّ	numerical sorting
أَمْر pl. أُمُور	command	تَرْقِيم	digitization
أَنالُوجِيّ	analog	تَسْطِير تَحْتِي	underlining
إِنْترانت	intranet	تَشْفِير	encryption
إِنْتَرْنَت	Internet	تَطْبِيق	application
إِنْجاز	execution, performance	تَعْدِيل pl. ـات	change
أَوْقَفَ	to shut down (computer, program)	تَعْمِية	see تشفير
		تَغْمِيق	to make bold (text)
إِيقونة	icon	تَوْقِيع رَقْمِيّ	digital signature
بايت	byte	جِسْر pl. جُسُور	bridge
بَرامِج مُلْحَقة	accessories		
بَرْمَجَ	to program	جِهاز pl. أَجْهِزة	device
بَرْمَجة	programming	جِهاز مُعالَجة النُّصُوص	word processor
بَرْمَجِيَّة	software		
بَرْنامِج pl. بَرامِج	program	جِيغابايت	gigabyte
		جِيغاهرتز	gigahertz
بَرِيد إِلِكْتْرونِي	electronic mail	جِهاز pl. أَجْهِزة	device, piece of hardware
بَرِيد صَوْتِيّ	voice mail		

جِهاز بَحْث	محرك البحث see	رابِطة	link
جِيل pl. أَجْيال	generation (e.g. of computers)	رائِد pl. رُوّاد	surfer (Internet)
حاجِز ناريّ	firewall	رِسالة الكترونيّة pl. رَسائِلُ –	e-mail message
حاسِب (إلِكْترونيّ) see كمبيوتر pl. حَواسِب (إلكترونيّة)		رِسالة قَصيرة	text message
حاسِب شَخْصيّ	personal computer	رَقَّمَ	to digitize
حاسوب	see كمبيوتر	رقْم المَرْجِع	reference number
حالة	mode	رَقْمي	digital, numerical
حِبْر	ink, toner (printer)	رَمْز	symbol
حَجْم الوَثيقة	document size	رُموز pl.	
حَرْف كَبير pl. حُروف كَبيرة	capital letter	سُرْعة	speed (computer, drive)
حَرَّرَ	to edit (text)	سُرْعة الاتِّصال	connection speed
حِساب المُسْتَخْدِم	user account	سلّة المُهْمَلات	recycle bin
(a) حَفِظَ	to save	شاشة	screen
حَقْل pl. حُقُول	field (on screen)	شاشة مُساعَدة	help screen
حَمَّلَ	1. to load (e.g. page) 2. upload	شَريط الأَدوات pl. شَرائطُ	toolbar
حَوَّلَ	to convert	شَريط المهامّ	task bar
خاصّيّة pl. خَصائِصُ	property	شَقَّرَ	to encrypt
(u) خَرَجَ	to exit (a program)	شَبَكة	network
خَزَّنَ	to store	شبكة العَنْكَبُوت العالَميّة	World Wide Web
(u) خَلَقَ	to create (document, etc.)	صَفْحة pl. صَفَحات	page
(u) دَخَلَ	to enter (e.g. words)		
دَرَجة الوُضُوح	resolution (e.g. scanner)	صَفْحة رئيسيّة	home page
ذاكِرة	memory	صُنْدُوق النُّصُوص	dialog box
ذاكِرة حَيّة	RAM (Random Access Memory)		

ضَغَطَ (a)	1. to press (key)	قُرْص (مَرِن)	diskette
	2. click (mouse)	pl. (مَرِنة) أقْراص	
طِباعة	printer	قُرْص جامِد	hard disk
pl. ـات		قُرْص رَقْمِيّ	DVD
طِباعة لَيْزَر	laser printer	قُرْص مُدَمَّج	CD-ROM
طاقة	capacity	قُرْصان الحاسُوب	computer hacker
عَدَّلَ	to edit (a document)	قَطَعَ (a)	to cut (text)
عَرَضَ (u)	to display	قَوائِم البَريد	mailing list
عَرْضة الحُزْمة	band width	كارت صوت	sound card
عَلامة	sign, mark	كَلِمة المُرور	password
pl. ـات, عَلائِمُ		كُمْبيوتر	computer
عُلْبة الحِبْر	toner cartridge	كمبيوتر مَحْمُول	laptop computer
pl. عُلَب		كوكي	cookie
غَلَقَ (i)	to close (file, document)	كِيان صَلْب	hardware
غُرْفة المُحادَثة	chatroom	كيلوبايت	kilobyte
pl. غُرَف		لَصِقَ (a)	to paste (text)
غَيْر مُتَّصِل	off-line	لَعْبة الكمبيوتر	computer game
غَيَّر اسْم	to rename (e.g. file)	لُغة بَرْمَجِيّة	programming language
فَأْرة	mouse	لُغة رَقْمِيّة	numerical language
فارِغ	free, available (e.g. space)	لَوْحة الأُمّ	motherboard
فَتَحَ (i)	to open (a document)	لَوْحة التَّحَكُّم	control panel
فَكَّ رُمُوز الشَّفْرة (u)	to decode	لَوْحة المَفَاتيح	keyboard
فيروس	virus	ماسِح ضَوْئِيّ	scanner
قائِمة	menu	مُبَدِّل	switch
pl. قَوائِمُ		pl. ـات	
قائِمة مُنْسَدِلة	drop-down menu	مُبَرمِج	programmer
قارِئ	1. drive	مُتَصَفِّح	browser
	2. reader (device)	pl. ـات	
قارِئ الأقْراص المُدَمَّجة	CD-ROM drive		

مُتَّصِل	on-line
مُتَطَلَّبَات	requirements
مُجَلَّد	folder, directory
ـات .pl	
مجلد البريد الصّادِر	outbox (e-mail)
مجلد البريد الوارِد	inbox (e-mail)
مجلد فَرْعِيّ	subfolder
مَجْمُوعة إخْبارِيّة	newsgroup
مُحَرِّك البَحْث	search engine
مَحَطّة عَمَل	workstation
مَخْزَن لِبَيانات	database
ـات .pl	
مُدَقِّق إمْلائِيّ	spell-checker
مُرفَق	attachment
مُزَوّد	server
مَساحة مُتَوَفِّرة	available space
مُسْتَخْدِم	user
مُسْتَنَد	وثيقة see
مُسَجِّل اسْطُوانات	CD writer
مُعلِج	processor
مُعالَجة النَّصُوص	word processing
مُعْطَيات	data
مَعْلُومات (.pl)	information
مِعْيار	criterion
مَعايِيرُ .pl	
مَفاتِيح الأسْهَم	arrow keys
مَفاتِيح الدّوال	function keys

مِفْتاح	key (keyboard)
مَفاتِيحُ .pl	
مِفْتاح إدْخال	ENTER key
مُفَرّع	موجّه see
مَكْتَب	desktop
مَكاتِبُ .pl	
مِلَفّ	file
ـات .pl	
من دون سِلْك	wireless
مُنَسَّق	arranged
مُواصَفات	product information
مُوَجّه	router
مودم، موديم	modem
مُؤَشِّر	cursor
مَوْقِع	(web) site
مَواقِعُ .pl	
مِيزة	characteristic, feature
مِيغابِيت	megabyte
نافِذة	window
نَوافِذُ .pl	
نَزَّلَ	to download
نَسَخَ (a)	to copy
نُسْخة احْتِياطِيّة	backup file
نَصَبَ	to install (e.g. software)
نِطاق	domain
نُطُق .pl	
نِظام التَّشْغِيل	operating system
نِظام	system
أنْظِمة .pl	
نَقْرة	click

نَقَل (u)	to move (text, document)	وَسيط التَّخْزين	storage device
نَقْل المَعْلومات	data transfer	وَسائطُ – .pl	
نَهِيَ (a)	to end, quit (e.g. program)	وَصْلة	see رابطة
وَثيقة وَثائقُ .pl	document	وَصلات هايبر تاكست	Hyper Text Protocol (http)

The media

أَبْلَغَ بِ/عَن	to inform s.o. of s.thing	اعْتَقَد	to believe
أجاب (على)	to reply, respond (to)	أَعْرَبَ (عن)	to express
الأَخْبار	the news	أَعْلَنَ	to announce, declare
أَخْبار حالِيَّة	current affairs	إعْلان ـات .pl	1. declaration, announcement 2. advertisement
أَخْبار دُوَلِيَّة	international news		
أَخْبار مَحَلِّيّة	local news	إعْلانات مُبَوَّبة	classified ads
أذاعَ (على)	to broadcast (to)	اقْتَضَبَ	to abridge
إذاعة	broadcast (radio, tv)	أَكَّدَ	to confirm
اسْتَطْرَدَ	to go on to say	أَلْقَى مُحاضَرَةً	to deliver a speech
أشارَ إلى	to point to	أَمْر أُمُور .pl	matter
إشارة	sign, indication		
إشاعة	rumour, gossip	انْتَشَرَ	to be widespread
اشْتِراك	subscription	انْتِقاد	review
اشْتَرَكَ (في)	to subscribe (to)	أَنْكَرَ	to deny
أَصْدَرَ	see نَشَرَ	إيجابِيّ	positive
أعادَ الطَّبْع	to reprint	بالنِّسْبة إلى	with regard to
إعادة الطَّبْع	reprint	بَيان ـات .pl	statement, declaration
اعْتَبَرَ	to consider, regard		
اعْتَرَفَ	to acknowledge, recognize	تَحْت الطَّبْع	in press

تَحْليل	analysis
pl. ـات	
تَسَرَّبَ	to circulate (news)
تَصْريح	see بيان
تَعْليق	commentary
pl. ـات	
بدون تَعْليق	'no comment'
تَغْطية تليفزيونونية	television coverage
تَقْرير	report
pl. تَقارِيرُ	
تَلْفَزَ	to televise
تِليفِزْيُون	television
تليفزيون مُلَوَّن	colour television
تَنْضيد	typesetting
جَريدة	newspaper
pl. جَرائدُ	
حَدَث	event
pl. إحْداث	
حَديث	interview
pl. أحاديث	
حَديث إذاعيّ	radio interview
حَديث تِليفِزْيُونيّ	television interview
حَديث صُحُفيّ	newspaper interview
حَمْلة صُحُفيَّة	press campaign
خَبَر	news item
pl. أخْبار	
دار النَّشْر	publishing house
ذَكَرَ (u)	to mention
راديو	radio

الرَّأي العامّ	public opinion
رَدَّ (على) (u)	see أجاب
رَقابة	censorship
رَقيب	censor
pl. رُقَباءُ	
زَعَمَ (u)	to claim
سَجَّلَ	to record
سَلْبيّ	negative
سِلْسِلة أحْداث	chain of events
سِياق	context
شاعَ (i)	to spread, disseminate
شَأْن	see قضية
pl. شُؤُون	
شَبَكة إخْباريّة	news network
شَدَّدَ عَلَى	to stress, emphasize
شَهَرَ (a)	to publicize, make well known
شَهير	well known
صِحافة	journalism
الصِّحافة	the press
صِحافيّ	1. journalistic
	2. journalist
صُحُفيّ	see صِحافيّ
صَحيفة	see جريدة
pl. صَحائفُ, صُحُف	
صحيفة صَباحيّة	morning newspaper
صحيفة مَسائيّة	evening newspaper
صحيفة يَوْميّة	daily newspaper

صَدَّرَ (i, u)	to publicize	كُشْك الجَرائد أكْشاك .pl	news-stand
صَرَّحَ بِ	to state	كَلِمات مُتَقاطِعة	crossword
طِباعِيّ	typographic	لَمَّحَ إلى	to allude to
طَبْع الحَجَر	lithography	لَوْحة إعْلانات	billboard
طَبْعة	edition	مَجَلَّة	magazine
عارٍ مِن/عَن	devoid of	مُحَرِّر	newspaper editor
عامُود عَوامِيدُ .pl	column	مَحَطَّة الإذاعة	radio station
عَبَّرَ بِ	see أعرب	محَطَّة الإرْسال	transmitter
عَدَم كَشْف الهُوِية	anonymity	مُحَلِّل	analyst
عَلَّقَ عَلى	to comment on	مُذِيع	announcer
عُنْوان عَناوِينُ .pl	headline	مُراسِل	reporter, correspondent
غَلْطة مَطْبَعِيَّة	misprint	مراسِل حَرْبِيّ	war correspondent
غِيبة	slander	مراسِل خاصّ	special correspondent
فَتْرة الإعْلانات	commercial break	مراسِل رِياضِيّ	sports correspondent
فِعْلِيّ	factual	مُرْسِلة	transmitter (radio)
فِيما يَتَعَلَّق بِ	concerning, as regards	مَسْأَلة مَسائِلُ .pl	see قضية
قابَلَ	to interview	مُسَوَّدة الطَّبْع	galley proof
قالَ (إن) (u)	to say (that)	مُشْتَرِك	subscriber
قانون المَطْبُوعات	press law	مَصادِر مُطَّلَعة	informed sources
قَضِية قَضايا .pl	issue, question	مَصادِر مَوثُوقة بِها	reliable sources
قَناة قَنَوات .pl	channel (tv)	مَصْدَر مَصادِرُ .pl	source
قَناة فَضائِيَّة	satellite channel	مَطْبَعة مَطابِعُ .pl	printing press
كاريكاتير ات- .pl	cartoon	مَطْبُوعات	printed material
كَشَفَ (i)	to expose, reveal	مُفاد	gist (e.g. of an article)

مُقابَلة	see حديث		2. publication
مَقالة	article		3. leaflet
مقالة افْتِتاحِيّة	editorial		4. see إعلان
مُقْتَضَب	concise	نشرة إخْبارِيّة	newscast (radio)
مِن جِهة أُخْرَى	on the other hand	نشرة أُسْبوعِيّة	weekly publication
مِن المُحْتَمَل أن	it is probable that	نشرة دَوْرِيّة	periodical publication
مِن المُتَوَقَّع أن	it is expected that	نشرة رَسْمِيّة	official bulletin
مُنْتَشِر	widespread, prevalent	نشرة شَهْرِيّة	monthly publication
مُؤْتَمَر صُحُفِيّ	press conference	نَضَّدَ	to typeset, compose
مُوجَز	summary	نِطاق	scope, sphere
ناشِر	publisher	pl. نُطُق	
ناقِد	critic	نَظَراً إلَى	in view of
pl. نَقَدة, نُقَّاد, ‑ون		نَقْد	criticism
نُبْذة	section (in newspaper)	نَقَلَ (u)	to convey
pl. نُبَذ		نَضَّدَ	to compose (typeset)
نَشَرَ (u)	to publish	واقِعة	incident
		pl. ‑ات	
نَشْر	publishing	وَسائِل الإعْلام	the media
نَشْرة	1. broadcast	وَكالة الأنْباء	news agency

Sports

إبْعاد	exclusion (player)	إسْتاد	stadium
أبْعَدَ	to expel	اسْتَأْنَفَ	to resume (play)
اتِّحاد الشَّطْرَنْج	chess federation	أغْرَمَ بـ	to support (e.g. a team)
اتِّحاد الكُرّة	football association	أقْلَعَ	to sail
أحْرَزَ نَصْراً	to win a victory	الْتَقَى	to meet (teams)
إسْباتِي	clubs (playing cards)	ألْعاب القُوى	track and field

ألْعاب ناريّة	fireworks	تَفَوُّق على	superiority over
أُنْشُودة أناشيدُ .pl	anthem, hymn	تَمَتَّع بِ	to enjoy
أهَّلَ لِ	to qualify for (e.g. other round)	تَمْرِير	pass (football)
بَسْتُونِي	spades (playing cards)	تَمْرِين ـات .pl	exercise, training
بَطَل أبْطال .pl	champion	تِنِس	tennis
بُطُولة	championship	جائِزة جَوائِزُ .pl	prize
بطولة العالَم	world championship	جَدَّفَ	to row
بُنْدُقِية الصَّيْد بَنادِقٌ- .pl	hunting rifle	جَرَى (i)	to run
بَيْدَق بَيادِقُ .pl	pawn (chess)	جُنْباز	gymnastics
تَجْدِيف	rowing	جُنْبازِيّ	gymnast
تَخَلَّفَ	to lag behind	جولف	golf
تَرْخِيص تَراخِصُ .pl	licence	حاذَ (u)	to spur on (animals)
تَزاحَمَ	to compete with one another	حارِس المَرْمَى	goalkeeper
تَزَحْلَقَ على الجَلِيد	to ice-skate	حِزام نَجاة	swimming belt
تَزَحْلُق على الجَلِيد	ice-skating	حَسْم	decider
تَزَلَّجَ	to ski	حِصان	1. riding horse 2. knight (chess)
تَسابُق	competitiveness	حَكَم حُكّام .pl	referee, umpire
تَسَلَّقَ	to climb (mountain)	حُكْم نِهائِيّ	final judgement
تَسَلُّل	offside (football)	حَلْبة حَلَبات .pl	race track
تَشَقْلَبَ	to do a somersault	حلبة المُصارعة	wrestling ring
تَصْفِية	elimination	خَرْطُوش خَراطِيشُ .pl	cartridge (rifle)
تَعادَلَ	to draw, be equal	خَرْفُوشة خَرافِيشُ .pl	discard (card playing)
تَعادُل	draw, tie		

خَسِرَ (a)	to lose	رَمْى الرُّمْح	javelin throwing
خَصْم	adversary	رَمْى القُرْص	discus throwing
pl. خُصُوم		رَمْى كُرة حَدِيدِيَّة	shotput
خَطَأ	fault	رِياضة	sport
خَطَفَ (i)	to throw	رِياضات	athletics
خَلَفَ عَن (u)	to stay away from	رِياضِيّ	athlete, sportsman
الدَّاما	draughts, checkers	زاحَمَ	to compete with s.o.
دِفاع	defence	زَحَافة	1. sled
دَوْر	round (n.)		2. see زحلوقة
pl. أَدْوار			
دِيناريّ	diamonds (playing cards)	زَحْلُوقة	1. skate
راكِب الدَّراجة	cyclist		2. ski
رامِي الرُّمْح	javelin thrower	زَهْر الطَّاوُلة (coll.)	dice
رامِي القُرْص	discus thrower	سابِح	swimmer
راهَنَ على	to bet on	pl. سُبَّاح, سُبَّاح, -ون	
رُتْبة	class, category	ساحة الأَلْعاب	athletic track
رَفَسَ (i, u)	to kick	سِباق	race, contest
رَفَعَ (a)	to lift	سِباق البَدَل	relay race
رَفَعَ الأَثْقل	to lift weights	سِباق الحُصُن	horse race
رَقْم قِياسِيّ	record	سِباق رالي	rally
رَكِبَ (a)	to ride (horse, bicycle, etc.)	سِباق القَوارِب	boat race
رَكِبَ الدَّراجة	to cycle	سِباق الهُجُن	camel race
رُكْبي	rugby	سَبَحَ (a)	to swim
رَكَضَ (u)	to run (race), sprint	سَجَّلَ	to score
رُكُوب الدَّرَجات	cycling	سَجَّلَ رَقْماً قِياسِيّاً	to set a record
رُكُوب الخَيْل	horseriding	سِجْل هَدَفِيّ	score (football)
رُمْح	javelin	سَرَج	saddle
pl. أَرْماح, رِماح		pl. سُرُوج	

سَقَطَ (u)	to fall (down)	ضَرْبة	kick (football)
سِلْك السِّنَّارة	fishline	ضَرْبة الجَزاء	penalty kick
سِنّارة	fishing tackle	ضَرْبة حُرَّة	free kick
سَنانيرُ .pl		ضَرْبة رُكْنِيَّة	corner kick
سَوْط	whip	ضَرْبة المَرْمَى	goal kick
أَسْواط .pl		طَبَقة	division, league
سيَّارة سباق	racing car	طَرَحَ (a)	to eliminate (e.g. from competition)
شَبَكة	net (fishing)		
شِراع	sail	طَرْح	elimination
شُرُعَ .pl		طُعْم	bait (e.g. fishing)
شَطْرَنْج	chess	عدّاء	runner (race)
شَقْلَبة	somersault	عَصا الصِّنَّارة	fishing rod
شَوْط	round, half (game)	عَصا الجُولف	golf club (stick)
أَشْواط .pl		عَصا الهوكى	hockey stick
شيش	rapier, foil	غاصَ (u)	to dive
صاحب الرَّقْم القِياسِيّ	record holder	غاوٍ	fan, amateur (of something)
		غُواة .pl	
صادَ (i)	to hunt	غَطَّا	to cover (e.g. the goal)
صاد السَّمَك	fishing	غَوَّاص	diver
صارَعَ	to wrestle	غَوْص	dive
صِراع	wrestling	أَغْواص .pl	
صفَّارة	whistle	فارس	horseman
صفارة البِداية	starting whistle	فُرْسان .pl	
صفارة النِّهاية	final whistle	فازَ (u)	to win
صيَّاد	hunter	فازَ عَلَى ب (u)	to beat s.o. at s.thing
صَيْد	hunting	فائز	winner
صَيْد السَّمَك	fishing	فَريق	team
ضَرَبَ رقماً قياسيّ	to beat a record	فُرُوق .pl	

كرة تَنِس	tennis ball
كرة السَّلَّة	basketball (game)
كرة الطَّاوُلة	table tennis
كرة القَدَم	football (game)
كرة اليَد	handball (game)
كُرْباج كَرابِيجُ .pl	(riding) whip
كريكيت	cricket
كِشّ (المَلِك)	check! (chess)
كَشّاف	boy scout
كَمال الأجْسام	bodybuilding
كوبة	hearts (playing cards)
لاعِب	player
لانش ـات .pl	launch, motorboat
لاكَمَ	to box
لِجام لُجُم, ألْجِمة .pl	rein(s), bridle
لَجَمَ	to bridle (horse)
لَعِبَ (a)	to play (e.g. tennis, golf)
لَعْب البردج	bridge
لَعِبَ الكُرة بالرَّأْس	to head (ball)
لَعْبة	game
لعبة الشِّيش	fencing
لَعْبة الطَّاوُلة	backgammon
لَكَمَ (u)	to box
لَكْمة	punch

فَنّ الانْزِلاق على الجَليد	figure skating
فَنّ القِتال	martial arts
فَوْز	victory
فَوْز بالنُّقَط	victory on points
فولى بول	volleyball
في الهَواء الطَّلْق	outdoors
فيل أفْيال, فُيُول, فِيَلة .pl	bishop (chess)
قَبْقاب الانْزِلاق قَباقيبُ ـ .pl	see زحلوقة (1)
قارِب تَجْديف	rowing boat
قارِب سِباق	racing boat
قُرْص	discus
قِطْعة قِطَعَ .pl	piece (e.g. chess)
قُفّاز المُلاكَمة	boxing glove
قَفَزَ (i)	to jump
قَفْز طَويل	long jump
قَفْز عالٍ	high jump
قَفْز عالٍ بالعَصا	pole vault
قَلْعة قُلُوع, قِلاعٌ .pl	rook (chess)
كَأس كَئاس, كُؤوس .pl	cup
كَأس العالَم	World Cup
كَبَحَ (a)	to rein in (horse)
كُرة كُرى ً, ـات .pl	ball

لَوْجه	offside (football)	مَرَّن	to train, exercise
لَوْح مُتَحَرِّك	springboard	مِزْلَج	see (2) زَحلوقة
لوحة الدّاما	draughts board	pl. مَزالِج	
لوحة الشَّطْرَنج	chessboard	مَشّاء	walker (athletics)
مارَسَ	to practise (a sport)	مُشاغِب	(football) hooligan
مُباراة	match, tournament	مُشَجِّع	supporter, fan
مُباراة أَرْبَع نهائيّة	quarter-final	مَشْهُور	famous
مُباراة الذَّهاب	away game	pl. مَشاهيرُ	
مُباراة زَوْجيّة	doubles	مُشَوَّق	fascinating
مُباراة فَرْديّة	singles	(i) مَشَى	to walk
مُباراة نُصْف نهائيّة	semi-final	مُصارِع	wrestler
مُباراة نهائيّة	final	مُصارَعة	wrestling match
مُتَزَحْلِق	skater	مِضْرَب	racket (e.g. tennis)
مُتَزَلِّج	skier	pl. مَضارِبُ	
مُتَقَدِّم	senior	مَعْرُوف	known
مِجْداف	oar	مُغْطَى	indoor
pl. مَجاديفُ		مَغْلُوب	loser
مُجَدِّف	rower	مَقْعَد	seat
مُحاوَرة	dribble (football)	pl. مَقاعِدُ	
مُدافِع	defender (e.g. football)	مِقْوَد	leading rein
مُدَرِّب	coach	pl. مَقاوِدُ	
مُراقِب الخُطُوط	linesman (football)	مَكْشُوف	open-air, outdoor
مُراهَنة	bet, wager	مُلاكِم	boxer
مَرْتَبة هَوائيّة	air mattress	مُلاكمة	boxing
pl. -مَراتِبُ		مَلْعَب التَّنِس	tennis court
مَرَّر	to pass (ball)	مَلِك	king (chess)
مَرْمًى	goal (structure)	pl. مُلُوك	
pl. مَرامٍ		مِنْطَقة	area (pitch), side
		ميداليّة	medal

مَيْدان السِّباق	race track	هداجة pl. هَدائِجُ	camel saddle
نادى pl. نَواد, أَنْدِية	club	هَدَف pl. أهْداف	goal
نادي الرِّياضة	sports club	هَزيمة pl. هَزائِمُ	defeat
نُزْهة pl. نُزه	excursion, outing	هوكى	hockey
نَطّ الحَبْل	rope skipping	هوكى الانْزِلاق	ice-hockey
نُقْطة pl. نُقَط	point	وَرَق اللَّعْب	playing cards
نَهْب	gallop	وَزير pl. وُزَراءُ	queen (in chess)
هاجَمَ	to attack	وَصَفَ (يَصِفُ)	to describe
هَتَفَ (i)	to cheer (crowd)	وَصْف	description
هَجَّان pl. هِجَّانة	camel rider	وَقْت إضافيّ	extra time
هُجُوم	attack	يودو	judo

Arts and entertainment

إخْراج	production (film, theatre)	آلة مُوسيقيَّة	musical instrument
أدَب، آداب	literature	أُوبِرا	opera
أُرْغُن pl. أراغِنُ	organ	إيقاع	rhythm
اِسْتِعْراض	revue, parade	بالون	balloon
اسْتُغْمَاية	hide-and-seek	باليه	ballet
أُسْطُوانة	phonograph record	بُوق pl. أبْواق, ـات	trumpet
أُغْنِية pl. أغانٍ	song	بَوَّقَ	to blow the trumpet
آلة لَعْب القِمار	slot machine	بيانو pl. بِيانات	piano

بيبة	pipe	دَوَّرَ	to wind
تِبْغ	tobacco	دَوْزَنَ	1. to tune an instrument
			2. to tune in (radio)
التَّرْقيم الدُوَليّ المِعْياريّ لِلْكُتُب	International Standard Book Number (ISBN)	ذُرْوة	climax (e.g. novel)
تَسْرِية	pastime	رَئيس الفِرْقة	conductor (orchestra)
تَسَلَّى	to be amused, to enjoy oneself	رَخيم	melodious
		رَسَمَ (u)	to draw, paint
تَسْلِيَّة	entertainment	رَقَصَ (u)	to dance
تَصْفيق الاسْتِحْسان	applause	رَقْص شَرْقيّ	belly dancing
		رَقْص شَعْبيّ	folk dancing
تَصْوير	photography	رَقْصة	dance
تَصْوير رَقْميّ	digital photography	pl. رَقَصات	
تَناغُم	harmony (music)		
جِهاز تَحَكُّم من بُعْد	remote control (e.g. tv)	رَنّانة	tuning fork
		رِواية	novel
حَبْكة	plot (e.g. book, play)	رواية غِنائِيَّة	musical
حَفْلة مُوسيقِيّة	musical concert	رواية مُحْزِنة	tragedy
حُقُوق النَّشْر والطَّبْع	copyright	رواية مَسْرَحِيَّة	play (theatre)
		رواية مُضْحِكة	comedy
حِكاية	see قصة	زَمَرَ (i, u)	to blow (a wind instrument)
حَلْبة الرَّقْص	dance floor	سَحّار	sorcerer, magician
حَمّام	bathhouse	سِحْر	magic
pl. ـات		pl. سُحُور, أسْحار	
حمام البُخار	steam bath	سَلَّمَ	to award (e.g. prize)
دَخَّنَ	to smoke (cigarette, cigar)	سُلَّم	scale (music)
دُفّ	tambourine	pl. سَلالِم	
pl. دُفُوف		سَلَّى	to entertain
دَنْدَنَ	to hum	سُمْعة	reputation
دَوّامة	top (toy)	سيرك	circus

Arabic	English	Arabic	English
سينما	cinema	طَبَلَ (u)	to drum
شاشة	screen (e.g. cinema)	طَبْل	Western drum
شاعر pl. شُعراءَ	poet	pl. أَطْبال, طُبُول	
		طَبْلة	traditional drum
شُخْشيخة pl. شَخاشخُ	rattle (toy)	عُود pl. أَعْواد	lute
شَريط pl. شَرائطُ	audiocassette tape	عَرّاف	fortune teller
		غَنَّى	to sing
شَريط الفيديو	videotape	فانُوس سحْريّ	magic lantern
شَعْبَذَ	to practise juggling, sleight of hand	فرْقة	band (music)
		فرْقة مَسْرَحيّة	theatre company
شَعْبَذة	sleight of hand, juggling	فُكاهة	merriment, joking
شعْر	poetry	فلْم pl. أَفْلام	film
شُغْل الإبْرة	needlework	فِلِم بُوليسيّ	crime drama
شُهْرة	fame	فَنّ pl. فُنُون	art
شَهْوة pl. شَهَوات	pleasure	فَنّيّ	artistic
شيشة	hookah	فيديو	videocassette recorder
صالة الموسيقى	concert hall	قامَرَ	to gamble
صَفّ pl. صُفُوف	row (e.g. theatre)	قُرْعة pl. قُرَع	(lottery) draw
صَفَّرَ	to whistle	قصّة pl. قصَص	story
صَفَّقَ الأَيادي	to clap one's hands	قصّة بُوليسيّة	detective story
صنْج pl. صنُوج	cymbal	قصّة قَصيرة	short story
ضَرَبَ البيانو (i)	to play the piano	قَوْس pl. أَقْواس	violin bow
ضَيْف الشَرَف	guest of honour	قيتار pl. قَياتيرُ	guitar
طَبّال	drummer		
طَبّاع	printer		

كازينو	casino	مُصَوِّر	photographer
pl. كازينوهات		مُضْحِك	funny
كِتاب مَسْمُوع	audiobook	مُضَخِّم	amplifier
كَمان	violin	pl. ـات	
كُورَس	choir	مُضَخِّم الصَّوْت	loudspeaker
كَوْكَب	star (music, film)	مَعْرَض	exhibition
pl. كَواكِب		pl. مَعارِضُ	
كُولِيس	wings (theatre)	مُغَنٍّ	singer
pl. كَوالِيس		مِقْرَعة	baton
لَحْن	tune, melody	pl. مَقارِعُ	
pl. أَلْحان		مُغَنٍّ	singer (male)
لَعْب القمار	game of chance	مُغَنِّية	singer (female)
لُغْز	riddle	مُفَرْقِعات	fireworks
pl. أَلْغاز		مُقامِر	gambler
لَهْو	amusement, diversion	مَقْمَر	gambling house
لَوْحة	painting (object)	pl. مَقامِرُ	
pl. أَلْواح, ـات		مُكَبِّر الصَّوْت	microphone
لوحة زَيْتِيَّة	oil painting	مَكْتَبة عامة	public library
مَتْحَف	museum	مُلَحِّن	composer
pl. مَتاحِفُ		مَلْهى	amusement centre, funfair
مُخْرِج	director (e.g. film)	pl. مَلاهٍ	
مَرْقَص	dance hall	مُمْتِع	enjoyable
pl. مَراقِصُ		مُمَثِّل	actor
مَزَّاح	jester	مُنْتِج	producer (e.g. film)
مَزَّحَ	to joke	مُنْتَزَه	recreational area, park
مُسَجِّل	tape recorder	مَنْدُولِين	mandoline
pl. ـات		مِنَصَّة	platform (stage)
مَسْرَح	theatre	مُهَرِّج	jester, clown
pl. مَسارِحُ			
مَسْرَحِيّة	(theatre) play		

مَهْزَلة	farce	نَغْمة	tone
pl. مَهازِلُ		pl. ـات	
مَوْجة الإرْسال	transmission frequency	نَقَرَ (u)	to engrave
مُوسيقار	musician	نَقَشَ (u)	1. to sculpt
			2. to paint
مُوسيقَى	music	نُكْتة	joke
موسيقى راقصة	dance music	pl. نُكَت	
نادى لَيْليّ	nightclub	نُوتة (الموسيقيّة)	musical note
ناقُوس	gong	هَنْدَسَ	to sketch
pl. نَواقيسُ		وَتَر	string (e.g. guitar, violin)
ناي	flute	pl. أوْتار	
pl. ـات		وقْت فارِغ	leisure time
نَشيط تَرْفيهيّ	recreational activity	يا نَصيب	lottery
pl. أنْشِطة تَرْفيهيّة			

Politics

أبْرَمَ	to ratify (pact, treaty)	اِجْتَمَعَ	to meet (conference)
اتّحاد	unity, solidarity	إجْراء	1. measure
اتّفَقَ على	to agree on	pl. ـات	2. procedure
إتفاق	agreement	إجْراء احْتِياطيّ	precautionary measure
pl. ـات		إجْراء اسْتِثْنائيّ	exceptional measure
اتّفاقيّة	convention (agreement)	أجْرَى انْتِخابات	to hold elections
اتّفاقيّة سَلام	peace agreement	إجْماع	unanimity
أثارَ	to incite	إجْماعيّ	unanimous
أثَّرَ	to influence	أجْمَعَ على	to agree unanimously
أجارَ	to grant asylum	احْتَجَّ على	to protest against
اجْتِماع	meeting	احْتِجاج	protest
		pl. ـات	

احْتِكاك	controversy	اسْتَفَزَّ	to incite, provoke
احْتِياط pl. ـات	precaution	اسْتِفْزاز	incitement, provocation
احْرار	Liberals	اسْتَقالَ (من، عن)	to resign (from) (an office)
إحْصاء السُّكّان	census	اسْتِقْلال	independence
اخْتَتَمَ	to conclude (an agreement)	اسْتَوْزَرَ	to appoint as minister
أدارَ	to administer	اسْتَوْلى على السُّلْطة	to seize power
إدْراج في	entry (e.g. on a list)	أسْقَطَ	to topple (e.g. ruler)
أدَّى إلى	to lead to	إشاعِيّة	collectivism
إذْن كِتابيّ	written permission	اشْتِراك pl. ـات	contribution
ارْتِباك	see تورط	اشْتِراكيّ	socialist
ارْتَشا	to be corrupt	اشْتِراكِيّة	socialism
ارْتِشاء	venality	اضْطِراب pl. ـات	political unrest, riot
أزالَ	to get rid of	إصْلاح pl. ـات	reform
أزْمة pl. إزَم	crisis	أعادَ العَلاقات الدِّبْلُوماسِيّة مَعَ	to resume diplomatic relations with
اسْتِبْداد	despotism	إعادة الإسْكان	resettlement
اسْتَخْلَفَ	to appoint as successor	اعْتَرَض على	1. to resist, oppose 2. to veto
اسْتِشاريّ	advisory	اعْتَرَف	to recognize, acknowledge
اسْتَطْلاع الرَّأْي	opinion poll	اعْتَزَلَ	to be deposed
اسْتِعْمار	colonialism	اعْتِماد pl. ـات	1. approbation 2. credit, loan
اسْتِعْمارِيّة	imperialism	أعَدَّ	to prepare, compile (e.g. report)
اسْتَعْمَرَ	to colonize	العِزّة القَوْمِيّة	national pride
اسْتَغاثَ	to call for help		
اسْتِغاثة	appeal for aid		
اسْتِغْلال	exploitation		
اسْتِفْتاء (شَعْبيّ)	referendum		

أَعْلَنَ	to declare	امتيازات دبلوماسيّة	diplomatic privileges
إعْلان	declaration, statement	أمَّمَ	to nationalize
أَعْمَرَ	to develop (a country)	أمانة عامّة	general secretariat
إقامة عَلاقات دِبْلُوماسيَّة	establishment of diplomatic relations	أُمَّة pl. أُمَم	nation
أَغْلَبية	majority	أمْن	security, safety
أَغْلَبيَّة مُطْلَقة	absolute majority	أمْن داخِليّ	internal security
أَفْسَحَ المَجال	to clear the way	أمير pl. أُمَراءُ	prince
أقالَ	see عزلَ		
اقْتِراع pl. ـات	ballot	أميرة	princess
اقْتِراع ثقة	vote of confidence	أمين عامّ	secretary-general
إقْطاعيَّة	feudalism	أمين المال	treasurer
أَقَلّيَّة	minority	انْتِخاب pl. ـات	election
أقلية عُنْصُريَّة	ethnic minority	انْتِخابات تَشْريعيَّة	legislative elections
إقْليم pl. أقاليمُ	province	انْتِخاب جُزْئيّ	by-election
إقْليميّ	regional	انْتِخابات حُرّة ونَظيفة	free and fair elections
الْتَحَقَ بالحزْب	to join a party	انْتِخابات رَئيسيّة	presidential elections
التحق بالحُكُومة	to go into government service	انْتِخابات عامّة	general elections
إلْتِزام pl. ـات	obligation, commitment	انتِخاب فَرْعيّ	see انتخاب جزئي
ألْغى	to annul, abolish	انْتِخابات مُبَكِّرة	early elections
إلْغاء	annulment, abolition	انْتَخَبَ	to elect
آليّ	instrumental	انْتِصار ساحِق	overwhelming victory
إمارة	1. power 2. principality	انْتِعاش	revival
		انْتِقائيّ	selective, eclectic
امْتِياز pl. ـات	privilege	انْتِقائيَّة	eclecticism
		إنْتَقَلَ السُّلْطة	to transfer power

اِنْتِماء الى	membership of	بالغ الأهْميَّة	of the utmost importance
اِنْتَمى إلى	to be a member of	بَرَّرَ	to justify
اِنْخَرَطَ	see انضم	بَرْلمان	see مجلس النواب
إنْذار نِهائيّ	ultimatum	بروتوكول	protocol
اِنْسِجاماً مَعَ	in conformity with	بِطاقة الاقْتِراع	ballot paper
أَنْشأ علاقة دبلوماسيَّة	to establish diplomatic relations	بَعْثة	1. delegation 2. mission
اِنْشَقَّ عن	to break away from	بِلاد pl. بُلْدان	country
اِنْضَمَّ إلى	to join, become a member of	بَلاط	(royal) court
اِنْضِمام (إلى)	accession (to)	بَلاغ pl. ـات	communiqué
اِنْعِزال	seclusion, isolation		
اِنْعِزاليَّة	isolationism	بَلَديَّة	municipality
اِنْعَقَدَ	to be convened (e.g. meeting)	بالنِّسْبة لِ	with respect to
اِنْفِصاليّ	separatist	بَنْد pl. بُنُود	clause (e.g. contract, treaty)
اِنْفِصاليَّة	separatism		
اِنْقِلاب	coup	بيروقراطية	bureaucracy
اِنْهِيار	downfall, collapse	تَأَثَّرَ بِ	to influenced by
أَوْراق الاعْتِماد	see وثائق الاعتماد	تَأْثِير	influence
أَوْساط سِياسيَّة	see دوائر سياسية	تاج pl. تِيجان	crown
أَوْصى بِ	1. to advise 2. to recommend	تَآمَرَ	to plot
أَوَّليَّة	priority	تأْميم pl. ـات	nationalization
اِئْتِلاف pl. ـات	coalition	تَبادَلَ	to exchange (e.g. views)
اِئْتَمَرَ (ب)	to conspire, plot (against)	تَبْرِير pl. ـات	justification
أَيَّدَ	see دعم	تَجَنَّسَ	to become naturalized
بارِز	prominent	تَجَنُّس	naturalization

تَحالُف	alliance	تَظاهَرة	demonstration
تَحْتَ رِعاية	under the auspices of	تَعارَضَ	to oppose
تَحَدّ	challenge, provocation	تَعامُل	collaboration
pl. تَحَدِّيات		تَعاوَنَ	to cooperate
تَحَدَّ	to provoke, to challenge	تَعايَشَ	to live together
تَحْديث	modernization	تَعايُش	coexistence
تَحْريض	inflammatory propaganda	تَعايُش سِلْمِيّ	peaceful coexistence
التَحَفُّظ	conservatism	تَعَدُّدِيَّة	pluralism
تَخَلُّف	backwardness	تَعَدُّدِيَّة ثَقافِيَّة	multiculturalism
تَدْعيم	strengthening	تَعْديل وِزارِيّ	cabinet reshuffle
تَدَهْوُر	decline	تَعْزيز عمل	reinforcement of action
تَراضٍ	compromise	تَعَصُّب عُنْصُرِيّ	racism
تَرَشَّحَ	to be nominated	تَعَلَّقَ بـ	to be related to
تَرْشيح	nomination, candidature	تَعْليل	argumentation, motivation
تَزْوير الانْتِخابات	election rigging	pl. ـات	
تَسامُح	tolerance	تَفَكَّكَ	to disintegrate
تَسْمِية	designation	تَفْويض	delegation of authority
تَسْوِية سِلْمِيَّة	peace settlement	تَفاهُم	agreement
تَشْريعِيّ	legislative	تَقارُب	rapprochement
تَشْكيل	establishment, foundation	تَقَدُّم	progress
تَصْريح	declaration	تَقْديم	memorial
تَصْويت الِكْتروني	electronic voting	تَقْرير	report
		pl. تَقاريرُ	
تَطْبيع العَلاقات	normalization of relations	تَقْرير مَصير (ه)	self-determination
تَطْبيق	application	تَكَتُّل	formation of blocs
تَطَرُّف	extremism	تَمْثيل نِسْبِيّ	proportional representation
تَطَوَّعَ	to volunteer	تَمْييز	discrimination

تَمْييز عُنصُرِيّ	racial discrimination	جُزْئِيّ	partial
تَناقُض	incompatibility	جَلْسة	session
تَناوَلَ	to deal with s.thing	جَلْسة عامّة	plenary meeting
تَنَوُّع	diversity	جَمْعِيّة	society, assembly
تَوَتُّر	tension	جَمْعية تَشْريعِيّة	legislative assembly
تَوَّجَ	to crown	جُمْهُورِيّ	republican
تَوَجُّه	orientation	جُمْهُورِيّة	republic
تَوَرُّط في	involvement in	جِنْس	race
تَوَسَّطَ	to mediate	pl. أَجْناس	
تَوَسُّط	intercession, mediation	الجِهاز السِّياسِيّ	the political apparatus
تَوْصِية	recommendation	جَوْر	injustice, oppression
تَوْطيد الرَوابِط	strengthening of ties	حارِس	guardian, custodian
تَيّار	current (n.)	حاسِم	decisive
pl. ـات		حال	situation, circumstance
ثَبَّتَ	to stabilize	pl. أَحْوال	
ثُلاثِيّ	tripartite	الحالة الرّاهِنة	status quo
ثُنائِيّ	bilateral	حالة الطَّوارِىء	state of emergency
ثَوْرة	revolution	حُبّ السَّلام	pacifism
ثَوْرِيّ	revolutionary	حَدّ	border
جادّ	serious	pl. حُدُود	
(u) جارَ على	to oppress, tyrannize	حَذَّرَ	to warn
جَبْهة	front	حُرّ	liberal
(i) جَبَى	to collect taxes	حِراسة	custodianship, administration
جَدَل	argument, controversy	حَرِج	critical
جَدْوَل زَمَنِيّ	timetable (deadlines by which goals have to be met)	حَرَكة	movement
		الحَرَكة النِّسائِيّة	the feminist movement
جَدْوَل الأَعْمال	agenda	حُرّيّة	freedom, liberty

حرية الصّحافة	freedom of the press	حكْم ذاتيّ	self-determination
حرية العبادة	freedom of worship	حكْم لامَرْكَزيّ	decentralized rule
حرية الفكْر	freedom of thought	حكْم جمْهوريّ	republicanism
حرية الكَلام	freedom of speech	حكْم مطْلَق	absolute rule
حزْب pl. أحْزاب	party	حكْم نيابيّ	parliamentarianism
الحزْب الجمْهوريّ	Republican Party (US)	حكوميّ	governmental
الحزْب الحاكم	the ruling party	حكومة	government
الحزْب الدّيموقراطيّ	Democratic Party (US)	حكومة انْتقاليّة	transitional government
الحزْب الدّيموقراطيّ الليبراليّ (UK)	Liberal Democrat Party (UK)	حكومة مؤقّت	provisional (interim/ caretaker) government
حزْب العمّال	Labour Party (UK)	(i) حلّ	to dissolve
حزْب المُحافظين	Conservative Party (UK)	حلّ وَسَط see تراض	
حزْبيّ	party member	حمْلة انْتخابيّة	election campaign
(i) حَصَلَ على	to obtain	حَوْزة	territory
(u) حَضَرَ	to attend	حَياة عامّة	public life
حَظْر	embargo, blockade	حياد	neutrality
(a) حَفّى بـ	to receive s.o. with honours	حياديّ	neutral
حقّ الاقْتراع	suffrage, right to vote	خَزينة الدّوْلة	Treasury
حقّ الفيتو	power of veto	خطاب pl. ـات	speech
حقيبة pl. حقائبُ	portfolio (minister)	خَطير	grave, momentous
حقيقة pl. حقائقُ	truth, fact	خَفَّفَ	to moderate
حقيقيّ	real	خلافيّ	controversial
(u) حَكَمَ	to govern	(a) خَلَعَ من الحكْم see عزل	
حكْم pl. أحْكام	rule, governance	خَلَف pl. أخْلاف	successor
		خيار pl. ـات	choice, option

داخِليّ	domestic	دِيبلوماسِيَّة	diplomacy
داعِيَة السَّلام	peace activist	دِيموقراطِيَّة	democracy
دافِع pl. دَوافِع	incentive, motive	دِيموقراطِيّ	democratic
دائِرة انْتِخابِيَّة	constituency	رابِطة pl. رَوابِطُ	confederation
دَسَّ (u)	to plot, scheme	راقَبَ	to supervise
دَسَّاس	conspirator, schemer	الرَّأي العامّ	public opinion
دُسْتُور pl. دَساتيرُ	constitution	رائِج	current, common, widespread
دَسِيسة pl. دَسائِسُ	intrigue, plot	رائِد pl. رُوَّاد	pioneer
دعا (يَدعُو إلى)	to call on s.o. (to do s.thing)	رَأْسمالِيّة	capitalism
دِعاية	propaganda	رجَعَ إلى (i)	to stem from
دَعَمَ (a)	to support	رَجعِيَّة	reaction
دَوائِر الحُكُومة	government circles	رَسْمِيّ	official (adj.)
دَوائِر سِياسِيّة	political circles	رَشا (u)	to bribe
دَوْرة	session	رِشْوة pl. رَشاوى, رُشى	1. bribe 2. bribery, corruption
دَوْرة بَرْلَمانِيّة	parliamentary session		
دَوْرة تَشْريعِيّة	legislative period	رَشَّحَ (ل)	to nominate (for an office)
الدُّوَل الأَعْضاء	member states	رفَضَ (i, u)	to reject
الدُّوَل العُظْمَى	the Superpowers	رفَعَ عُقوبات (a)	to lift sanctions
دَوْلة pl. دُوَل	state	رُوح الهَزِيمة	defeatism
دَوْلة قَوْمِيّة	nation-state	رِئاسة	1. presidency 2. see قِيادة
دَوْلة مُتَعاقِدة pl. دُوَل-	contracting state	رَئيس pl. رُؤَساءُ	president
دُوَليّ	international	رَئيس الحِزْب	party chairman, leader
دِيبلوماسِيّ	diplomatic	رَئيس الوُزَراء	Prime Minister

رَئِيسِيّ	principal, main
زَعِيم pl. زُعَماء	see قائِد
السَّاحة الدُّوَلِيّة	the international stage
ساحِق	overwhelming (e.g. majority)
سامَح	to be tolerant (towards s.o.)
سانَد	see دعم
سائِد	prevailing
سَبَب pl. أَسْباب	cause, reason
سِجِلّات	records
سِفارة	embassy
سَفِير pl. سُفَراء	ambassador
سُلْطان pl. سَلاطِين	sultan
سُلْطة	1. power, rule 2. authority
السُّلْطات	the authorities
السُّلْطات المُخْتَصَّة	competent authorities
السُّلْطة التَّنْفِيذِيّة	the Executive
السلطة التَشْرِيعِيّة	the Legislature
سُلْطة مُؤَقَّتة	interim authority
سَلْطَنة	sultanate
سَلَّم السُّلْطة	to hand over power
سِلْمِيّ	pacifist
سَوَّى	to settle (dispute)

سِيادة	sovereignty
سِياسة	1. politics 2. policy
سِياسة الالْتِجاء	asylum policy
سِياسِيّ	politician
سَيْطَرَ عَلَى	to rule over, to dominate
سَيْطَرة	supremacy
شامِل	comprehensive
شاوَرَ	to consult
شائِع	widespread
شِعار	slogan
شَعْب (a) pl. شُعُوب	people
شَعْبِيّ	popular
شَعْبِيّة	popularity
شَمَلَ (a)	to include, comprise
شُمُولِيّة	totalitarianism
شِيُوعِيّ	communist
شِيُوعِيّة	communism
صادَرَ	to confiscate, seize
الصَّالِح العامّ	public welfare
صَدَد	topic (e.g. discussion)
فِي هذا الصَّدَد	in this respect
صَرَّحَ	to declare, announce
صَهْيُونِيّة	Zionism
صَوَّتَ (عَلى/ضَدّ)	to cast a vote (in favour / against)

صُورة	image	عَريضة	petition
pl. صُوَر		pl. عَرائِض	
صَوَّتَ	to vote	عِزّة	might
ضَغْط	pressure	عَزَّزَ	to consolidate
pl. ضُغُوط		عَزَلَ (i)	to dismiss, depose
ضَلَعَ مع (a)	to side with	عَزْل	dismissal, deposition
طائِفيّة	sectarianism	عَزَمَ (i)	to decide
طالَبَ	to demand	عَزْمة	decision
طالِب اللُجُوء	asylum seeker	عَصَى (i)	to rebel, revolt
طَرَف مَعْنِيّ	concerned party	عُضْو	member
طَلَبَ عَضَوِيّة (u)	to apply for membership	pl. أَعْضاء	
ظاهَرَ	to demonstrate	عُضْو مُنْتَسِب	associate member
ظَرْف	circumstance	pl. أَعْضاء مُنْتَسِبُون	
pl. ظُرُوف		عَضَوِيّة	membership
ظَلَمَ (i)	to oppress	عُقُوبات (pl.)	sanctions
ظُلْم	oppression, tyranny	عَقَبة	obstacle
عارَضَ	to resist, oppose	pl. عِقاب, -ات	
عاصِمة	capital (country)	عَقَدَ (i)	to hold (a meeting)
pl. عَواصِمُ		عَكَسَ (i)	to reflect
عاقِبة	outcome	عَلاقات ثُنائِيّة	bilateral relations
pl. عَواقِبُ		عَلاقات مُتَعَدِّدة	
عامِل	factor	الأَطْراف	multilateral relations
pl. عَوامِلُ		عَلاقات وَثيقة	close ties
عاهِل	monarch	عَلْمانِيّة	secularism
pl. عَواهِلُ		عَلَناً	in public
عَدَم الانْحِياز	non-alignment	عَلَنِيّ	public (adj.)
عَرْش	throne	عُمْران	prosperity, civilization
pl. عُرُوش		عَمَلِيّة السَّلام	peace process
عِرْقِيّ	ethnic, racial		

عَميل	1. agent	فَشَل	failure, fiasco
عُمَلاءُ .pl	2. collaborator	(i) فَصَلَ مُنازَعة	to settle a dispute
عُنْصُر	race	فَضّ	1. settlement (dispute)
عَناصِرُ .pl			2. closure (session)
عُنْصُرِيّة	see تعصب عنصري	فَقْرَة	paragraph
عَهْد	mandate	فَكَّكَ	to disband
عُهُود .pl		فَوَّضَ	to authorize
عَيَّنَ	to appoint	فَوْضَى	anarchy
غَرَّبَ	to banish, exile	فَوْضَوِيّة	anarchism
غُرْبة	banishment, exile	في إطار	in the framework of
غَضينة عُنْصُرِيّة	racial hatred	(u) قاد	to lead, rule
غَوْغاء	mob, rabble	قاد بالمثال	to lead by example
غَيْر دُسْتُورِيّ	unconstitutional	قائِد	leader
غَيْر رَسْمِيّ	unofficial	قادات, قادة, قُوَّد, قُوَّاد .pl	
غَيْر مَسْبُوق	unprecedented	قائِم بالأعْمال	Chargé d'Affaires
غَيْر مَسْؤُول	irresponsible	قَبَلِيّ	tribal
(u) فازَ	to win (an election)	قَبيلة	tribe
فِئة	faction	قَبائِلُ .pl	
فِئَوي	factional	قَرار	decision, resolution
فِئَوِيّة	factionalism	ـات .pl	
فَرْدِيّة	individualism	قَرَّرَ	to resolve, decide
فُرْصة	opportunity	قِسْم	service, department
فُرَص .pl		أقْسام .pl	
فُرْصة نادِرة	unique opportunity	قُطْر	region, province
(i) فَرَضَ (على)	to impose s.thing (on)	أقْطار .pl	
(u) فَرَضَ عُقُوبات	to impose sanctions	قَطَعَ العَلاقات الدِّبْلُوماسِيّة مَعَ	to sever diplomatic relations with
فُرْقة	separation	(i) قَلَبَ	to overthrow
فَشَّلَ	to thwart, foil	(a) قَمَعَ	to repress

قُنْصُل	consul	لجنة مُشْتَرَكة	joint committee
pl. قَناصِلُ		لُجوء	asylum (refuge)
قنصل عامّ	consul general	لجوء سياسيّ	political asylum
قُنْصُلِيَّة	consulate	لَعِبَ دَوْراً في	to play a role in
قنصليَّة عامّة	consulate general	لُغة عَمَل	working language
قَواعد السِّرِّيَّة	the rules of confidentiality	الليبراليّة	Liberalism
قُوَّة	strength	الليبراليُّون	the Liberals
pl. قُوى		مادة	1. rule
قَوْم	see شعب		2. see بند
pl. أَقْوام		مَأْمُور	official (n.)
قَوْميّ	national (of the people)	مُباحَثات	talks
قَوْميَّة	see وطنية	مُبادَرة	undertaking, initiative
قِيادة	leadership	مَبْدَأ	principle
كارثة	catastrophe	pl. مَبادِئُ	
pl. كَوارِثُ		مُبَرِّر	justification, excuse
كامِل	complete	مَبْعَث	see سبب
كِبار المَسْؤُولين	high-ranking officials	pl. مَباعِثُ	
كُتْلة	bloc	مَبْعُوث	envoy
pl. كُتَل		مَبْعُوث ديبلوماسيّ	diplomatic agent
لاجِئ	refugee	مَتاريس	barricades
لامَرْكَزِيَّة	decentralization	مُتَحَدِّث (باسْم)	see ناطق
لَجَأَ (a)	1. to take refuge	مُتَشَدِّد	bigot, radical
	2. to seek asylum	مُتَصَلِّب	hard-line
لَجْنة	committee, commission	مُتَطَرِّف	extremist
pl. لِجان		مُتَظاهِر	demonstrator
لجنة الاتصال	liaison committee	مُتَعاطِف	sympathizer
لَجنة اسْتِشاريّ	advisory committee	مُتَقَدِّم	predecessor
لَجنة التَّوْجيه	steering committee		
لَجْنة الطُّعُون	appeals committee		

مُتَوافِق مَعَ	compatible with	مُخَطَّط السَّلام	peace plan
مُثِير لِلجَدَل	see خلافي	مُخَيَّم	camp (refugees)
مُجْتَمَع	society	pl. ـات	
المُجْتَمَع الدُّوَلِيّ	the international community	مُداوَلة	deliberation, consultation
		مَذْهَبِيّة	see طائفية
مَجْلِس	council	مُراقِب	observer
pl. مَجالِسُ		مُرْتَبِك	involved, implicated
مجلس تَنْفِيذِيّ	executive board	مَرْجِع	authority (person)
مجلس النُّواب	Parliament	pl. مَراجِعُ	
مجلس الوُزَراء	Council of Ministers, Cabinet	مَرْحَلة	stage, phase
مُحْتَجّ	protestor	pl. مَراحِلُ	
مُحايِد	neutral	مَرْسُوم	decree
مَحْضَر	minutes (meeting)	pl. مَراسِيم	
pl. مَحاضِرُ		مُرَشَّح	nominee, candidate
مَجْمَع	assembly	مُرَشَّح مُسْتَقِلّ	independent candidate
pl. مَجامِعُ		مُساعِد	aide, assistant
مُحادَثة	talk, negotiation	مُسْتَبِدّ	despot, tyrant
مُحاذَرة	precautionary measure	مُساعَدة إنْسانِيّة	humanitarian aid
مُحاضَرات حَرْفِيّة	proceedings, verbatim records	مُساعَدة دُوَلِيّة	international aid
مُحافِظ	1. conservative	مُسْتَجِير ·	see طالب للجوء
	2. governor	مُسْتَشار	advisor, consultant
مَحْسُوبِيّة	favouritism	مُسْتَعْمَرة	settlement, colony
مُحَلِّل	analyst	مُسْتَقِلّ	independent
مَحَلِّيّ	local	مُسْتَنَد	document
مِحْوَر الشَّرّ	the Axis of Evil	pl. ـات	
مِحْوَرِيّ	pivotal	مُسْتَوْطِن	settler
مُخْبِر	informant	مُسْتَوْطَنة	settlement (site)
مُخْتَصّات	competences	مَسْؤُول	official (n.)

مُشاركة	participation	مُقاوَمة	resistance
مُشاوَرة	consultation	مُقتَرَح pl. ـات	proposal
مَشْروع pl. مَشاريعُ	1. project, scheme 2. legitimate, lawful	مَقَرّ pl. ـات	seat, centre
مَشْروع قَرار	draft resolution	مَقْعَد pl. مَقاعِدُ	seat (elections)
مَشْروع قانون	bill (draft law)	مُكافحة الإرْهاب	counter-terrorism
مَشْروعِيّة	legitimacy	مَلاء (i)	to fill (e.g. a position)
مُشاوَرة	consultation	مُلائم	suitable
مَشيخة	sheikhdom	مِلّة pl. مِلَل	religious community
مُصادَرة	confiscation, seizure	مُلْحَق	attaché
مُصالَحة	settlement (peace), conciliation	مُلْحَق ثَقافِيّ	cultural attaché
المَصلَحة العامّة	public interest	ملحق عَسكَرِيّ	military attaché
مَضْمُون	guaranteed	مَلِك pl. مُلُوك	king
مَطْلُوب pl. مَطالِبُ	demand	مَلِكة	queen
مُظاهَرة	demonstration	مَلَكِي	royalist
مُعاداة السّامِيّة	anti-Semitism	مَلَكِيّة دُسْتُورِيّة	constitutional monarchy
مُعارَضة	opposition	مُمَثِّل	representative
مُعاهَدة	treaty	مَمْلَكة pl. مَمالِكُ	kingdom
مُعِدّ	compiler (e.g. of report)	مَناعة دِبلُوماسِيّة	diplomatic immunity
مُعَيَّن	specific	مُنافِس	rival
مُفاوِض	negotiator	مُناقَشة	debate, discussion
مُفاوَضة	negotiation, discussion	مُنتَدىً pl. مُنتَدَيات	meeting place
مُفَوَّض	commissioner		
مُفَوَّض سامٍ	High Commissioner		
المَقامات المُخْتَصّة see السلطات المختصة		مُنتَقىً	select (adj.)

مَنَحَ (a)	to award, grant	مُؤْتَمَر القِمَّة	summit meeting
مَنْدُوب	delegate, representative	مُوَظَّف حُكُومِيّ	1. government official
			2. civil servant
مندوب خاصّ	special envoy	مَوْقِف	position, stance
مندوب فَوْق العادة	ambassador extraordinary	pl. مَواقِفُ	
مَنْدُوحة	alternative	مُؤَيِّد	supporter
pl. مَنادِحُ			
مَنْشَأ	native country	مِيثاق	charter
		pl. مَواثيقُ	
مُنَشِّط	activist	مَيَّزَ	to discriminate
مُنْشَقّ	dissident	ناطِق (بِاسْم)	spokesman
مَنْصِب	office, position	نائِب	Member of Parliament
pl. مَناصِبُ		pl. نُوَّاب	
مَنْصُوص عَلَيْه	stipulated, provided for	نائِب القُنْصُل	vice-consul
مُنَظَّمة	organization	ناخِب	voter
مُنَظَّمة دُوَلِيَّة غَيْر حُكُومِيَّة	non-governmental organization	نازِيّة جَديدة	neo-Nazism
		ناشِط	see منشط
مُنَظَّمة دُوَلِيَّة حُكُومِيَّة	intergovernmental organization	ناظِر	inspector
		pl. نُظَّار	
مُهاجِر	emigrant	ناقَشَ	to discuss
مُهاجَرة	emigration	نَخْبَوِيّ	electoral
مُهاظَرة	demonstration	نَسَّقَ	to arrange
مَهَّدَ الطَّريق	to pave the way	نَشيد حَماسِيّ	rallying song
مُهِمّ	important	pl. نَشائِدُ حماسِيَّة	
مُواطِن	compatriot	نشيد وَطَنِيّ	national anthem
مُواطِنِيَّة	citizenship	pl. نشائِدُ وطنيَّة	
مُؤَامَرة	conspiracy, plot	نَصَحَ بِ (a)	see أوصى (1)
مُؤْتَمَر	conference	نَصيحة	see وصية
pl. ـات		pl. نَصائِحُ	
مُؤْتَمَر السَّلام	peace conference	نِظام	regime
		pl. أَنْظِمة	

نِظام الأَحْزاب المُتَعَدِّدة	see نظام التعددية الحزبية
نِظام التَّعَدُّدِيّة الحِزْبِيّة	multiparty system
نظام الحِزْب الواحِد	one-party system
نظام الحُكْم	political system
نَفَّذَ	to implement, execute
نَفَى (i)	1. to exile 2. to deny
نقاش	debate
نُقْطة التَّحَوُّل	turning point
هاجَرَ	to emigrate
هَمَّشَ	to marginalize
هَيْئة	body (organization)
هَيْئة الوُزَراء	Cabinet
هَيْئة ناخِبة	electorate
هَيْبة	prestige
واسِع النِّطاق	far-reaching
وافَقَ على	to approve
والٍ pl. وُلاة	governor
وَثائق الاِعْتِماد	credentials
واقِعيّ	realistic
وَثيقة pl. وَثائق	document (official)
وَجْهة النَّظَر	point of view
وَحَّدَ	to unite

وَحْدانيّ	unilateral
وَحْدة	unity
وِزارة	ministry
وزارة الاِسْتِعْلامات	Ministry of Information
وزارة الأَشْغال العُمُوميّة	Ministry of Public Works
وزارة الأَوْقاف	Ministry of Religious Endowments
وزارة البَحْرِيّة	Ministry of the Navy
وزارة التِّجارة	Ministry of Trade
وزارة التَّخْطيط	Ministry of Planning
وزارة التَّعْليم	Ministry of Education
وزارة الثَّقافة	Ministry of Culture
وزارة الحَرْب	Ministry of War
وزارة الخارِجيّة	Foreign Office
وزارة الدَّاخِليّة	Home Office
وزارة الدِّفاع	Ministry of Defence
وزارة الزِّراعة	Ministry of Agriculture
وزارة السِّياحة	Ministry of Tourism
وزارة الشُّؤُون الاِجْتِماعيّة	Ministry of Social Affairs
وزارة الصِّحّة العُمُوميّة	Ministry of Public Health
وزارة الطَّيْران	Ministry of Aviation
وزارة العَدْل	Ministry of Justice
وزارة العَمَل	Ministry of Employment
وزاة الماليّة	Ministry of Finance
وزارة المُواصَلات	Ministry of Communications

وَزِير pl. وُزَراءُ	minister	وَطَن pl. أوْطان	homeland, nation
وزير بلا وِزارة	minister without portfolio	وَطَنيّ	nationalist
وزير مُفَوَّض	minister plenipotentiary	وَطَنيّة	nationalism
وَسِيط pl. وُسَطاءُ	intermediary	وَطِيد	solid (e.g. ties)
وِصاية	mandate	وَظِيفة pl. وَظائفُ	office, appointment
وَصَلَ (يَصِلُ) إلى السُّلْطة	to come to power	وَفْد pl. أوْفاد, وُفُود	delegation, deputation
وَصَّى بِ	see أوصى	وِلاية وَطَنيّة	national jurisdiction
وَصِي على العَرْش pl. أوْصِياءُ	regent	وَلِي العَهْد	Crown Prince
وَصِيّة pl. وَصايا	advice, counsel	اليَسار	the Left
		يَسارِيّ	left-wing
وَضْع pl. أوْضاع	see موقف	اليَمِين	the Right
		يَمِينيّ	right-wing

Law and order

ابْتَزَّ	to blackmail	اخْتِطاف	1. kidnapping, abduction 2. hijacking
ابْتِزاز	blackmail	اخْتَطَفَ	1. to kidnap, abduct, take hostage 2. to hijack
أبْرَأ	to acquit		
إبْراءُ	acquittal, release (e.g. from liability)	اخْتِلاس	embezzlement
اتَّهَمَ ه بِ	to accuse s.o. of s.thing	اخْتَلَسَ	to embezzle
أثْبَتَ	to prove	أدان (بِ)	to convict s.o. of s.thing
أثَر القَدَم pl. آثار-	footprint	ارْتَكَبَ	to commit (a crime)
احْتَجَزَ	to detain	إرْهاب	terrorism

إِرْهابِيّ	terrorist	اِغْتِصاب	rape
أَرْهَبَ	to terrorize	اِغْتَصَبَ	to rape
أَساءَ المُعامَلَة	to mistreat	اِغْتِيال	assassination, murder
اِسْتِئْناف	appeal	اِفْتِراض	hypothesis, assumption
اِسْتَأْنَفَ	to appeal (against a sentence)	اِفْتِراضِيّ	hypothetical
اِسْتِئْنافِيّاً	by appeal	أَفْرَجَ عَن	to release
اِسْتَجْوَبَ	to interrogate, question	اِقْتَفَى أَثَرَه	to follow s.o.'s tracks
اِسْتِجْواب pl. ـات	interrogation	أَقْسَمَ	to take an oath, swear
		أَلْغَى	to abrogate
اِسْتَدْعا	to summon, subpoena	اِنْتِهاك pl. ـات	violation
اِسْتِدْعاء	summons, subpoena		
اِسْتَذْنَبَ	to find guilty of a crime	اِنْحِراف	delinquency
اِشْتِباك pl. ـات	clash	أَوْقَفَ	see اعتقل
		بِأَثَر رَجْعِيّ	with retroactive force
اِشْتَبَهَ فِي	to suspect (s.o.) of s.thing	بَرِيء أَبْرِياء .pl	innocent
اِشْتَرَطَ	to stipulate		
أَشْغال شاقّة	hard labour	بَصْمة الأَصابِع بَصَمات .pl	fingerprint
أَصْدَرَ حُكْماً	to hand down a sentence	بَلْطَجِيّ بَلْطَجِيّة .pl	gangster
إِضْراب عَن الطَّعام	hunger strike		
أَطْلَقَ (سَراحَهُ)	to release, set free	بَنْد بُنُود .pl	article
أَظْهَرَ	to demonstrate, show		
إِعادة الحُقُوق	rehabilitation	بَيْت الدَّعارة	brothel
اِعْتِداء عَلى	attempt on s.o.'s life	تَبْرِئة	exoneration
اِعْتَرَفَ بِ	to confess	تَحْقِيق pl. ـات	investigation
اِعْتَقَلَ	to arrest		
أَعْدَمَ	to execute	تَحْقِيق جِنائِيّ	criminal investigation
اِغْتالَ	to assassinate	تَرافَعَ إِلى الحاكِم	to bring one's case before a judge

تَرْخيص	1. licensing
	2. licence
تَزْوير	forgery
تَسْجيل	registration
تَسْوية حُبِّيَّة	amicable settlement
تَعْذيب	see عذاب
تَقْرير الشُّرْطة	police report
تَلاءَمَ مَعَ	to comply with
تَهْريب	smuggling
تَهْريب البَشَر	people smuggling, trafficking
تُهْمة، pl. تُهَم	accusation, charge
جَريمة، pl. جَرائِمُ	crime
جَلْسة المَحْكَمة	court hearing
جِناية، pl. جِنايا	felony
جُنْحة، pl. جُنَح	misdemeanour
جِهاز قَضائيّ	judicial instrument
حَبْس احْتِياطيّ	remand
حَبْس انْفِرادِيّ	solitary confinement
حاكَمَ	to prosecute s.o.
حَتَّمَ (i)	to impose, prescribe
حَصانة	immunity
حُقُوقيّ	legist, jurist
حَكَمَ على (u)	to sentence s.o.

حَكَمَ عَلَيْهِ بِالإعْدام	to sentence s.o. to death
حُكْم، pl. أحْكام	1. judgement 2. sentence
حكم بالاعْدام	death sentence
حكم البَراءة	acquittal
حكم غِيابيّ	trial *in absentia*
حُكْميّ	legal
حَلَفَ يَميناً (i)	to take an oath
حَوالة	assignment, cession
خالَفَ	to break (rule)
خَبير، pl. خُبَراءُ	expert
خَصْم، pl. خُصُوم	adversary
خيانة	treason
خيانة عُظْمَى	high treason
دار الشُّرْطة	police station
دَعْوة	summons
دَعْوَى، pl. دَعاوى	lawsuit
دعوى مَدَنيّ	civil suit
دَلَّ عَلَى	see أثبت
ذُو سَوابِق	s.o. with a criminal record
رافَعَ عن	to act as s.o.'s defence counsel
رَجْعي	revocable
رَخَّصَ	to license
رَفَعَ اسْتِئْناف (أمام) (a)	to lodge an appeal (before a court)

رَفَعَ الدَعْوَى على (a)	to file a complaint against s.o.	شُرْطة الأدب	vice squad
رفع قَضية على	to bring legal action against	شكاية	complaint
رَهينة pl. رَهائِن	hostage	شَنَقَ (u)	to hang
رئيس النِّيابة	chief prosecutor	شَنْق	hanging
زِنْزانة	cell (prison)	صادَقَ على	to authenticate (e.g. signature)
زَوَّرَ	to forge	صَكّ قانُونيّ pl. صُكُوك قانُونيّة	legal instrument
زَيَّفَ	to counterfeit (money)	صَلاحيّة	jurisdiction
ساري المَعْقُول	valid	صُلْح تَحَفُّظيّ	preventive settlement
سَجَّان	warder, prison guard	طارَدَ	to chase, pursue
سَجَنَ (u)	to imprison	عاقَبَ (ب)	to punish s.o. (for)
سِجْن pl. سُجُون	prison	عبْء الإثْبات	burden of proof
سَجين pl. سَجْنَى, سُجَناءُ	prisoner, inmate	عَدَسة	magnifying glass
		عَدْل pl. عُدُول	notary public
سَجين سياسيّ	political prisoner	عَدُو قَوْميّ رقْم ١	public enemy No 1
سارق pl. سُرَّاق, سَرَقة	thief	عَديم الأهْليَّة	legally incompetent
سَرَقَ (i)	to steal	عَذاب pl. ـات, أعْذِبة	torture
سَرِقة	theft	عَذَّبَ	to torture
سُفَّاح	killer	العِصابة	the Mob
السُّلْطة القَضائيَّة	the Judiciary	عِصبة	(criminal) gang
سَيَّاف	executioner	عَفْو	1. pardon 2. amnesty
شاهِد pl. شُهُود	witness		
شاهِد العِيان	eye-witness	عِقاب	punishment
شُرْطة	police	عِقابيّ	penal
شُرْطِيّ	policeman	عُقُوبة	punishment, sanction

عُقُوبة الإعْدام	death penalty	قَسَم	oath
		pl. أقْسام	
عُنْف	violence	قَضية	lawsuit
عَنيف	violent	pl. قَضايا	
pl. عُنُف		قَفَص الاتِّهام	prisoner's dock
غَرامة	1. fine	قَوّاد	pimp
	2. damages	قَيْد	handcuff
(a) غَرِمَ	to pay (a fine)	pl. قُيُود	
غَرَّمَ	to fine	كاتب	court secretary
غَيْر قانونيّ	illegal	pl. كُتَّاب, ون-	
غُسْل الأمْوال	money laundering	كاتب اخْتِزال	stenographer
غَسيل الأمْوال	see غسل الأموال	كامِل الأهْليّة	legally competent
غَشٌّ, غِشٌّ	fraud	كَشّاف كَهْرَبائيّ	searchlight
(u) فَضَحَ	to expose, uncover	pl. كَشّافة كَهْرَبائيّة	
فَضيحة	scandalous act, infamy	(i, u) كَفَلَ	to guarantee
pl. فَضائِح		كَفالة	bail
قاتل	murderer	كَلِمة الشَّرَف	word of honour
pl. قُتّال		لَجْنة التَّحْليف	jury
قاضٍ	judge	(u) لَصَّ	to rob
pl. قُضاة		لِصّ	robber
قانُون	law	pl. لُصُوص	
pl. قَوانين		لُصُوصيّة	robbery
قانون جِنائيّ	criminal law	لِقاء كَفالة	on bail
قانون دُسْتُوريّ	constitutional law	مُتَرْجِم مُحَلَّف	sworn translator
قانون دُوَليّ	international law	مُتَّهَم بـ	accused of
قانون مَدَنيّ	civil law	المُتَّهَم	the accused
قانونيّ	legal, lawful	مُجْرِم	criminal
قانونيّة	lawfulness	مُحاكَمة	court hearing
(i) قَبَضَ عَلَى	see اعتقل		

مُحامٍ	lawyer	مَسْرُوقات	stolen goods
مُحاوَلة الاغْتِيال	assassination attempt	مُسَلَّح	gunman
مُحْضِر	court usher	مُشْتَبَه فيه	suspect
مُحَقِّق	detective	مُشْتَبَه ب	suspected of
مَحْكَمة	court, tribunal	مَشْبُوه	suspicious, dubious
pl. مَحاكِمُ		مُشَرِّع	lawmaker
مَحْكَمة جِنائيّة	criminal court	مَشْرُوعيّ	see قانوني
المَحْكَمة الجِنائيّة الدَّوْليّة	International Criminal Tribunal	مَشْرُوعيّة	legality
محكمة عُرْفيّة	court martial	مِشْنَقة	gallows
مَحْكُوم عَلَيْه ب	sentenced to	pl. مَشانِقُ	
مُحَلَّف	juror	مَشْهَد	scene (crime)
		pl. مَشاهِدُ	
مُخالَفة	infringement, violation	مُطْلَق السَّراح	at large
مُخْتَلِس	embezzler	مُعْدٍ	aggressor
مُخَدِّر	illegal drug	مُعْتاد الجَرائم	habitual criminal
pl. ـات		مُعَلَّق	pending
مُدانٍ ب	convicted of	مُغْتَصِب	rapist
المُدَّعَى عَلَيْه	defendant	مُفْتَرَض	alleged (adj.)
المُدَّعِي	plaintiff	مُفَتِّش	inspector
مَدَنيّ	civil	المُدَّعِي العامّ	public prosecutor
مُدِير السِّجْن	prison governor, warden	مُفَوَّض شُرْطة	police commissioner
مُذْنِب	guilty party	مَمْنُوع	forbidden
مُرافَعة	1. proceedings at law	مَنَع (a)	to prohibit
	2. speech for the defence	مُهَرِّب	smuggler
مُرْتَكِب	criminal	مُهَرَّب	contraband
مَزاعِمُ	allegations	pl. ـات	
مُزَيِّف	counterfeiter	مُهْلة	respite, delay

مَوادّ جِنائِيَّة	criminal cases	هِراوة	truncheon
مواد مَدَنِيَّة	civil cases	هَراوى .pl	
مُوفَد	delegate	هَرَب (u)	to escape
نَشّال	pickpocket	هَرَّب	1. to free (a prisoner)
			2. to smuggle
نَشْل	pickpocketing	هُرُوب	flight, getaway
النِّيابة	the prosecution	هَوادة	leniency, clemency
نِيابة عُمُومِيَّة	public prosecution service	وَصايا	regulation, ordinance
هارِب	fugitive, runaway	يَمين	oath
		أَيْمان ,أَيْمَن .pl	

The military

أَبادَ	to annihilate	اسْتَرْجَعَ	to recover
إبادة جَماعِيَّة	genocide	اسْتِرْجاع	recovery
إجْراءات أمْنِيَّة	security measures	اسْتَرَقَ	to monitor (communications)
أجْلَى	to evacuate (trans.)	اسْتِسْلام	surrender
احْتِلالَ	occupation	اسْتَسْلَمَ	to surrender
احْتَلَّ	to occupy	اسْتِطلاع	reconnaissance
احْتِلال عَسْكَرِيّ	military occupation	اسْتَعْرَضَ	to review (troops)
أحْكام عُرْفِيَّة	martial law	اسْتَلَّ	to draw (a sword)
أداة التَّفْجير	explosive device	اسْتَهْدَفَ	to target
الأراضي المُحْتَلَّة	the Occupied Territories (Palestine)	اسْتَوْلَى	to confiscate
أرْكان الجَيْش	general staff	أَسَرَ (i)	to take prisoner
اسْتِخْبارات	see مخابرات	أُسْطُول	fleet
		أساطيلُ .pl	
اسْتَخْلَصَ المَعْلُومات	to debrief	أَسْلِحة خَفيفة	small arms
		أَسير	captive, prisoner of war
		أَسارَى ,أَسْرَى ,أَسْراء .pl	

إِشْعاع	radiation	اِنْفَجَرَ	to explode, detonate
أَطْلَقَ	to launch (e.g. missile)	اِنْهَزَمَ	to be defeated, routed
أَطْلَقَ النّارَ على	to shoot, open fire at	بارِجة	warship, man of war
اِعْتَقَلَ	to intern (prisoner)	pl. بَوارِج	
أَغْمَدَ	to sheathe (sword)	بارُود	gunpowder, saltpetre
اِقْتَحَمَ	to storm	بَطَل	hero
آلة حَرْبِيّة	instrument of war	pl. أَبْطال	
اِلْتَحَقَ بالجَيْش	to join the army	بُلُوك	company
أَمَرَ (u)	to command	pl. ـات	
أَمْر	command	بَنْد	banner
pl. أوامِر		pl. بُنُود	
آمِر	commanding officer	بُنْدُقِيّة	gun, rifle
أمير اللِواء	brigadier	بُنْدُقِيّة آلِيّة	automatic rifle
اِنْتِشار الأَسْلِحة النَّوَوِيّة	nuclear proliferation	تَبادَلَ إطْلاق النّار	to exchange fire
		تَجْريد من السِّلاح	disarmament
اِنْتِصار	victory	تَجَسَّسَ	to spy
اِنْتَصَرَ على	to be victorious over	تَجَسُّس	espionage
اِنْدَلَعَ	to break out (war)	تَجْنيد	enlistment, mobilization
إِنْذار	alarm	تَجْنيد إجْباريّ	conscription
pl. ـات		تَحْرير	liberation
إنذار بوُقُوع غارات جَوِّيّة	air-raid warning	تَخْريب	sabotage
اِنْسِحاب	withdrawal	تَدَخَّلَ (في)	to intervene (in)
اِنْسَحَبَ	to withdraw (troops)	تَدَخُّل (عَسْكَريّ)	(military) intervention
اِنْضِباط	discipline	تَدْريب عَسْكَريّ	military training
اِنْعِكاسات	repercussions	تَدْمير	destruction
اِنْغَلَبَ	to be defeated	تُرْس	shield
اِنْفِجار	explosion	pl. أتْراس, تُرُوس	
pl. ـات			

تَرْسانة	arsenal	جَلاء	evacuation
تَسَرُّب	see تسلُّل	جَلا (يَجْلُو) عَن	to evacuate from
تَسَلَّلَ إِلى	to infiltrate	جَنَّدَ	to conscript, draft
تَسَلُّل	infiltration	جُنْد (coll.)	soldiers
تَشْكِيل	formation (order)	pl. جُنُود	
تَسَلَّحَ	to arm oneself	جُنْدِيّ	1. soldier
تَطْهِير إِثْنِيّ	ethnic cleansing		2. private (rank)
تَعْبِئة	mobilization	جَيْش	army
تَعْزِيزات عَسْكَرِيّة	military reinforcements	pl. جُيُوش	
تَفْتِيش	inspection	جيش الاحْتِلال	occupation force
pl. تَفاتِيشُ		حارَبَ	to wage war
تَفَجَّرَ	to explode (intrans.)	حارِس	sentry
تَفَقَّدَ	to inspect	pl. حُرّاس	
تَقاتَلَ	to fight one another	حاصَرَ	to besiege
تَكْتِيكات عَسْكَرِيّة	military tactics	حافَظ (على)	to protect against
تَمَرُّد	1. rebellion	حالة التَّأَهُّب	state of alert
	2. mutiny	حالة الحَرْب	state of war
تَوَغَّلَ فِي	to penetrate deeply into	حامِلة الطّائِرات	see ناقلة الطّائِرات
ثائِر	see متمرد	حامِية	garrison
pl. ثُوّار		حَرِبَ (a)	to wage war against
جاسُوس	spy	حَرْب (f.)	war
pl. جَواسِيسُ		pl. حُرُوب	
جَبان	coward	حَرْب الأَدْغال	jungle warfare
pl. جُبَناءُ		حَرْب أَهْلِيّة	civil war
جَبانة	cowardice	الحرب البارِدة	the Cold War
جَرِيح	injured person	حرب خاطفة	blitzkrieg
pl. جَرْحى		حرب العِصابات	guerrilla warfare
جُلّة	cannon ball	حَرَّرَ	to liberate
pl. جُلَل			

حَشَدَ (i, u)	to mobilize	دَرَجة الاسْتِعْداد	state of readiness
حِصار	blockade, cordon	دِرْع	coat of mail
حِصار جَوّيّ	air blockade	pl. أَدْرُع, أَدْراع, دُرُوع	
حَصيلة القَتْلَى	death toll	دِرع واقٍ	protective armour
حَظْر التَّجَوُّل	see منع للتجول	دِفاع	defence
حِلْف	league, alliance	دَمَّرَ	to destroy
pl. أَحْلاف		دَوْرِيَّة	patrol
حِلْف عَسْكَرِيّ	military alliance	ذَخيرة	ammunition
حَليف	ally	رائِد	major
pl. حُلَفاءُ		pl. ون, رُوَّاد	
حِماية	protection	رَئيس الأَرْكان	see رئيس أركان الجيش
حَمْلة	campaign	رَئيس أَرْكان الجَيْش	chief of general staff
حَمَى (i)	to protect		
خائِن	traitor	رُتْبة	rank
pl. خُوَان		pl. رُتَب	
خِدمة عَسْكَرِيّة	military service	رَشاش قَصير	submachine gun
خَرَبَ (i)	to destroy, lay waste	رَصاصة	bullet
خَرْطُوش	cartridge	رَقيب	sergeant
pl. خَراطيشُ		pl. رُقَباءُ	
خَنْجَر	dagger	رَقيب أَوَّل	sergeant major
pl. خَناجِرُ		رُكْن	military staff
خَنْدَق	trench	pl. أَرْكان	
pl. خَنادِقُ		رُمْح	lance
خِيانة	treason	pl. رِماح	
دارِعة	armoured cruiser	زَحَفَ (a)	to advance (army)
pl. دَوارِعُ		زَحْف	advance, march
دافَعَ عن	to protect against	زَوْرَق حَرْبِيّ	gunboat
دَبّابة	tank	ساحة القتال	battlefield
دُبّانة	sight (e.g. rifle)	سِباق الأَسْلِحة	arms race

سِرْب pl. أَسْراب	squadron	شَنَّ هُجُوماً	to launch an attack
سَفِينة حَرْبِيّة	see بارجة	شَهَرَ (a)	to draw (a weapon)
سِلاح pl. أَسْلِحة	weapon	شهر البندقِيّة على	to level a gun at
سِلاح الدَّمار الشامِل	weapon of mass destruction	شهر الحَرب على	to declare war on
سِلاح ذَرّيّ	see سِلاح نَوَويّ	صاروخ pl. صَواريخُ	rocket, missile
سِلاح قَذّافِيّ	ballistic weapon	صاروخ بَعيد المَضَى	long-range missile
سِلاح نَوَويّ	nuclear weapon	صارُوخ سَطْح- جَوّ	surface-to-air missile
سَلام	peace	صاروخ طَوّاف	cruise missile
سَلَّح	to arm	صاروخ عابِر القارات	intercontinental ballistic missile (ICBM)
سُلْطة عَسْكَرِيّة	military authority		
سِلْك شائِك	barbed wire	صاروخ قَصير المَدَى	short-range missile
سَهْم pl. سِهام	arrow	صاروخ مُضادّ للطائرات	anti-aircraft missile
سَيّارة مُدَرَّعة	armoured car	صالَحَ	to make peace
سَيّارة مُفَخَّخة	car bomb	صِراع	conflict
سَيْف pl. سُيُوف	sword	صُلْح	peace, reconciliation
شارِد pl. شَوارِد, شُرَّد, شُرُد	deserter, defector	صَليل السِّلاح	clatter of weapons
شُجّاع pl. شَجَعة, شُجْعان	brave	ضابِط pl. ضُبّاط	officer
شَجاعة	bravery	ضابِط الصَّفّ	non-commissioned officer
شَجُعَ (u)	to be brave	ضَحية pl. ضَحايا	victim
الشُّرْطة العَسْكَرِيّة	the Military Police	ضَرَبَ (i)	to strike
شَظايا (pl.)	shrapnel	ضَرْبة pl. ضَرَبات	strike
شَنَّ حَرْباً (u)	to start a war		

ضَرْبة عَسْكَرِيّة	military strike	عَفْو عامّ (عن)	general amnesty (for)
ضَرَبة وِقائِيّة	pre-emptive strike	عَقيد	colonel
ضَرْب النّار	see قصف	pl. عُقَداء	
طائرة دَوْرِيّة	reconnaissance plane	عَمَلِيَّة انْتِحارِيّة	suicide attack
طائرة عَمُودِية	helicopter	غارة جَوِّيّة	air raid
طائرة القتال	combat plane	غارات مُتَواصِلة	rolling attacks
طائرة مِرْوَحِيّة	see طائرة عمودية	غالب	victor
طائرة مُقاتِلة	fighter plane	pl. غَلَبة	
طَرّادة	cruiser	غَزا (u)	to raid, attack
طُرْبيد	see نسيفة	غَزْو	raid, incursion
طَرَدَ (u)	to expel, drive out	pl. غَزَوات	
طَرَف	side, party	غِطاء جَوِّيّ	air cover
pl. أَطْراف		غِمْد	sheath
طَلَق	shot	pl. أَغْماد	
pl. أَطْلاق, -ات		غَنِمَ (a)	to plunder
طَيّار	pilot	غَنيمة	(war) booty
		pl. غَنائمُ	
عادَ	to treat as an enemy	غَوّاصة	submarine
عَبَّأَ (جَيْشاً)	to mobilize (an army)	فَتَحَ (a)	to conquer
عَدّ تَنازُلِيّ	countdown	فَتَحَ النّار	see أطلق النّار
عَداوة	hostility, animosity	فَتَّشَ	see تفقد
عَدُو	enemy	فُتُوح	conquest
pl. أَعْداء		pl. -ات	
عُدْوان	1. see عداوة	فَجَّرَ	to explode (trans.)
	2. aggression, hostile action	فِدائي	1. guerrilla fighter
			2. fedayeen
عَريف	corporal	فَرَّ (من) (i)	to escape (from), run away
pl. عُرَفاءُ		فِرْقة	company (army)
عَريف أَوَّل	lance corporal	pl. فِرق	
عَسْكَرِيّ	military (adj.)	فَرْقَعَ	to explode, burst

فَرِيق pl. أَفْرِقاءُ, فُروق	lieutenant general	قَصْف	bombardment, shelling
فَصيلة pl. فَصائِلُ	squad	قَصْف جَوِّيّ	air bombardment
فَصيلة الإعْدام	firing squad	قَصْف دَقيق	precision bombing
فَكَّ (u)	to ransom, liberate	قَصْف مِدْفَعيّ	artillery fire
فَكاك	ransom	قَلَّدَ	to confer, award (a decoration)
فَوْج (عَسْكَرِيّ) pl. أَفْواج (عَسْكَرِيّة)	regiment	قِناع واقٍ	gas mask
في حالة الحَرْب	in a state of war	قَنْبَلَ	to bomb
فَيْلَق pl. فَيالِقُ	army corps	قُنْبُلة pl. قَنابِلُ	bomb, shell
قاتَلَ	to fight	قُنْبُلة حارقة	incendiary bomb
قاذفة الصَّواريخ	rocket launcher	قنبلة ذَرّيّة	A-bomb
قاعدة عَسْكَرِيّة	military base	قُنْبُلة عُنْقوديّة	cluster bomb
قانص pl. قُنّاص	sniper	قُنْبُلة غازِيّة	gas shell
قاوَمَ	to resist	قُنْبُلة مائِيّة	depth charge
قَتَلَ (u)	to kill, murder	قُنْبُلة مُحْرِقة	see قنبلة حارقة
قَتيل pl. قَتْلى	casualty (dead)	قُنْبُلة مُنْفَجِرة	high-explosion bomb
قَذَفَ بالقَنابِل (i)	to bomb	قُنْبُلة نَوَوِيّة	nuclear bomb
قَذيفة pl. قَذائِفُ	1. projectile, shell 2. detonator	قُنْبُلة هيدروجينيّة	hydrogen bomb
قذيفة اللَهَب	flame thrower	قُنْبُلة يَدَوِيّة	hand grenade
قَذيفة هاوُن	mortar bomb	قُوّات احْتِياطِيّة	reserves
قِراب pl. أَقْرِبة, قُرُب	scabbard	قُوّات الأمْن	security forces
		قُوّات بَرِّيّة	Army, ground forces
قَشْلة pl. قِشَل	barracks	قُوّات بَحْرِيّة	Navy
		قُوّات التَّحالُف	the Allied Forces
		قُوّات جوِّيّة	Airforce
		قُوّات حِفْظ السَّلام	peacekeeping forces
		قُوّات خاصّة	special forces

قُوَّة دِفاعِيّة	defence force	مُتَفَجِّرات	explosives
قُوّات الصّاعقة	commandos	مُتَمَرِّد	rebel, insurgent
قُوّة مُتَعَدِّدة الجِنْسِيات	multinational force	مَجْزَرة pl. مَجازِر	massacre
القُوّات المُسلَّحة	the armed forces	مُجَنَّد	recruit, conscript
قُوّات هَنْدَسِيّة	engineering corps	مُخابَرات	intelligence service, secret service
قُوّة مُدَرَّعة	tank corps	مَدافِع ضَخْمة	heavy artillery
قَوْس pl. أَقْواس	bow	مِدْفَع pl. مَدافِعُ	cannon, gun
كافَحَ	to combat	مدفع رَشّاش	machine gun
كَبَتَ (i)	to crush, repress	مدفع هاوُن	mortar
كَتيبة pl. كَتائِبُ	battalion	مِدْفَعيّ	artilleryman
كُلّة pl. كُلَل	1. see جِلة 2. shell, grenade	مِدْفَعيّة	artillery
كُلِّيّة الحَرْب	military academy	مدفعيّة مُضادة الطّائِرات	anti-aircraft artillery
كَمين pl. كُمَناءُ	ambush	مُدَمِّرة	destroyer (ship)
لَغَمَ (a)	to mine	مَدَنيّ	civilian
لُغْم pl. لُغْم، أَلْغام	mine	مَرَّدَ على	to revolt, rebel against
		مُساعِد	adjutant
لِواء	1. general (rank) 2. flag	مُسَدَّس pl. ـات	revolver
مَأْذُونية	leave, furlough	مَسْرَح الحَرْب	theatre of war
مارِد pl. مُرّاد، مَرَدة، ـون	see متمرد	المُشاة (pl.)	the infantry
		مَصْرَع pl. مَصارِعُ	battleground
مارشال	marshal	مِظلّة	parachute
مُباغَتة	surprise attack	مِظلّيّ	paratrooper
مُتَطَوِّع	volunteer	مُعْتَقَل pl. ـات	concentration camp

مَعْرَكة	battle	مَيْدان العَمَلِيّات	field of operations
pl. مَعَارِك		ناقلة جُنُود مُدَرَّعة	armoured personnel carrier (APC)
مُعَسْكَر	military camp		
pl. ـات		ناقلة الطَّائِرات	aircraft carrier
مُعْنَوِيات	morale	نِزاع	conflict
مَفَرّ	escape	(i) نَزَعَ السِّلاح	to disarm
pl. مَفَارّ		نَزْع السِّلاح	disarmament
مُقاتِل	fighter	نَسِيفة	torpedo
مُقَدَّم	lieutenant colonel	pl. نَسائِف	
مُكافَحة	struggle, combat	نِصاب	hilt, handle (of weapon)
مُلازِم	second lieutenant	pl. ـات, نُصُب	
مُلازِم أوّل	first lieutenant	نَصْل	blade
مَلْجَأ	shelter, dugout	pl. نِصال	
pl. مَلاجِىء		نِضال	struggle
مَلْجَأ مَضادّ للغارات الجَوَّيّة	air-raid shelter	نَفّاثة	jet (plane)
مُناوَرة	manoeuvre	نَفَر القُرْعة	draftee
مَنْصُور	conqueror	pl. أنْفار	
مِنْطَقة حَظْر جَوّيّ	no-fly zone	(i) نَفَى	to exile, banish
مِنْطَقة خالية من الأسْلِحة النَّوَوِيّة	nuclear-free zone	نَقِيب	captain
		pl. نُقَباءُ	
مِنْطَقة القتال	combat zone	نَهّاب	plunderer
مَنْع للتَجَوُّل	curfew	نَوْط	medal
مَنْفَى	place of exile	pl. نِياط, أنْواط	
مُهادَنة	truce negotiations	نَوَوِيّ	nuclear
المُؤَسَّسة العَسْكَرِيّة	the military	نِيشان	decoration
مَيْدان التَدْرِيب	drill ground	pl. نَياشِينُ	
pl. مَيادِينُ		هادَنَ	to conclude a truce with
ميدان الحَرْب	see مسرح الحرب	(i) هَجَمَ	to attack
		هُجُوم	attack
		هُجُوم إرهابيّ	terrorist attack

هُجُوم بَرِّيّ	ground offensive	هَزِيمة	defeat
هُجُوم مُضادّ	counter-offensive	pl. هَزائِمُ	
هَدَف	target	هَليكُبْتَر	see طائرة عمودية
pl. أَهْداف			
هُدْنة	truce	وَحْدة	unit
(u) هَرَبَ	to flee	pl. وَحَدات	
هرب مَن الخِدْمة العَسْكَرِيّة	desertion, draft dodging	وَرْطة	critical situation
		pl. وِراط, وَرَطات	
(i) هَزَمَ	to rout, defeat	وَقْف إِطْلاق النّار	ceasefire

Economics and commerce

اتِّفاق	contract	اِحْتِكار	monopoly
		pl. ـات	
اِتِّفاق تِجارِيّ	trade agreement	اِحْتَكَرَ	to monopolize
اتِّفاقِية	see اتّفاق	اِحْتِياطات النَّقْد الأَجْنَبِيّ	foreign currency reserves
أَساسِيّ	basic, fundamental		
إِجابة	transfer, conveyance	اِحْصائِيّ	statistician
إِجازة	licence, permit	اِخْتِراع	invention
أَجْر	salary, wages	pl. ـات	
pl. أُجُور		اِخْتَرَعَ	to invent
أجر السَفَر	fare (coach, etc.)	اِدَّخَرَ	to save, put by
إِجْرائِيّ	operational	اِرْتَقى (الى)	to be promoted (to)
أُجْرة	1. rate	اِرْتَهَنَ	to receive in pledge
	2. fare (taxi)	اِسْتَبْضَعَ	to trade
أجرة النَّقْل	transport charges	اِسْتِثْمار	investment
إِجْمالِيّ	total, gross	pl. ـات	
اِحْتَسَبَ على	to charge (money) for	اِسْتَثْمَرَ	to invest

اِسْتَحَقَّ	to deserve
اِسْتَرَدَّ	to reclaim
اِسْتِرْداد	refund
اِسْتَعْرَضَ	to examine, inspect
اِسْتِغاثة	appeal for aid
اِسْتَغَلَّ	to exploit
اِسْتَفاد من	to benefit from
اِسْتِقْرار الأسْعار	price stability
اِسْتَلَفَ	to borrow
اِسْتَلَمَ	to receive
اِسْتِمارة طَلَب	application form
اِسْتِهلاك	consumption
اِسْتَهْلَكَ	to consume
اِسْتَوْدَعَ	to store
اِسْتَوْرَدَ	to import
أَسَّسَ	to set up, establish
أَسْنَدَ إلى	to entrust to
أسْواق الصَّرْف	exchange markets
أسْواق العُمْلة الأجْنَبِيّة	foreign currency markets
اِشْتِراء	purchase
اِشْتِراك	subscription
اِشْتَرَكَ	to subscribe
اِشْتَرى	to buy
اِشْتَغَلَ	to work
أشْرَفَ على	to supervise
إشْهار	advertising, publicity

اِصْطَلَحَ (على)	1. to agree on
	2. to adopt
اِصْطِناعِيّ	artificial
اِصْطَنَعَ	to manufacture
أَصْل pl. أُصُول	asset
أضاعَ	see بدد
إضْراب pl. ـات	strike
أضْرَبَ	to strike
إضْطَلَعَ بـ	to be skilled in
اطار pl. أُطُر, ـات	framework
إعادة جَدْوَل الدُّيُون	debt restructuring
إعادة الإعْمار	reconstruction
إعانة	subsidy
اِعْتِماد	credit
إعْلان pl. ـات	advertisement
أعْلَنَ	to advertise
إغاثة	aid
اِغْتَشَّ	to be cheated, duped
أغْنى	to enrich (s.o.)
إفادة التَّسْليم	acknowledgement of receipt
اِفْتَقَرَ	to become poor
أفْضَلِيَّة	precedence, priority
إفْلاس	bankruptcy, insolvency
أفْلَحَ	to thrive

أَفْلَسَ	to be(come) bankrupt	إيصال	receipt, voucher
أَقالَ	to dismiss	باعَ (i)	to sell
اِقْتِراح	proposal	باع بالمَزاد	to sell at auction
اِقْتِصاد	economy	بائع	seller, salesman
اِقْتِصاد الحَجْم	economy of scale	pl. باعة	
اِقْتِصاديّ	1. economist	بائع مُتَجوّل	travelling salesman
	2. economic	بالتَقْسيط	in instalments
اِكْتَسَبَ	to acquire	بالجُمْلة	wholesale
اِلْتِماس	job application	بالدَيْن	on credit
إِلْغاء الدُيُون	debt cancellation	بَدَّدَ	to squander
أمانة	deposit	بضاعة	merchandise
اِمْتِياز	concession, licence	pl. بَضائعُ	
pl. ـات		بطاقة اِئْتِمان	credit card
أمَّمَ	to nationalize	بالقَطَاعِي	retail
أمَّنَ	to insure	بالمائة	per cent
أمين الصُنْدُوق	treasurer	بَدَل السَفَر	travelling expense
إِنْتاج	production	بطالة	unemployment
إِنْتاج على السَيْر	assembly line production	بَنْدَر	commercial centre
		pl. بَنادر	
أَنْتَجَ	to produce, result in	بَنْك	bank
اِنْدِماج	merger, amalgamation	pl. بُنُوك	
اِنْدَمَجَ	to amalgamate, merge	بُنْية تَحْتِية	infrastructure
إِنْسانيّ	humanitarian	بُورصة	Stock Exchange, Bourse
إِنْشاء	foundation, establishment	بُوليسة الشَحْن	bill of lading
أَنْفَقَ	to spend	بَيْت المال	Treasury
اِنْهِيار	crash	بيع	sale
		pl. بُيُوع, بُيُوعات	
أَهْدى	to give as a present	تاجر	trader, merchant
		pl. تُجّار	

تاجِر المُفَرَّق	retailer
تارِيخ الاسْتِحْقاق	due date (e.g. repayment)
تَأْمِيم	nationalization
تَأْمِين	insurance
تَأْمِين ضِدَّ الحَرِيق	fire insurance
تَأْمِين ضِدّ الحَوادِث	accident insurance
تَأْمِين على الحَياة	life assurance
تَبادَلَ	to barter
تَبادُل تِجارِيّ	trade exchange
تَبَرَّعَ	to donate
تَبَرُّع	donation
تَبَضَّعَ	to shop
تِجارة	trade, commerce
تِجارِيّ	commercial
تَجْمِيد الأمْوال	freezing of assets
تَحَرَّشَ	see ضايق
تَحَسَّنَ	to improve (*intrans.*)
تَحَوَّلَ	to change (*intrans.*)
تَحْوِيل pl. ـات	transfer, remittance (money)
تَخْزِين	storage
تَخْفِيض pl. ـات	reduction
تَخْفِيض القِيمة	devaluation
تَداوُل	circulation (money)
تَذَبْذَبَ	to fluctuate
تَراوَحَ بَيْن	to range between

تَرْخِيص pl. تَراخِيصُ	authorization, concession
تَرْقِية	promotion (position)
تَرْوِيج	promotion (marketing)
تَسْدِيد	settlement of a debt
تَسْلِيف	credit
تَسْلِيم	delivery
تَسَوَّغَ	to take a lease on s.thing
تَسَوُّق	shopping
تَسَوَّلَ	to beg
تَسْوِية	settlement
تَسْوِيغ	leasing
تَسْوِيق	marketing (of merchandise)
تَشاغَلَ	to pretend to be busy
تَصْرِيح pl. ـات, تَصارِيحُ	official permit
تَصْفِية	1. liquidation 2. clearance (sale)
تَصْفِية الحِسابات	settlement of accounts
تَصْمِيم آلِيّ	computer-aided design (CAD)
تَضاءَلَ	to dwindle
تَضَخُّم (مالِيّ)	inflation
تَطَوَّرَ	to develop (*intrans.*)
تَطَوُّر pl. ـات	development
تَعامَلَ مع	to do business with
تَعْرِيفة	tariff

تَعَيَّشَ	to earn a living	تَوَسُّع	expansion
تَعْليمات الدَّفْع	payment instructions	تَوَظَّفَ	to be employed
تَعَهَّدَ ب، ل	to commit oneself	تَوْظيف	employment, appointment
تَعْويض pl. ـات	damages, compensation	تَوَلَّى	to undertake
تَغَيَّرَ	see تحوّل	ثَرْوة	wealth
تَفْتيش pl. تَفاتيشُ	inspection	ثَمَن pl. أَثْمان	price
تَفْويض	proxy, power of attorney	جِبائيّ	fiscal
تَفْويض مُطْلَق	general power of attorney	جَدَّدَ	to modernize
تَقاضَى	to claim, demand payment	جَرْد	stocktaking, inventory
تَقاعُد	pension	جَمَّدَ	to freeze (e.g. assets)
تَقْدير	estimate, valuation	جَمْعيَّة	society, association
تَقْليد	imitation	جَمْعيَّة تَعاوُنيَّة	cooperative society
تَكامُل اقْتِصاديّ	economic integration	جَمْعيَّة خَيْريَّة	charitable organization
تَكَلَّفَ على	to spend (money) on	جُنَيْه pl. ـات	pound (Egyptian currency)
تَكْليف pl. تَكاليفُ	cost, expense	جُنَيْه اِسْتِرْلينيّ	pound sterling
تَمَسُّك	IOU	جِهاز الكَسْب	cash cow
تَمْويل	financing, funding	حاسَبَ على	to charge for (s.thing)
تَنافُس	competition	حاصِل pl. ـات, حَواصِلُ	product
تَنْزيلات	sales (shops)	حَجَزَ (u, i)	to seize, confiscate
تَهَرُّب من الضَّرائب	tax evasion	حَجْز	seizure, confiscation
تَهْريب العُمْلة	currency smuggling	حَجْم التِّجارة	volume of trade
تَوَتُّر	stress	حَرْب تِجاريّة	trade war
تَوْزيع	distribution	حِرْفة pl. حِرَف	profession, craft
تَوَسُّط	mediation		
تَوَسَّعَ	to expand (intrans.)	حِرَفيّ	craftsman

حَرَكة البَيْع	turnover
حِرْمان	deprivation, dispossession
حِساب pl. ‑ات	1. account (e.g. bank) 2. bill, invoice
حِساب جارٍ	current account
حِساب تَوْفير	savings account
حِساب مُجَمَّد	frozen account
حَسَّنَ	to improve (*trans.*)
حصة في الرِّبْح	dividend
حَصَّلَ	1. to collect (payment) 2. to levy (taxes)
حَصيلة pl. حَصائِل	yield, income
حَظْر	embargo, ban
حَظْر اِقْتِصاديّ	economic boycott
حَظْر تِجاريّ	trade embargo
حَقَّقَ	1. to realise, achieve 2. to verify
حَمْلة التَّسْويق	marketing campaign
حَوّالة	1. bill of exchange 2. promissory note
حَوّالة سَفَر	traveller's cheque
حَوّلَ	1. to transform, change (*trans.*) 2. to change (money) 3. to transfer, remit (money)
خِبْرة	experience
خَبير pl. خُبَراء	expert
خَدَمَ (i, u)	to serve

خِدْمة pl. خَدَمات	service
خَرْج	outlay, expenditure
خَزْنة مُحَصَّنة	safe (*n.*)
خَسارة pl. خُسْران	loss
خَسِرَ (a)	to incur losses
خَصَّصَ	to privatize
خَصْخَصة	privatization
خَصْم pl. خُصوم	discount
خُصوم	liabilities
خَطّ الفَقْر	poverty line
خَفَّضَ	to lower (e.g. prices, taxes)
خِلافات	differences
خَيْمة البَيْع pl. ‑ خِيَم	market stall
دائِن	creditor
دَجّال pl. دَجاجِلة, ‑ون	swindler, cheat
دَجَلَ (u)	to deceive, dupe, cheat
دَخَلَ حَيِّز التَّنْفيذ	to come into effect
دَجْل	deceit, trickery
دَخْل	income, revenue
دِرْهَم pl. دَراهِمُ	dirham (currency)
دَفْتَر pl. دَفاتِر	ledger, register
دفتر حِسابيّ	1. account book 2. bankbook

دفتر الشِّيكات	cheque book	رائج	in demand (product)
دفتر الصُّنْدُوق	cashbook	رِباء	usurious interest
دفتر اليَوْميّة	journal	رِبْح	profit
(a) دَفَعَ	to pay	pl. أرْباح	
دَفْع	payment	رِبْح إجْماليّ	gross profit
دُكَّان	shop, store	رِبْح صافٍ	net profit
pl. دَكاكينُ		(a) رَبِحَ من	to profit from
دُوَل مُتَخَلِّفة	underdeveloped (lit. 'backward') countries	رِبَويّ	usurious
دُوَل مُتَقَدِّمة	developed countries	رَجُل آليّ	robot
		pl. رِجال آليُّون	
دُوَل ناميّة	developing countries	رَجُل الأعْمال	businessman
دَوْلة الرَّفاه	welfare state	رَخاء	prosperity
دولار	dollar	رَخيص	cheap
pl. ـات		pl. رُخاص	
دَيْن	debt	رَدّ	reimbursement
pl. دُيُون		pl. رُدُود	
دَيْن مُسْتَحَقّ	outstanding debt	رَسْم	1. customs duty (tax)
دَيْن مُوَحَّد	consolidated debt	pl. رُسُوم	2. charge
			3. regulation
دينار	dinar	رَسْم دُخُوليّ	import duty
pl. دَنانيرُ		رسم الصَّادِر	export duty
رابِح	lucrative	رَسْم قيميّ	ad valorem duty
رَأْس مال	capital	رُسُوم البَلَديّة	municipal tax
pl. رُؤُوس أمْوال			
رَأسمال	see رَأس مال	(i) رَصَدَ	to monitor
pl. رَساميلُ		رَصَّدَ	to allocate (funds)
رَأس ماليّ	capitalist	رَصيد	1. balance
راقَبَ	to supervise	pl. أرْصِدة	2. stock
راهِن	mortgager	(يَرْعَى) رَعَى	to sponsor
راوَحَ بَيْنَ	to fluctuate between	(a) رَفَعَ	to raise (e.g. prices, taxes)

رَفاهة	luxury	ساهَمَ في	to contribute to
رَقِيَ (a)	to rise to (rank)	ساوَمَ	to haggle
رقّى	to promote	سبَّبَ	to cause
رَقِيب	supervisor	سَحَبَ (a)	to withdraw (e.g. money)
pl. رُقَباءُ		سدَّدَ دَيناً	to settle a debt
ركَّبَ	to assemble	سعْر	see ثمن
ركَدَ (u)	to stagnate	pl. أسْعار	
رُكُود	1. sluggishness, stagnation	سِعْر البَيْع	retail price
	2. recession	سعر التَّحْويل	exchange rate
رَمْزِيّة	logo	سِعْر التَّشْغيل	running cost
رَهَنَ (a)	1. to pawn	سِعْر الصَّرْف	see سعر التحويل
	2. to deposit as security		
	3. to mortgage	سِعْر الفائدة	interest rate
رَهْن	1. mortgage	سِكْرِتيرة	secretary
pl. رُهُون,	2. pledge, security	سِلَع استِهْلاكِيّة	consumer goods
رِهان, رُهُونات		سِلْعة	commodity
رَهْنِية	mortgage (deed)	pl. سِلَع	
رَواج	marketability	سَلَف	advance payment
رَوَّجَ	to bring on the market	pl. أسْلاف	
رِيال	riyal (currency)	سلَّفَ	to lend
pl. ـات		سلَّمَ (إلى، لـ)	to deliver (to s.o.)
زايَدَ	to outbid someone	سِمْسار	broker
زِبانة	clientele	pl. سَماسِرُ, سَماسِرة	
زَبُون	customer, client	سَمْسَرَ	to act as a broker
pl. زَبائنُ,		سَمْسَرة	brokerage
زَبُون دائم	regular customer	سِنّ التَّقاعُد	pensionable age
زَميل	colleague	سَنَد	1. document
pl. زُمَلاءُ		pl. أسْناد, ـات	2. bond, debenture
زَوَّدَ	to distribute	سَهْم	share
زِيادة	increase	pl. أسْهُم	

سهم التَّأْسِيس	founders' share	شِعار	1. slogan, motto
سُوء اسْتِعْمال	misuse, abuse	pl. أَشْعِرة، شُعُر	2. badge, emblem
سُوبِرماركت	supermarket	شُغْل	work, occupation, profession
سُوق	market	pl. أَشْغال	
pl. أَسْواق		شَغَّلَ	see وظَّف
السُوق الحُرَّة	duty free (market)	شَغَّلَ رَأْسمالاً	to invest capital
السوق السَوْداء	the black market	شيك	cheque
السوق المُشْتَرَكة	the Common Market	pl. ـات	
سيَّارة مُصَفَّحة	armoured car	صاحِب الامْتِياز	concessionaire
سَيْر مُتَحَرِّك	assembly line	صاحِب العَمَل	employer
سيرة ذاتيَّة	curriculum vitae	صادِرات	exports
سُيُولة	liquidity	صافٍ	net
شاغِر	vacant (pl. 'vacancies')	صافِي المَبْلَغ	net amount
pl. ـات		صانِع	manufacturer
شاوَرَ	to consult	pl. صُنَّاع	
شَحْن	freight	صَدَّرَ	to export
pl. شُحُون		صَرَّاف	1. banker, money changer
شَراكة	partnership		2. cashier
شَرِكة	company	صرَفَ (على) (i)	1. to spend (money) (on)
			2. to pay (for)
شركة التَّأْمِين	insurance company	صَفْقة	deal, bargain
شركة تِجاريَّة	trading company	pl. صَفَقات	
شركات صَغِيرة و	small- and medium-	صَمَّمَ	to plan, design
مُتَوَسِّطة	sized companies	صناعة	1. industry
شركة مَحْدُودة			2. manufacturing
(المَسْؤوليَّة)	limited liability company	صُنْدُوق التَّوْفِير	savings bank
شركة المُساهَمة	joint-stock company	صُنْع	production, workmanship
شَرِيك	partner	صنَعَ (a)	to make, manufacture
pl. شُرَكاء		صنْع اليَد	handwork
		صَنْعة	craftsmanship

صِنْف pl. صُنُوف, أَصْناف	category	عالِق	pending, remaining
صِيانة	maintenance	عامِل pl. عُمّال	1. worker 2. manual worker, labourer
ضارَبَ	to speculate (e.g. Stock Exchange)	عامِل الإغاثة	aid worker
ضايَقَ	to harass	عامِل مُهاجِر	immigrant worker
ضَرَر pl. أَضْرار	damage	عائِدة pl. عوائِدُ	return (fin.)
ضَرِيبة pl. ضَرائِبُ	tax	عائِدة	return (on investment), dividend
ضَرِيبة الأَرْباح الرَّأْسماليّة	capital gains tax	عَجْز	deficit
		عَجْز تِجاريّ	trade deficit
ضَرِيبة الاسْتِهْلاك	value added tax (VAT)	عُرْبون pl. عَرابينُ	down payment
ضَرِّيبة التَّرِكات	inheritance tax	عَرْض و طَلَب	supply and demand
ضَرِيبة الدَّخْل	income tax	عَزَلَ (i)	to dismiss (s.o.)
ضَرِيبة الطَّاقة	energy tax	عَصْر الصِّناعة	industrial age
ضَرِيبة القيمة المُضافة	see ضريبة الاستهلاك	عَطاء pl. ـات	offer, tender
ضَمان	1. guarantee, warranty 2. collateral, security	عَطِلَ (a)	to be unemployed
ضَمِنَ (a)	to guarantee	عُطْلة pl. عُطَل	holiday, vacation
طَرْز pl. طُرُوز	brand	عُطلة رَسْمِيَّة	public holiday
طَرِيقة pl. طُرُق, طَرائِقُ	method	عَطِية pl. عَطايا	gift
طَلَبَ (u)	1. to demand 2. to order	عَقَدَ (i)	to hold (a meeting)
		عقد صَفْقة	to conclude a bargain
طَلَب pl. ـات	1. demand 2. order	عَقْد pl. عُقُود	contract, agreement
طَوَّرَ	to develop (trans.)	عقد البَيع	sales contract
عاطِل	unemployed	عقد إيجار	lease

عَقِيم	ineffective, unproductive	فاتُورة	invoice
pl. عِقام, عُقُم		pl. فَواتيرُ	
عُقُوبة اقْتِصاديّة	economic sanction	فاوَضَ	to negotiate
عَلاقة تِجاريّة	trading link	فائدة	benefit, advantage
علامة تِجاريّة	trade mark	pl. فَوائدُ	
عَمِلَ (a)	to work	فائض	surplus
عَمَل	trade, craft	pl. فَوائضُ	
pl. أَعْمال		فَعّال	effective
عَمَل فَريقيّ	teamwork	فَعّاليّة	effectiveness
عَمَل مُتَطوّعيّ	volunteer work	فَقْر	poverty
عَمَليّ	practical	فَقير	poor
عَمَل يَدَويّ	manual work	pl. فُقَراءُ	
عُمْلة	currency	فَكّة	change (money)
عُمْلة زائفة	counterfeit money	فَلّسَ	to declare bankrupt
عُمْلة سَهْلة	soft currency	فَوّضَ	to authorize
عُمْلة صَعْبة	hard currency	قابِل للتَّفاوُض	negotiable
عُمُولة	commission	قاطَعَ	to boycott
عُمُولة بَنكيّة	bank charges	قافِلة الأَغْذِيّة	food convoy
عَنْوان بَريديّ	mailing address	قَدّرَ	to estimate, value
عَوّضَ عَن	to compensate for	قَدْر	see مبلغ
عَيّنة	sample	pl. أَقْدار	
عَيْنى	in kind (payment)	قُدْرة تَنافُسيّة	competitiveness
غالي	expensive	قَدّمَ	to present
غُرْفة تِجاريّة	Chamber of Commerce	قَدّمَ عَطاء	to make an offer
غَنِي	rich	قَرْش	piaster (Egyptian currency)
pl. إغْنِياء		pl. قُرُوش	
غَيّرَ	see حَوّل	قَرْض	loan
غَيْر مُؤَهّل	unqualified	pl. قُرُوض	
		قَسّطَ	to pay in instalments
		قِسْط	instalment
		pl. أَقْساط	

قِسْم التَّوْظيف	personnel department	مَأمُور التَّصْفية	official receiver, liquidator
قُشُور	formalities, trivialities	ماهِر pl. مَهَرة	skilful
قطاع خاصّ	private sector	مُبادَرة	initiative
قطاع عامّ	public sector	مُبْتَكَر	new, original
قَلَّد	to imitate	مُبْضِع	limited partner
قُوّات السُّوق	market forces	مُبَعْثَر	scattered, widespread
قُوّة الشِّراء	purchasing power	مُبَعْزِق	squanderer
القُوَى العاملة	see اليد العاملة	مَبْلَغ pl. مَبالِغ	amount
قيمة	value	مُتَداوَل	in circulation, common
كَبَّد	to cause (losses, damage)	مُتَرَكِّم	accumulated
كَثَّف	to consolidate (e.g. loans)	مُتَسَوِّل	beggar
(i) كَسَبَ	1. to gain, earn 2. to acquire	مُتَشَرِّد	homeless person
كَسْب	earnings	مُتَعَد	contractor
كَسَل	idleness	مُتَقاعِد	pensioned, retired
كُشْك pl. أَكْشاك	stall, stand	مُثْمِر	productive
كَفيل pl. كُفَلاء	sponsor	مَجال pl. ـات	field, domain
كَلَّف	to cost	مَجّاناً	free (of charge)
كُلْفة pl. كُلَف	cost	مُجَرَّب	experienced, practised
لُقْطة	bargain, lucky find	مَجْلِس الإدارة	board of directors
لَيْرة	pound (currency of Syria, Lebanon)	مَجْمُوعة	conglomerate
ماركة مُسَجَّلة	registered trade mark	مُحاسِب	accountant
مال pl. أَمْوال	assets, wealth	مُحاسَبة	accounting
		مُحاكاة	imitation
مال احْتياطيّ	reserve fund	مُحال على التَّقاعُد	pensioner
		مُحْتَرِف	professional (adj.)

مَحَلّ رُهُونات	pawn shop	مُساوَمة	haggling
مُخاطِر	risk taker	مُسْتَثْمِر	investor
مُخْتَبَر	laboratory	مُسْتَجِدّات	innovations
مُدير	director, manager	مُسْتَحْدَث	novelty, innovation
		pl. ـات	
مدير عامّ	general manager		
		مُسْتَعير	borrower
مدير مُساعِد	deputy director/manager	مُسْتَفيد	beneficiary
مَدين	debtor	مُسْتَلِم	recipient
مَدْيون	indebted	مُسْتَهْلِك	consumer
مَدْيونِيّة	indebtedness	مُسْتَوْدَع	warehouse
مُراب	usurer	مُسْتَوَى العَيْش/ المَعيشة	living standard
مُراسَلة	correspondence		
مُراقِب	supervisor, foreman	مُسَجِّلة النُّقُود	till, cashbox
مُراقَبة	supervision	مَسْك الحِسابات	accountancy
مُرْبِح	profitable	مَسْك الدَفاتِر	book-keeping
مُرْتَهِن	1. mortgagee	مَسْؤُولِيّة	responsibility
	2. pawnbroker	مُسيء إلَى	harmful to
مَرْكَز	centre	مُشْتَرٍ	purchaser
pl. مَراكِزُ		مُشْتَقّات	derivatives
مَرْكَز الإدارة	head office	مَشْروع	project
مَرْكَز تجارِيّ	emporium	pl. مَشاريعُ	
مَرْكَزِيّ	central	مَشْغُول	busy
مَزاد	auction	مِشْوار	errand
pl. ـات		pl. مَشاويرُ	
مَساءة	shortcoming	مَشْوَرة	consultation
pl. مَساوِئُ		مَصْرُوف	expenditure
مُساعَدات غَذائِيّة	food aid	pl. مَصاريفُ	
مُساهِم	shareholder	مَصْنَع	factory
مُساهَمة	corporation	pl. مَصانِعُ	

مَصْنُوع pl. ـات	manufactured product
مُضارِب	speculator
مُضارَبة	speculation
مُعادَلة	adjustment
مَعاش pl. معاشة	1. livelihood 2. pension (payment)
مَعاش مُبكِّر	early retirement
مُعامِل	trader (Stock Exchange)
مُعامَلة	transaction
مُعاوِن	assistant
مَعْرِض تِجاريّ pl. مَعارِضُ تِجاريّة	trade fair
مَعْمَل البَحْث	research institute
مَعُونة	see إغاثة
مُعير	lender
مُفاعِل	reactor
مُفْتَعَل	forged, fabricated
مُفرَّق	retail (adj.)
مُفْلِس pl. مَفاليسُ	bankrupt, insolvent
مُفاوِض	negotiator
مُفاوَضة	1. negotiation 2. partnership (Islamic law)
مُفَوَّض	authorized agent
مُفيد	useful, beneficial, advantageous
مُقاطَعة	boycott
مُقْتَضًى pl. مُقْتَضَيات	requirement

مُقدَّم	advance, deposit
مَكْتَب pl. مَكاتِبُ	office
مَكْشُوف	uncovered
مُلْتَمِس	applicant
مَلَكَ (i)	to own
مُلكيّة فِكْريّة	intellectual property
مُمَوِّل	financier
مُنافِس	competitor
مُنافَسة	see تنافس
مُناقَصة	public invitation for tender
مِنْحة السُّكْنى	housing benefit
مُنْشَأة	installation, plant
مَنْصِب pl. مَناصِبُ	see وظيفة
مِنْطَقة صِناعيّة	industrial zone
مِنْطَقة مَنْكُوبة	disaster area
مُنظَّمة خَيْريّة	charitable organization, charity
مَهارة	skilfulness, expertise
مَهَرَ (u, a)	to be skilful, proficient, experienced
مَهَمّة pl. مَهامّ	duty
مِهْنة	profession
مِهْنيّ	vocational
مَوادّ تِجاريّة	commercial articles
مَوادّ اسْتِهْلاكيّة	consumer goods
مَوادّ خام	raw materials

مواد مَصْنوعة	manufactured goods	نَشَّطَ	to stimulate
مَوارِد الدَوْلة	government revenues	نَشيط	lively, dynamic
مُودِع	depositor	نَظَّمَ	to organize
المُودَع عليه	consignee	نَفَعَ (a)	to be useful
مَوْرِد	income, revenue	نَفَقات	expenses
pl. مَوارِدُ		نِقابة العُمّال	trade union
مُؤَسَّسة	1. establishment	نَقْد	money
	2. organization, business	pl. نُقُود	
		نَقْداً	in cash
مُؤَشِّر	indicator		
مُوَظَّف	employee	نَقْدِيّة	cash
مُوَظَّف الاسْتِقْبال	receptionist	نُمُو	growth, development
مَوَّلَ	to finance	هداية	see عطية
مُؤْنة، مَؤُونة	provisions, supplies	pl. هَدايا	
pl. مُؤَن		هَواء	amateur
مُؤَهَّل	qualified	هَواية	amateurism
مُؤَهِّل	qualification (training)	هَيْكَل	structure
مَيْدان	see مجال	pl. هَياكِلُ	
pl. مَيادينُ		هَيْكَلِيّ	structural
ميزان تِجارِيّ	trade balance	هَيْكَل تَمْويلِيّ	financial institution
ميزانِيّة	budget	هَيْئة المَعُونة	aid organization
ناقَصَ	to invite bids (for projects)	واجِهة	shop window
نائِب مُدير	deputy director	وادِع	depositor
نَدْوة	symposium	وارِدات	imports
نِسْبة التَّصْنيع المَحَلِّيّ	local content ratio	والَسَ	to double-cross
		وَدَعَ (a)	to deposit
نِسْبة مِئَوِّية	percentage	وَديعة	deposited amount
نَسَّقَ	to coordinate	pl. وَدائعُ	
نَشاط	activity	وَرْشة	workshop
pl. أَنْشِطة، -ات		pl. وِرَش، -ات	

ورشة التَّصْليح	repair shop	وَظيفة خاليَّة	vacancy
وَرَقة بَنْك	bank note	وَفاء	loyalty
وَزَّعَ	to distribute	وَكالة	representation, agency
وَسَّعَ	to expand (trans.)	وَكالة الإشْهار	advertising agency
وَسيط pl. وُسَطاءُ	middle man	وَكَّلَ	to appoint someone as an agent
وَسيطة pl. وَسائطُ	means	وَكيل pl. وُكَلاءُ	representative, agent
وَسيلة pl. وَسائلُ	see وسيطة	اليَد العاملة	the workforce
وَظَّفَ	to hire, employ	يُورُو pl. ـات	Euro (currency)
وَظيفة pl. وَظائفُ	post, position	يَوْم الحِساب	settlement day

Agriculture and farming

إبالة	bale (e.g. hay)	بَيْطار pl. بَياطِرة	veterinarian
اجْتِناء	harvest (yield) (esp. fruit)	تِبْن	straw
احْتَشَّ	to mow	تُراب pl. أتْرِبة	soil
أراض بُور	fallow land	تَرْبِيَّة الحَيَوان	cattle farming
إصْطَبْل pl. ـات	stable	تَرْبِية النَّحْل	beekeeping
أقْطَعَ	to allot (land)	تُرْعة pl. تُرَع	canal
آلة الجَرّ	tractor	تُرْعة التَصْريف	drainage canal
بَدَالة	culvert	تُرْعة الإيراد	irrigation canal
بَذَرَ (u)	to sow	جَثّ الحِراج	deforestation
بُرْج المِياه	water tower	جَذَرَ (u)	to uproot
بَقَّار	cowhand		

جَرَّ (u)	to pull, tow		خَصَّبَ	to make fertile (soil)
جَرَّافة pl. جَرَارِيفُ، ـات	rake, harrow		خِصْب	fertility
جُرْن pl. أَجْران	threshing floor		خَصيب	fertile
			خَنْدَق pl. خَنَادِقُ	trench
جَفاف	drought		دَفيئة	greenhouse
جَنَى (i)	to pick		دَلو الرَّيِّ	watering can
حارث	ploughman		راعٍ pl. رُعاة	shepherd
حَجَر الرَّحَى	millstone		رَبَّى	to breed (animals)
حَدَّاء	camel driver		رَدَمَ (i)	to fill up with earth (e.g. pond)
حَرَثَ (i)	to plough, cultivate (land)		رَعَى (a)	to graze
حَرْثة	arable land		رَيّ	irrigation
حِصاد	harvest (time)		ريف pl. أَرْياف	countryside
حَصَّادة	mower			
حَصَّادة دَرَّاسة	combine		زارِع	sower
حَصَدَ (u, i)	to harvest, reap		زِراعة	agriculture, farming
			زَرَبَ	to corral, pen
حَصيدة pl. حَصائِدُ	harvest (yield) (esp. wheat)		زَرَعَ (a)	1. to plant 2. see بذر
حَطَّاب	lumberjack			
حَظيرة pl. حَظائِرُ	enclosure, coop, pen		زَرْع pl. زُروع	plantation
حَفَرَ (i)	to dig		زَريبة pl. زَرائِبُ	cattle pen
حُفْرة pl. حُفَر	pit, hollow			
حَقْل pl. حُقُول	field		سَبْلة	manure, dung
			سَرَحَ (i)	to graze
حَلَبَ (u)	to milk		ساقية pl. سَواقٍ	water wheel
حَمَّار	donkey driver			
خَصَبَ (i)	to be fertile (soil)		سَقَى (i)	to water, irrigate

سَماد pl. أَسْمِدة	fertilizer	قَحْط	drought
سَمَّدَ	to fertilize	قادُوس pl. قَوادِيسُ	water-wheel bucket
صِهْرِيج pl. صَهارِيجُ	cistern, water tank	قِطاف	harvest (picking) (fruit)
ضَيْعة pl. ضِياع	country estate	قَطَفَ (i)	to pick (flowers, fruit)
طاحُون pl. طَواحِين	mill	كُدَّاس pl. كَدادِيسُ	stack (grain)
طاحون الهَواء	windmill	كَرْم pl. كُرُوم	vineyard
طارِد الحَشَرات	insect repellent	ماشية pl. مَواشٍ	cattle, livestock
طَحَنَ (a)	to mill, grind	مُبيدات الحَشَرات	insecticides
عَزَقَ (i)	to dig (up)	مَجاعة	famine
عَقيم	barren	مِحْراث pl. مَحارِيثُ	plough
عَلَفَ (i)	to feed (cattle)	مَحْصُول pl. مَحاصِيلُ، ـات	crop (yield)
عَلَف pl. عُلوفة، عِلاف، أَعْلاف	fodder, forage	مَخْلة pl. مَخالى، مِخَل	nosebag
غابة	forest	مِذْوَد pl. مَذاوِدُ	manger
غِراسة	cultivation	مُرَبِّي الماشية	cattle breeder
غَلَّ (u)	to yield crops	مَرْبَط pl. مَرابِطُ	stud farm
غَلَّة pl. غِلال	crop	مَرْج pl. مُرُوج	meadow
غَيْط pl. غيطان	field	مَرْعىً pl. مَراعٍ	pasture
فَأْس pl. أَفْؤُس، فُؤوس	axe	مَزْرَعة pl. مَزارِعُ	farm
فَزَّاعة	scarecrow		
فَلَّاح	farmer		
فَلَحَ (a)	to cultivate (land)		
فَيَضان	flood, inundation	مِساحة الأراضي	acreage

مُسَمَّدات	fertilizers	نافِ	yoke
مِعْزَقة	hoe	نَبَذَ (i)	to press (grapes)
pl. مَعازِقُ		نَحَّال	beekeeper
مِعْوَل	pick (tool)	نَقَّبَ	to drill (e.g. oil)
pl. مَعاوِلُ			
مَغْرِس	grove (olives)	نَمَى (i)	to grow
pl. مَغارِسُ		نَوْرَج	thresher
مُغِلّ	fertile, productive (land)	pl. نَوارِجُ	
مِنْجَل	sickle	هَنْدَسة الرَّيِّ	irrigation engineering
pl. مَناجِلُ		هندسة زراعيَّة	agronomy
مَواد كَريهيَّة	weedkiller	وافِر	abundant
ناعُورة	noria	يابِس	dry
pl. نَواعِيرُ		يُبْس	see جفاف

Natural resources

إسْبِيداج	white lead, ceruse	بلوتويوم	plutonium
اِسْتِياتِيت	steatite, soapstone	بلَّوْر، بِلَّور	crystal
أكْسِجين	oxygen	pl. ـات	
أمْطار سَوْداء	black rain	بلور صَخْريّ	rock crystal
ألْماس	diamond	بَنْزين	petrol, gasoline
ألُومْنِيا	aluminium	بَنْفْش	amethyst
أوزُون	ozone	بِئَر النَّفْط	oil well
بَخَّرَ	to evaporate	pl. بِئَار، آبَار	
بُرْج التَّبْريد	cooling tower	تَلَوُّث	pollution
بُرْج الحَفْر	derrick, oil rig	جاذِبيَّة	gravitation
بلاتين	platinum	جاذبيَّة الثِّقْل	gravitational force
بلاستيك	plastic	جَزْع	onyx

جُزَىءْ pl. ـات	molecule	رَمْل	sand
جِيَار	unslaked lime	زَبَرْجَد	chrysolite
جِير	lime	زِرْنِيخ	arsenic
حامِض الفَحْم	carbonic acid	زُمُرُّد	emerald
حامِض كِبْرِيتِيّ	sulphuric acid	زُنْجُفْر	cinnabar
حَجَر pl. حِجار, حِجارة, أَحْجار	stone	زِنْك	zinc
حَجَر ثَمِين	precious stone	زُجاج	glass
حَجَر جَهَنَّم	silver nitrate	زِنْجار	verdigris
حَجَر الجِير	limestone	زِيْبَق	mercury, quicksilver
حَجَر السُّمَّاقِيّ	porphyry	زَيْت pl. زُيُوت	oil
حَجَر الشَاذِنة	haematite	زَيْت حُلْو	sweet oil
حَجَر القَمَر	selenite, gypsum	زيت خام	crude oil
حَدِيد	iron	زَيْت الغاز	kerosene
حامِض كِبْرِيتِيّ	sulphuric acid	سَبَكَ (i, u)	to found, cast (metal)
حَطَب	firewood	سَبِيكة pl. سَبائِك	ingot
حَقْل النَّفْط	oil field		
حِماية البِيئة	environmental protection	سَبِيكة ذَهَب	gold bullion
حَمَّضَ	to oxydize	سَلْبِى	negative (el.)
حَمْض pl. أَحْماض	acid	سُلْفات	sulphate
خام pl. ـات	raw material	شَمْع pl. شُمُوع	wax
خَشَب pl. أَخْشاب	wood	صاج	sheet iron
		صاج مُضَلَّع	corrugated iron
ذَرَّة	atom	صُلْب	steel
ذَهَب	gold	صَمْغ pl. صُمُوغ	gum, resin
رُخام	marble		
رَصاص	lead	صمغ عَرَبِيّ	gum arabic

صِناعة سَبْك المَعادن	metallurgic industry	فَيْرُوز	turquoise
صُودا	soda	قَصْدير	tin
صُودا كاويّة	caustic soda	قَطَّرَ	to filter
صُوديوم	sodium	قَطْران	tar
طاقة	energy	كادْميوم	cadmium
طاقة الرِّيح	wind energy	كَبْرَتَ	to vulcanize
طاقة شَمْسيّة	solar energy	كِبْريت	sulphur
طاقة نَوَويّة	nuclear power	كَرَّرَ	to refine, filter
طَبقة الأوزون	ozone layer	كَلَّسَ	to whitewash, calcify
طَفْل	potter's clay	كلور	chlorine
طَبيعيّ	natural	كَهْرَباء	electricity
عاج	ivory	كَهْرَمان	amber
عِرْق اللُؤْلُؤ	mother-of-pearl	كيرُوسين	kerosene
عَقيق (coll.) عَقائقُ .pl	carnelian	لازُوَرْد	lapis lazuli
عُنْصُر عَناصِرُ .pl	element	لَمّاع	glistening, sparkling
		لُمْعة	gleam, glow
عِيار ات- .pl	1. standard (gold, silver) 2. carat (gold)	لِماع, لُمَع .pl	
		لُؤْلُؤ (coll.) لآلئ .pl	pearls
غاز	gas	لَيِّن ,-ون .pl أَلْيلانة	soft, flexible
غاز طبيعيّ	natural gas		
فَحْم (coll.) فُحُومات .pl	coal	لين	softness, flexibility
		مادّة مَوادّ .pl	material
فَحْم حَطَب	charcoal	مَحْجَر مَحاجِرُ .pl	stone quarry
فَحْم كُوك	coke	مَحَطّة تَوْليد الكَهْرَباء	power station
فِضّة	silver		
فُوسْفات	phosphate	مَحَطّة نَوَويّة	nuclear power plant
فُوصْفُور	phosphorus	مُخَصَّب	enriched (material)

مُذَهَّب	gilded	مُوجَب	positive (el.)
مُرْجان	coral	مَوْرِد pl. مَوارِدُ	resource
مَسْبَك pl. مَسابِكُ	foundry	ناعِم	fine, smooth
مَصْدَر الطَّاقة	energy source	نُحاس	copper
مَطَّاط	rubber	نُحاس أَصْفَر	brass
مَعْدِن pl. مَعادِنُ	mineral	نَفايا نَوَوِيَّة	nuclear waste
مُعَدِّن	miner	نَفْط	petroleum
مَعْرُوض نَفْطِيّ	oil supply	نَفْط خام	crude oil
مَعْمَل التَكْرير	refinery	نُقْطة التَجَمُّد	freezing point
مَغْنَطيس	magnet	نيتروجين	nitrogen
مُفاعِل نَوَوِيّ	nuclear reactor	نيكِل	nickel
مَنْجَم pl. مَناجِمُ	mine	هيدروجين	hydrogen
مَوادّ أَوَّلِيَّة	base materials	وَقُود	fuel
موادّ خام	raw materials	وَلَّدَ	to generate (energy)
موادّ مُلْتَهِبة	combustible materials	ياقوت (coll.) pl. يواقيت	ruby
مَوارِد طَبيعِيَّة	natural resources	يورانيوم	uranium
		يورانيوم مُخَصَّب	enriched uranium

Tools and equipment

إِزْميل pl. أَزاميلُ	chisel	آلة الحِياكة	power loom
إِشْفَى pl. أَشافٍ	awl	آلة الخِياطة	sewing machine
آلة	1. machine	آلة كابِسة	compressor
	2. tool, instrument	آلة لِحام	soldering iron
		آلِيّ	mechanical, mechanized

أُنْبُوب	pipe, tube	رافعة	hoist
pl. أَنابِيب		pl. رَوافِع	
بُرادة	iron filings	رَحًى (f.)	quern, hand mill
بَرَّامة	drilling machine	pl. أَرْحِية, رُحِي, أَرحَى	
بَرَدَ (u)	to file	رَفْش	shovel, spade
بَرِيمة	auger, gimlet	pl. رفوش	
بُرْشَمة	rivet	زَحَّافة	leveller (agriculture)
بَكَّارة	pulley	زَرْدِيَّة	pliers
تَعَطُّل	defect, flaw	سَدَّ (u)	to plug up
تَكَسَّرَ	to become broken	سداد	plug, stopper
تُورِبين	turbine	pl. أَسِدَّة	
pl. ـات		سِلْك	wire
ثَقَبَ (u)	to drill, pierce	pl. أَسْلاك	
جَلَخَ	to sharpen, whet	سِلْسِلة	chain
جَلْخ	whetstone	pl. سَلاسِلُ	
جهاز	device, appliance	سُلَّم	ladder
pl. أَجْهِزة		pl. سَلاليمُ, سَلالِمُ	
حَبْل	rope	سَنَّ (u)	to sharpen, whet
pl. حِبال		سِنْدان، سِنْدان	anvil
خِتام	sealing wax	pl. سَنادِينُ	
خَلَّاطة الأسْمَنت	concrete mixer	سِيخ	skewer
خُوذة	safety helmet	pl. أَسْياخ	
خَيْط	thread, string, cable	شَبَكة	net
pl. خُيُوط		pl. شُبُوكات, شِباك, شَبَك	
دَبُّوس رسْم	thumb tack	شَرِيط	tape, string
pl. دَبابِيسُ -		pl. أَشْرِطة, شَرائطُ	
دَلْو	bucket	شريط المِقْياس	measuring tape
pl. أَدْلاء, دِلاء, أَدْلٍ		صَفِيحة	can
دَوَّارة	vane	pl. صَفائحُ	
		صِمام	valve
		pl. ـات	
		صمام الأمان	safety valve

صَمُولة	nut
عَتَلة pl. عَتَل	crowbar
عَجَلة اليَد	wheelbarrow
عَدَّة pl. ـات, عَدَد	tool, instrument
عَرَبة قَلّابة	tipcart
عَصا (f.) pl. أَعْص, عُصِى	cane, stick
عُقْدة pl. عُقَد	knot
غُراب pl. أَغْرِبة, أَغْرُب, غِرْبان	blade (hatchet)
غِرْبال pl. غَرابيلُ	sieve
فارة	plane
قَبْضة	grip
قَدُوم pl. قُدُم, قَدائمُ	adze
قَدّاحة	lighter
قُطْب pl. أَقْطاب	pivot
قطب سالب	cathode
قطب مُوجَب	anode
قَلّاب	skip
قَلاب خَلّاط	rotary mixer
قَلاووظ	screw
قَلْوَظَ	to screw together
كابَل	cable
كِبْريت	matches

كرنك pl. ـات	crank
كَسَرَ (i)	to break
كَمّاشة	pincers
لَوْح pl. أَلْواح	board, plate
مالَج pl. مَوالِجُ	trowel
مَبْرَد pl. مَبارِدُ	file, rasp
مِطْرَقة pl. مَطارِقُ	hammer
مُعَطَّل	broken, out of order
مِثْقَب pl. مَثاقبُ	drill
مثقب بالهَواء المَضْغُوطة	pneumatic drill
مِجَزّ	shears
مِخْرَطة pl. مَخارِطُ	lathe
مِدَقّة pl. مَداقُّ	mortar (cf. pestle)
مِدَقّ الرَّكائزُ	piledriver
مِرْفَعة pl. مَرافِعُ	crane
مِرْوَحة pl. مَراوِحُ	fan
مِسْحاة pl. مَساحٍ	spade
مِسْلَفة	harrow
مِسْمار pl. مَساميرُ	nail

مَشْعَل pl. مَشاعِلُ	torch
مِصْباح مُفَلْوِر	fluorescent lamp
مِضَخَّة	pump
مِضَخَّة رافعة	suction pump
مِضْرَب pl. مَضارِبُ	mallet
مُعَدّ pl. ـات	equipment, appliance
مِفْتاح صَمُولة	spanner
مِفْراك	twirling stick
مِفَكّ pl. ـات	screwdriver
مَقْبِض pl. مَقابِضُ	handle
مِقَصّ pl. مِقاصّ	scissors
مِقْياس pl. مَقاييسُ	gauge
مقياس التَّيّار	ammeter
مقياس الجَهْد	voltmeter
مقياس الزَّوايا	protractor
مقياس الكَهْرَبائِيَّة	electrometer
مِكْبَس pl. مَكابِسُ	1. press 2. piston

مكبس مائيّ	hydraulic press
مِلْزَمة pl. مَلازِمُ	vice, clamp
مِنْجَل pl. مَناجِلُ	scythe
مَنْجَلة	vice
مِنْشار pl. مَناشيرُ	saw
مِنْصَبة	trestle
ميزان pl. مَوازينُ	scales
ميزان طَبْلى	weighbridge
ميزان الماء	spirit level
ناقِص	faulty
نَفَخَ (u)	to inflate
نَوْل pl. أَنْوال	loom
هاوُن	mortar
وَرَق السَّنْفَرة	emery paper, sandpaper
وُصْلة pl. وُصَل, ـات	joint
وِنْش pl. أَوْناش, ـات	winch
يَد الهاون	pestle

Time

General

أَبَداً	1. never (on its own; with negation)	بَعْد الظُّهْر	afternoon
	2. always	بُعَيْد	shortly after
أَثْناء	during	بُكْرة	tomorrow
أَجَّلَ (إلى)	to postpone (until)	بَكير	early
أَحْياناً	sometimes	بَنْدُول السَّاعة	pendulum
أَخَّر	1. to delay	بَيْن فترة وأُخْرى	now and then
	2. to set back (clock)	بَيْنَما	while, during
أَخير	last, recent	تَأَخَّر	to be delayed, lag behind
أَخيراً	at last	تَقَدَّم	to run fast (clock/watch)
أُسْبُوع pl. أَسابِع	week	تَقْويم pl. تَقاويمُ	calendar
أُسْبُوعِيّ	weekly (adj.)	تَوْقيت جرينتش	Greenwich Mean Time (GMT)
اسْتَغْرَق	to take, last (an amount of time)	ثانية pl. ثَوانٍ	second
أَضاع الوَقْت	to waste time	ثُلْث	twenty minutes to/past the hour
ألآن	now		
أَمْس	yesterday	ثُمَّ	then
آن pl. آونة, أَوان	time	جيل pl. أَجْيال	generation
آنِفاً	formerly	حاضِر	present
أَنْقَضَى	to pass, elapse (time)	حالاً	immediately
أَوَّل أَمس	the day before yesterday	حالِيّ	present, current
بِإسْتِمْرار	continuously, constantly	حَتْماً	definitely, inevitably
بُرْهة	a short time	حَتَّى	until
بَعْد	after	حَديث pl. حَداث	recent, modern
بَعْدَ ذلكَ	afterwards		

حِين pl. أَحْيان	time	السَنة الماضِيَّة	last year
حِينَئِذٍ	at that time, then	سَنة مَسيحِيَّة	Year in the Christian era (A.D.)
حِينَما	whenever	سَنة هِجرِيَّة	year in the Muslim era (A.H.)
خاطِف	fleeting	شَرَقَ (u)	to rise (sun)
خِلال	see أَثناء	شُروق	sunrise
دامَ (u)	to last	شَهْر pl. أَشْهُر, شُهور	month
دائِم	permanent		
دائِماً	always	شَهْرِيّ	monthly
دَقَّ (i)	to strike (clock)	صَباح	morning
دَقيقة pl. دَقائِق	minute	صَباحاً	in the morning
		صَباح غَدّ	tomorrow morning
رَأْس السَنة	New Year's Day	صَباح اليَوْم	this morning
راهِن	see حالي	طَوْراً بعد طَوْر	time and again
رُبْع ساعة	quarter of an hour	ظُهْر pl. أَظْهار	midday
سابِق	previous, former		
سابِقاً	formerly	عاجِلاً أَو آجِلاً	sooner or later
ساعة	hour	عادَةً	usually
ساعة الحائِط	clock	عام pl. ـات, عْوام	see سنة
ساعة اليد	watch		
سَبَقَ له أَن (i, u)	to have experienced . . . (perf.) before	عَقْرَب pl. عَقارِبُ	hand (watch/clock)
		عقرب الثَواني	second hand
سَحْر	early dawn	عقرب الدَقائِق	minute hand
سَلَفاً	beforehand	عقرب الساعات	hour hand
سَنة pl. سِنون, سَنَوات	year	عَلَى المَدَى البَعيد	in the long term
السَنة القادِمة	next year	عَلَى المَدَى القَريب	in the short term
سَنة كَبيسة	leap year	عُمر pl. أَعْمار	age (person)

عَهْد	era, age	قَرِيباً	soon
pl. عُهُود		قَضَى (i)	to spend (time)
عِيد رَأْس السَّنَة	New Year	قَطُّ	never (with negative verb)
غُرَّة الشَّهْر	first day of the month	قَلَّمَا	rarely
غَرَبَ (u)	to set (sun)	كالمُعْتاد	as usual
غُرُوب	sunset	كَثِيراً	often
غَسَق	dusk, twilight	كُلَّمَا	whenever
فاتَ (u)	to elapse, pass (time)	لاحِقاً	afterwards
فَتْرَة	interval of time	لَحْظَة	moment
فُجَأَةً	suddenly	لَيْل (نهار > <)	night (نهار > <)
فَجْر	dawn	لَيْلاً	by night
فَصْل	season	لَيْلَة (يوم > <)	night (يوم > <)
pl. فُصُول		pl. لَيَال, ـات	
فَوْرَ	as soon as	اللَّيْلَةَ	tonight
فَوْراً	immediately	لَيْلَة أَمس	last night
فِي أَسْرَع وَقْت مُمْكِن	as soon as possible	الماضِي	past
فِي أَعْقاب	in the wake of	مُبَكِّراً	early in the morning
فِي المُسْتَقْبَل القَرِيب	in the near future	مُتَأَخِّر	late
فِيما بَعْد	subsequently	مَتَى	when
فِي نَفْس الوَقْت	at the same time	مَساء	evening
قادِم	see مقبل	pl. أَمْسِيات, أَمْساء	
قائِم	existing	مَساءً	in the evening
قَبْلَ	before (prep.)	مَساء اليَوْم	this evening
قَبْل الآن	previously	مُسْتَقْبَل	future
قُبَيْل	shortly before	مُسْتَمِرّ	continuous, continual
قَرْن	century	مَصِير	outcome
pl. قُرُون		مُفَكِّرة (يَوْمِيَّة)	diary
		مُقْبِل	forthcoming

مِن الآن وصاعداً	from now on	نَهار pl. أنْهُر	day (<> night)
مُنَبِّه pl. ـات	alarm clock	نَهاراً	by day
مُنْتَصَف اللَيْل	midnight	وَشيك	imminent
مُنْذُ	since	وَقْت pl. أوْقات	time
مُؤَخِّراً	lately, recently		
مُؤَقَّت	temporary	وَقَّتَ	to set a time
مُؤَقَّتاً	temporarily	يَوْم pl. أيَّام	day
نادِراً	seldom, rarely		
نِصْف ساعة	half an hour	اليَوْمَ	today
نِصْف أصْبوعيّ	biweekly (twice weekly)	يَوْميّ	daily (adj.)
نِصْف شَهْريّ	biweekly (fortnightly)	يَوْميّاً	daily (adv.)

Days of the week

(يوم) الأحَد	Sunday	(يوم) الخَميس	Thursday
(يوم) الإثْنَيْن	Monday	(يوم) الجُمْعة	Friday
(يوم) الثَّلاثاء	Tuesday	(يوم) السَّبْت	Saturday
(يوم) الأرْبِعاء	Wednesday		

The seasons

اصْطافَ	to spend the summer	خَريف	autumn
تَوْقيت صيْفيّ	daylight-saving time	خَريفيّ	autumnal
ربيع	spring	شِتاء pl. شُتِي، أشْتِية	winter
صَيْف pl. أصْياف	summer	شِتْويّ	wintry
		قائظ	scorchingly hot
صيْفيّ	summery	قَيْظ	summer heat

Months

Gregorian

	Middle East	N Africa	
كانون الثاني	يَنائِر	جانْفي	January
شُباط	فبْرائِر	فيفري	February
آذار	مارْس	مارس	March
نيِسان	أبْريل	أفْريل	April
أيَار	مايو	ماي	May
حَزيِران	يونيو	جُوان	June
تَمّوز	يوليو	جويليه	July
آب	أغُسْطُس	أوت	August
أيْلول	سِبْتمْبِر	سِبْتمْبِر	September
تِشْرين الأوّل	أكْتوبِر	أكْتوبِر	October
الثاني تِشْرين	نُوفمْبِر	نُوفمْبِر	November
كانون الأوّل	دِسمْبِر	دِسمْبِر	December

Islamic

1. مُحَرَّم	4. رَبيِع الثّاني	7. رَجَب	10. شَوّال
2. صَفَر	5. جُمادَى الأولَى	8. شَعْبان	11. ذو القَعْدة
3. رَبيِع الأوّل	6. جُمادَى الأخيِرة	9. رَمَضان (month of fasting)	12. ذو الحِجّة (month of the pilgrimage)

Coptic (Egypt)

1. توت	4. كيِهَك ,كيِهَك	7. بَرْمَهَات	10. بَؤونة
2. بابِه	5. طَوبة	8. بَرْمودة	11. أبيِب
3. هاتور	6. أمْشيِر	9. بَشَنْش	12. مِسْرَى

Geography

Natural geography

أَجْوَف f. جَوْفَاء ,pl. جُوف	hollow (*adj.*)	تسونامي	tsunami
أَحْفُور pl. أَحافيرُ	fossil	تَصَحُّر	desertification
أَرْخَبِيل	archipelago	تَلّ pl. تلال	hillock
أَرْض pl. أَراضٍ	earth (planet)	تَلّ رَمْلِيّ	sand dune
أُفْق pl. آفاق	horizon	جاذِبِيَّة أَرْضِيَّة	gravity
إِقْفار	desolateness	جَبَل pl. جِبال	mountain
بَحْر pl. أَبْحار ,بُحُور ,بِحار	sea	جَدْوَل pl. جَداوِل	brook, rivulet
بُحَيْرة pl. بَحائرُ	lake	جُرْف pl. أَجْراف ,جُرُوف	cliff, precipice
بَدْر	full moon	جَزَرَ (i, u)	to ebb
بَرّ	land (< > sea)	جَزْر	ebb
بَرْزَخ pl. بَرازِخُ	isthmus	جَزِيرة pl. جَزائِرُ	island
بُرْكان pl. بَراكِينُ	volcano	جَنُوب	south
بِرْكة pl. بِرَك	pool	حَجَر جَوِّيّ	meteor
بَطْحاء pl. بَطْحَوات ,بِطاح	plain, flatland	حَفْر	excavation (archaeology)
بُعْد	remoteness	حُفْرة pl. حُفَر	pit
		الخارِج	the outside world
بِئْر pl. بِئار ,آبار	well	خَرَّ (i, u)	to purl (water)
		خَطّ الاسْتِواء	the Equator
		خَلِيج pl. خُلْجان	gulf, bay
		الخَلِيج العَرَبِيّ	the Persian Gulf

الدَّلْتا	the Nile Delta	شَرْق	east
دَوَار	whirlpool, vortex	شَمَال	north
رَأْس pl. رُؤُوس	cape	شَمْس pl. شُمُوش	sun
رَاسِب غَرِينِيّ	alluvial deposit	صَبَّ (i)	to pour forth (water)
رُماد	ash	صَحْراء pl. صَحْرَوات, صِحار, صَحارَى	desert
رَمْل pl. رِمال	sand	صَخْر pl. صُخُور	rock, cliff
زَبَد pl. أَزْباد	froth (sea)	صَدَف (coll.) pl. أَصْداف	seashells
زَلْزَلة	earthquake		
ساحِل pl. سَواحِلُ	shore, coast	ضاحية pl. ضَواحٍ	surroundings
سَدّ pl. أَسْداد	dam	ضَحْضاج	shallow
سَطْح	surface	ضَفَّة pl. ضِفاف	bank (river)
سَطْح البَحْر	sea level	طَبيعة	nature
سَفْح pl. سُفُوح	foot (mountain)	طَمْى	alluvial mud
سِلْسِلة الجِبال	mountain chain	عالَم pl. عالَمُون	world
سَماء pl. سَمَوات	sky	عامِر	inhabited
سَهْل pl. سُهُول	plain	عَقيق pl. أَعِقّة	gorge, ravine
شاطِئٌ pl. شَواطِئُ	shore, beach	غابة	forest
		غَرْب	west
شِبه جَزيرة	peninsula	غَوْط pl. غِيطان, غِياط, غُوط, أَغْواط	cavity, depression
شَبْه قارة	subcontinent		
شَلَّل pl. ات-	waterfall	فَرْع pl. فُرُوع	tributary (river)

فَوْقَ سَطْح البَحْر	above sea level	ماء عَذْب	fresh water
فَيَضان	flood	ماء مالِح	salty water
قارة	continent	مَجْرى pl. مَجارٍ	current (stream)
قاع pl. أَقْواع, أَقْوُع, قيعان	bottom (e.g. sea)	مُحيط	ocean
قاع النَّهْر	river bed	مَدّ	rise (water)
قاع البَحْر	sea bed	مَدار الجَدْى	Tropic of Capricorn
قَرارة	depression	مَدار السَّرَطان	Tropic of Cancer
قَرْية pl. قُرىً	village	مُذَنَّب	comet
قُطْب pl. أَقْطاب	pole	مُرْتَفَعات	heights
القطب الجَنُوبيّ	the South Pole	مَساحة	area, surface
القطب الشَّماليّ	the North Pole	مَسافة pl. مَساوِف, -ات	distance
قَفْر pl. قفار	wasteland	مُسْتَنْقَع pl. -ات	marsh, swamp
قمّة pl. قِمَم	summit (mountain)	مَشْرِق	East
قَمَر pl. أَقْمارُ	moon	مَصَبّ pl. مَصابّ, -ات	mouth (river)
قَناة pl. قَنَوات	canal	مَضْيَق pl. مَضايِقُ, مَضائِقُ	strait, isthmus
كارِثة طَبيعيّة	natural disaster	مَطْرَح pl. مَطارِحُ	location, site
الكُرة الأرْضِيَة	the globe	مَغْرِب	West
كَثيب pl. كُثْبان, كُثُب, أَكْثِبة	dune	مُقْفِر	deserted, forsaken
كُسُوف	eclipse, solar eclipse	مِقْياس ريخْتَر	the Richter scale
كَهْف pl. كُهُوف	cave	مُنْحَدَر pl. -ات	slope
ماء pl. مِياه	water	مَنْظَر طَبيعيّ pl. مَناظِرُ طَبيعيَّة	landscape

مَوْجة pl. أمْواج	wave	هَضْبة pl. هِضاب	hill
نَبَع (a, i,u)	to originate (river)	هَواء طَلْق	open air
نَجْم pl. نُجُوم	star	هَزّة أرْضِيّة	earth tremor
نَهْر pl. أنْهُر	river	واحة	oasis
هاوِية	abyss	واد pl. وِدْيان, وُدْيان	valley
هائِج	rough (sea)	وَحْل pl. أوْحال, وُحُول	mud

Urban geography

ازْدَحَم	to be crowded	زِحام	crowd
أقام	to reside, live	زُقاق pl. أزِقّة	alley, lane
اكْتِظاظ	overpopulation	ساحة	square
بُرْج pl. أبْراج	tower	شارِع pl. شَوارِعُ	street
بَلَد pl. بِلاد	town	شارِع رئيسيّ	high street
بَلَدِيّة	municipality	ضاحِية pl. ضَواحٍ	city outskirts, suburb
تِمْثال pl. تَماثِيل	statue	ضَيّق	narrow
جِسْر pl. جُسُور	bridge	عاصِمة pl. عَواصِمُ	capital
جِسْر مُعَلَّق	suspension bridge	عائِق pl. عَوائِقُ	obstacle
حَدِيقة pl. حَدائِقُ	garden, park	عَطْفة	side street, alley
حديقة الحَيَوان	zoo	قَرَوِيّ	villager
حَيّ pl. أحْياء	city district	قَرْية pl. قُرى	village
رَصِيف pl. أرْصِفة	pavement		

قَطْر pl. أَقْطار	region, country	مُزْدَحِم	overcrowded
كَثافة السُّكّان	population density	مَصْرِف pl. مَصارِف	drain
لافتة	sign	مُقاطَعة	province
مَجْرًى pl. مَجارى	sewer	نافُورة pl. نَوافِيرُ	fountain
مَرْكَز المَدِينة	city centre	نَجْع pl. نُجُوع	hamlet
مَدِينة pl. مُدُن	city	واسِع	wide

Travel and mobility

General

أَبْطأ	to slow down	أَقْبَلَ	to go near
اتِّجاه pl. ـات	direction	أَكَّدَ	to confirm (e.g. flight)
أَجْذَب	pull (door)	الْتْحاق	connections
أَجْنَبِيّ pl. أَجانِب	foreigner	انْتَبِه	WATCH OUT!
اِخْتَتَمَ زِيارةً	to conclude a visit	انْتَحَى	to turn
أَدْفَع	push (door)	انْصَرَفَ	to leave, depart
اِسْتِعْلام pl. ـات	enquiry	انْقَلَبَ	to get knocked over
اِسْتَفْهَمَ عن	to inquire about	أَوْتاد الخَيْمة	tent pegs
اِسْتِقْبال	reception	باتَ (i)	to spend the night
اِسْتِمارة	form	بَطُؤَ (u)	to be slow
أَطَلَّ على	to look out onto (e.g. room)	بَطِىء pl. بِطاء	slow
إعادة المال	refund	بَعِيد pl. بِعاد، بُعْدان، بُعْد، بُعَداء	far
إقامة	stay	بَقِىَ (a)	to stay, remain
		بَلَغَ (u)	to reach

بَيْت الشَّبَاب	youth hostel	جِنْسِيَّة	nationality
تَأْخِير	delay	جِنْسِيَّة أَصْلِيَّة	nationality at birth
تَأْشِيرة	visa	جَواز السَّفَر	passport
تَبِعَ (u)	to follow	جَوْلة	tour, journey
تَجَمْرَكَ	to declare (to customs)	حَجَزَ (u, i)	to reserve, to book
تَحْتَ	underneath, below	حَجْز	reservation
تَحْذِير	WARNING!	حَذِرَ (a, i)	to be cautious
تَحَرَّكَ	to move, be in motion	حَذِر	cautious
تَخْيِيم	camping	حَذْر	caution, watchfulness
تَذْكار pl. ـات	souvenir	حَذَارى من	BEWARE OF . . .
تَذْكِرة pl. تَذاكِرُ	ticket	حَرَّكَ	to move (*trans.*)
		حَزَمَ (i)	to tie up, bundle
تَعَجَّلَ	to be in a hurry	حَصىً (*coll.*)	pebbles
تَقْلِيد pl. تَقالِيدُ	tradition	حَقيبة pl. حَقائِبُ	suitcase
تَوَجَّهَ إلى	to head for	حَمَّال	porter
جاءَ (i)	to come	حَمَلَ (i)	to carry
جاءَبِ	to bring	خارِج	outside (*prep.*)
جابٍ pl. جُباة	conductor (bus)	خاصّ	private
		خالٍ	free, available
جَدْوَل pl. جَداوِلُ	schedule	خِدْمة	service
		خِدْمة الغُرَف	room service
جَرَبَنْدِيَّة	knapsack	خَرَجَ (u)	to go out
جَرَى (i)	to run	خُروج	exit
جُمْرُك pl. جَمارِكُ	customs	خَرِيطة pl. خَرائِطُ	map
جِنْس	sex	خَلْفَ	behind

خَيْمة	tent	سرير مُخَيَّم	camp bed
خِيَم .pl		سرير مُزْدَوِج	double bed
داخِلاً	inside (adv.)	سَريع	quick
دارَ (u)	to turn around	سُرْعان, سِراع .pl	
دَخَلَ (u)	to enter	سَفَرَ (i)	to travel
دُخُول	entrance	سَفَر	journey, trip
الدُّخُول مَجاناً	free admission/access	أسْفار .pl	
دَرَجة	class (e.g. train, plane)	شَكْلِيات	formalities
دَليل السَّفَر	travel guide	شِمال	left (direction)
دليل العَناوين	address book	شَنْطة	1. bag
ذَهَبَ (a)	to go	شُنَط .pl	2. rucksack, backpack
رائِد	explorer	شَقّة	flat (apartment)
رُوَّاد .pl		شِقَق .pl	
رائِد الفَضاء	astronaut	صَرَفَ (i)	to change (money)
رَجَعَ (i)	to return	صَعَدَ (a)	to climb
رِحْلة	journey	ضاعَ (i)	to lose one's way
رحلة صَيْد	safari	طَلَعَ (u)	to go up, ascend
رَسْم الجُمْرُك	customs duty	طُول	length
زَلِقَ (a)	to slip, slide	عادَ (u)	see رجع
ساحَ (u)	to travel around	عادة	custom, habit
ساعَدَ	to help	عَوائِدُ, -ات .pl	
ساعٍ	delivery boy, porter	عالٍ	high
سُعاة .pl		عامود الخَيْمة	tent pole
سائِح	tourist	عَبَرَ (u)	to cross
سُوَّاح, سِيّاح .pl		عَثَرَ (u)	to stumble
سَرُعَ (u)	to be quick, to hurry	عَثَرَ عَلى	to find, discover
سَرير الأطْفال	cot	عَجَرِيّ	gipsy
		عَجَر .pl	

عَريض	broad	لَوَّحَ إلى	to wave at (someone)
عَرْض	width, breadth	لوكانْدَه	guesthouse
عَريق	deep-rooted (e.g. tradition)	ماء شُرْب	drinking water
عَفْش	luggage	مَبيت	overnight stay
pl. عُفوش		مَحْجوز	reserved
عَفْش اليَد	hand luggage	مَحْفَظة	wallet
على الأَقَلّ	at least	pl. مَحافظُ	
على الأكْثَر	at most	مُخَيَّم	campsite
عُمْق	depth	pl. ـات	
pl. أعْماق		مَرَّ (u)	to pass
عَميق	deep	مُرافِق	accompanying person
غادَرَ	to depart	مُراقِب الشّاطىء	beach guard
غُرْفة	room	مُرْشِد	guide
pl. غُرَف		مُسافِر	traveller
غرفة الطَّعام	dining room	مُساعَدة	help, assistance
غرفة مُفْرَدة	single room	مُسْتَوى	level
غرفة مُزْدَوِجة	double room	مَشَى (i)	to walk
غَرِقَ (a)	to drown	مِصْعَد	lift
غَيْر مُقيم	non-resident	pl. مَصاعِدُ	
فَوْقَ	above, on top	مُطِلَّة على	with a view of (room)
فِراش هَوائِيّ	air mattress	مُغْلَق	CLOSED
فُنْدُق	hotel	مَفْتوح	OPEN
pl. فَنادِقُ		مُقيم	resident
فَوْج	group	مكان	place
pl. أفْواج		pl. أماكنُ, أمْكِنة	
قَريب	close, near	مَكْتَب تَسْليم العُفوش	left-luggage office
قَعَدَ (u)	to sit	مَكْتَب الاسْتِعْلامات	information desk, enquiry office
كيس النَّوْم	sleeping bag		

مَكْتَب السِّياحة	1. travel agency	نَجْوَ	towards
	2. tourist agency	نَزَلَ (i)	1. to descend
مَلاحة جَوِّيَّة	aviation		2. to disembark (car, train, etc.)
مَمْنُوع الخُرُوج	NO EXIT		3. to dismount (horse)
مَمْنُوع التَّدْخِين	NO SMOKING	نَصْب تَذْكارِيّ	monument
مَمْنُوع التَّسَلُّق	NO CLIMBING	نَقَذَ (u)	to save, rescue
مَمْنُوع التَّصْوِير	NO PHOTOGRAPHS	هَزَّ (u)	to shake
ممنوع الدُّخُول	NO ENTRY	هُنا	here
مَمْنُوع قَطِيعاً	STRICTLY FORBIDDEN	هُناكَ	there
مَمْنُوع اللَمْس	DO NOT TOUCH	وَتَد	tent peg
مُنْخَفِض	low	pl. أوْتاد	
مَنْزَل اسْتِراحة	resthouse	وَثيقة السَّفْر	travel document
مَهَلَ (a)	to tarry	pl. وَثائِق-	
مَهَلاً	slowly	وَسَط	middle
مَوْعِد السَّفْر	departure time	pl. أوْساط	
pl. مَواعِدُ		وَصَلَ (يَصِلُ) إلى	to arrive in
مَوْقِع مُخَيَّم	camping site	وَصُول	arrival
		pl. وَصُولات	
موقِع المَقْطُورات السَّكَنِيَّة	trailer park	وَقَفَ (يَقِفُ)	to stop
		يَمِين	right (direction)

Communications

إتِّصال	1. communication	اسْتَعْلَمَ	to ask for information
	2. contact, connection	أشاعَ	to disseminate (news)
إتَّصَلَ ب	to telephone someone	إمْضاء	signature
أُجْرة البَريد	postage	أمْضَى	to sign
أخْبَرَ	to notify	أوْصَلَ	to put through (a phone call)
أرْسَلَ	to send (e.g. letter)	بَرْقِيَّة	telegram

بَرِيد	post, mail	خَطّ مُباشِر	direct line
pl. بُرُد		راسَلَ	to correspond, exchange letters
البَريد الجَوِّيّة	air mail		
البَريد السَّريع	express mail	رزَمَ (u)	to wrap
بَشْر	good news, glad tidings	رِزْمة	parcel, package
		pl. رِزَم	
بَعَثَ (a)	to send, dispatch		
بَلَّغَ	to inform	رِسالة	letter
		pl. رَسائِل	
تَراسَلَ	to exchange letters with one another	رِسالة مُسَجَّلة	registered letter
		رقْم الهاتِف	telephone number
تَسْجيل	registering (mail)		
pl. ـات		رقْم الفاكس	fax number
تَعْريفة بَريدِيَّة	postal rates	رَمْز البَريد	postal code, ZIP code
		pl. رُمُوز ـ	
تَعْليق	commentary		
تِليفون	telephone	ساعي البَريد	postman
		pl. سُعاة ـ	
تِليفون لاسِلْكِيّ	cordless phone	سَجَّلَ	to register (a letter)
تِليفون مَحْمُول	mobile phone	سَمّاعة	(telephone) receiver
تَوْقيع	see إمْضاء	صاحِب الإمْضاء	the undersigned
ثَمَن المُكالَمة	telephone call rate	صُنْدُوق البَريد	mailbox
جَواب	reply	طابِع	stamp
pl. أجْوِبة		pl. طَوابِعُ	
حَوّالة البَريد	money order	ظَرْف	envelope
خابَرَ	to contact s.o.	pl. ظُرُوف	
خَبَر	news	طابِع	stamp
pl. أخْبار		pl. طَوابِعُ	
خَتْم	seal	عاجِل	urgent
pl. خُتُوم		عامِل التِّليفونات	telephonist
خَتْم البَريد	postmark	عامِل فَنِّيّ	technician
خَطّ تِليفُونِيّ	telephone line	عُنْوان	address
pl. خُطُوط تِليفُونِيّة		pl. عَناوينُ	

عُنْوان بَيْتيّ	home address	مُسَجَّل	registered
عَنْوَنَ	to address (a letter)	مَشْغول	busy (telephone), taken (seat)
فاكس	1. fax machine	مُعَلَّق	commentator
pl. ـات	2. facsimile message	مُكاتَبات	correspondence
فَرَزَ (i)	to sort	مُكالَمة تليفونيّة	telephone conversation
قُرْص	dial	مكالمة خارجيّة	long-distance call
pl. أَقْراص		مكالمة دُوَليّة	international call
كابين التِّليفون	telephone booth	مَكْتَب البَريد	post office
لَصِقَ (a)	to stick	مَكاتِب .pl	
لَوْحة التَّوْزيع	switchboard	مِنْطقة بَريديّة	postal area
مِذْياع	microphone	مُواصَلات	communications
مَذاييعُ ,ـات .pl		مُوَظَّف البَريد	postal worker
مُراسَلة	correspondence	هاتف	see تليفون
المُرْسَل إليه	addressee	هَواتِفُ .pl	
مُرْسِل	sender	وَسيلة المُواصَلات	means of communication
مُرْفَق بِهِ	enclosed	وَسائلُ .pl	
مُرْفَقات	enclosures	وَكيل مَكْتَب البَريد	postmaster
مُسْتَعْجَل	express	وُكَلاء .pl	

Air

إقْلاع	take-off	رِحْلة	flight, journey
أَقْلَعَ	to take off	الشَّرِكة النّاقِلة	carrier
بِطاقة صُعود	boarding pass	صالِح	valid
حالة الحَجْز	booking status	طائرة	aeroplane
حُجْرة القِيادة	cockpit	طائرة شَحْن	cargo plane
حِزام الأَمْن	safety belt	طائرة رياضيّة	sports plane
خُطوط جَوّيّة	airline	طائرة مِيائيّة	water plane, sea plane
دُولاب الحَقائب	luggage locker	طَلَعَ (a, u)	to board

طَيَّار	pilot	مُفيضة	hostess
طَيَران	aviation	مَقْعَد	seat
طَيَران بَهْلَوانيّ	stunt flying	pl. مَقاعدُ	
طَيَران شراعيّ	glider flying	مَلاحون	crew
عنْد الاضطرار	in case of an emergency	مِنْضَدة	table, tray
القادمون	ARRIVALS	pl. مَناضدُ, ـات	
قاعة السَّفَر	departure hall	مَنْفَذ	exit
قاعة الوُصولات	arrivals hall	pl. مَنافذُ	
قناع أَكْسجين	oxygen mask	مَنْفَذ الهُروب	emergency exit
مُحَرّك	engine	مَهْبَط	landing strip
مَدْرَج	runway	pl. مَهابطُ	
pl. مَدارجُ		ميزان الحَقائب	baggage scales
مَطار	airport	نُزول	disembarkation
pl. مطارات		هَبَط (u, i)	to land, touch down
مظَلَّة	parachute	هُبُوط	landing
المُغادرون	DEPARTURES	هبوط الاضطرار	emergency landing
		وُصول	arrival

Sea

أَبْحَرَ	to set sail	بُوصلة	compass
إقْلاع	sailing, departure	تَسْتيف	stowage
أَقْلَعَ	to sail	جَدْوَل الأَبْحار	sailing schedule
بَحَّار	sailor	حَرَكة المَلاحة	shipping traffic
pl. ـون, بَحّارة		حزام النَّجاة	lifebelt
بَحْر	sea	جُنْدُول	gondola
pl. بُحُور, بِحار		pl. جَناديلُ	
تَحَطَّمَ	to be wrecked	جنْزير المَرْساة	anchor chain
بَنْدَر	seaport	حُطام	shipwreck
pl. بَنادرُ		حَوَّامة	hovercraft

حَوْض جافّ	dry dock		شِراع	sail
pl. أحْواض جافّة			pl. أشْرِعة, شُرُع	
حوض عَوّام	floating dock		شَرْم	inlet
pl. أحْواض عَوّامة			pl. شُرُوم	
خَفَر السَّواحِل	coastguard		شَمَنْدُورة	buoy
دَرابْزين	railing		صارية, صارٍ	mast
دَفّة	helm		pl. صَوارٍ	
دَفْتَر	logbook		صارى العَلَم	flagpole
pl. دَفاتِر			صالح للمَلاحة	navigable
دَوْخة	seasickness		طاقِم	crew
رابَطَ	to be moored (ship)		عَبور	crossing
راكِب	passenger		عَجَلة القِيادة	steering wheel
pl. رُكّاب			عَرْض السَّفينة	beam
رُبّان	captain, skipper		عُقْدة	knot
pl. رُبّانية, رَبابِنة			pl. عُقَد	
رِحْلة	journey, crossing		عَلَم	flag
رَسا (u)	to dock, to anchor		pl. أعْلام	
رُسُوم الإرْساء	berthage		على طُول الرَّصيف	alongside quay
رُسُوم الإرْشاد	pilotage		عَنْبَر	hold
رُسُوم الميناء	harbour dues		pl. عَنابِرُ	
رَصيف الميناء	quay		غَرِقَ (a)	to founder
رَفّاس	1. propeller		فَنّار	lighthouse
	2. steamboat		pl. ـات	
سَتَّفَ	to stow (goods)		قارِب	boat, skiff
سَطْح	deck		pl. قَوارِبُ	
pl. سُطوح			قارِب شِراعيّ	sailing boat
سَفينة	ship		قارِب النَّجاة	lifeboat
pl. سُفُن			قائِد	helmsman
سفينة البَضائِع	cargo ship		pl. قُوّاد	
شَحْن	cargo		قَبْطان	see ربان
pl. شُحُون				

قَناة pl. قَنَوات, أَقْنِيَّة	canal	مَعْدية pl. مَعادٍ	ferry
قَوارِبيّ	boatman	مِلاحة تِجارِيَّة	merchant shipping
قَيدُوم	bow (ship)	مِلاحة داخْليَّة	inland shipping
كَبينة	cabin	مِلاحة نَهْريَّة	river traffic
لَنْش pl. ـات	launch	مَوْجة pl. أَمْواج	wave
مانيفِستُو	ship's manifest	مِياه إقْليمِيَّة	territorial waters
مَرْبَط pl. مَرابطُ	hawser	ميناء pl. مَوانٍ	port, harbour
مَرْسًى pl. مَراسٍ	anchorage	ناقلة pl. نَواقِلُ	see سفينة البَضائع
مرساة pl. مَراسٍ	anchor	ناقلة النَّفْط	oil tanker
مُرْشِد	pilot	نَسيم pl. نَسائِمُ, نِسام	breeze
مَرْكَب pl. مَراكبُ	vessel, craft	هلْب pl. أَهْلاب	grappling iron, boathook
مركب ساحليّ	coaster	هويس pl. أَهْوِسة	(canal) lock
مركب الصَيْد	fishing vessel	يَخْت pl. يُخُوت	yacht

Rail

أَمْنيبوس	omnibus	رَبَطَ (i, u)	to brake (train)
تَخَلَّفَ الرِّحْلة	to interrupt the journey	رَصيف pl. أَرْصِفة	platform (train)
تَذْكِرة ذَهاب	one-way ticket	رَكِبَ (i)	to board (a train)
تذكرة ذهاب و إياب	return ticket	سِكَّة حَديديَّة	railways
جَدْوَل القِطارات	timetable	سِكَّة حَديدية مُرْتَفِعة	elevated railway
راكب pl. رُكَّب	passenger	شبّاك التَذاكِر pl. شَبابيك-	ticket office

عَرَبة	carriage	قطار الرُّكّاب	passenger train
عربة الأكْل	buffet car	قطار سَريع	express train
عربة الأمْتعة	luggage van	قطار فاخِر	luxury train
عربة النَّوْم	sleeper	قِيام	departure (train)
غُرْفة الانْتِظار	waiting room	مُحَصِّل	conductor (tram, train, bus)
غَيَّر	to change (trains)	مَحَطَّة	station
قاطِرة	locomotive	مَخْزَن الأمانات	left-luggage office
قِطار pl. قُطُرات, قُطُر	train	مَقْصُورة	compartment
قطار إكْسبريس	see قطار سريع	ناظِر المَحَطَّة pl. نُظّار -	station manager
قطار البِضاعة	freight train	نَزَل (i)	to get off
قطار دُوَلِيّ	international train	نِهاية الخَطّ	terminal (train)

Road

Traffic

إتِّجاه جاه	direction	تاكسي	see سيارة الأجرة
أُتوبيس، باص pl. -ات	bus	تَجاوَز	to overtake
إتجاه جَبْرِيّ	diversion	تَصْليح الطُرُق	road repairs
إتجاه واحد	one way	تَقاطُع	crossing, junction
إشارة المُرور	traffic lights	حادث pl. حَوادِث	accident
إصْطِدام pl. -ات	pile-up	حافلة سِياحة	coach
أعْمال الطُرُق	roadworks	حَد السُرْعة	speed limit
إلْزَم اليَسار	KEEP LEFT	حَرَكة المُرور	traffic
إلزم اليَمين	KEEP RIGHT	حَقّ المُرور	right of way
إنْحِدار	slope	حُوذي	coachman
باب للطَوارىء	emergency exit	خِدْمة جَرّ السَّيارات	breakdown/tow-away service
		خَطّ الباص	bus route

خَطّ سَيْر	lane (e.g. motorway)	عَرَبة سكَنِيّة	caravan
خَطَر	danger	عَرَّج	to zigzag
خَطِير pl. خُطُر	dangerous	قافلة pl. قَوافِل	convoy
دَرّاجة	bicycle	قُد سَيّارتك بِحذْر	DRIVE CAREFULLY
ذُرْوة pl. ذُرى	peak (fig.)	قف	STOP
رُخْصة القِيادة	driving licence	قَوانين المُرور	Highway Code
سالِم	safe	كَرُّوسة	carriage, hansom
سَوّاق	driver	لَوْحة المُرور	traffic sign
سَوّاق تاكْسي	taxi driver	مارّ pl. ūn, مارّة	passer-by
سَيّارة الأجْرة	taxi	ماشٍ pl. مُشاة	pedestrian
شاحِنة	lorry, truck		
شُرْطة المُرور	traffic police	مِترُو	underground railway
صِدام	collision	مُتَعَرِّج	winding (road)
طَريق pl. طُرُق	road	مُرْتَفَع	inclination
طَريق خاصّ	private road	مُرور دائِريّ	roundabout
طَريق دائِريّ	ring road	مَزْلَقان سِكّة حديديّة	level crossing
طَريق ريفيّ	country road	مَطَبّ pl. ـات	pothole
طَريق رَئيسيّ	main road		
طَريق للدَّرّاجات	bicycle lane	مَطَبّ اصْطِناعيّ	speed bump
طَريق سَريع	motorway	مَفْرَق pl. مَفارِق	intersection, crossroads
طَريق مَسْدود	cul-de-sac		
طَريق مُشّاة	pedestrianized road	مَمَرّ سُفْلِيّ	1. underpass 2. subway (pedestrians)
طَريق مُؤَقَّت	temporary road	مَمَرّ المُشاة	zebra crossing
عَجَلة ناريّة	motorcycle	مَمْنوع التَّجاوُز	DO NOT OVERTAKE
عَدّاد وُقُوف السَّيّارات	parking meter	ممنوع المُرُور	NO THROUGH TRAFFIC

مَمْنوع الوُقوف	NO PARKING	مَوْقف الباص	bus stop
مَمْنوع وُقوف الدَّرَّاجات	NO BICYCLE PARKING	مَوْقف التَّاكْسي	taxi rank
		مَوْقف السَّيَّارات	car park
مَمْنوع رُكوب الدَّرَّاجاة	NO BICYCLES	نَفَق pl. أَنْفاق	tunnel
مُنْتَصف الطَّريق	central reservation	هدِّئِ السُّرْعة	DRIVE SLOWLY
مُنْحَدِر	sloping (road)	وِنْش pl. ـات, أَوْناش	breakdown truck
مُنْحَنىً	bend		

The car

أَدارَ المُحَرِّك	to start the engine	تِرْس pl. تُروس	gear
إسْتِرْكاب	hitch-hiking	تِرْموسْتات	thermostat
أَسْطُوانة	cylinder	تَشْحيم	greasing, oiling
إشْعال	ignition	تَغْيير الزَّيْت	oil change
اصْطَدَم	to collide	تَغْيير العَجَلة	tyre change
إطار pl. أَطُر	1. see دولاب 2. rim (wheel)	تَكْييف	air conditioning
إطار داخِليّ	tube (tyre)	تَنْك البَنْزين	petrol tank
آلة كابِسة	compressor	تَنْكة بَنْزين احْتِياطيّ	jerrycan
بَخَّاخة	nozzle	جامعة كَهْرَبائيَّة	accumulator
بَطاريَّة	battery	جسْم السَّيَّارة	bodywork
بُقْعة pl. بِقاع	place (for passenger)	جِهاز التَّبْريد	radiator
بَنْزين	petrol	جَهاز الأَشْعال	ignition
بنزين عادِيّ	regular petrol	حَقْن الوُقود	injection pump
بنزين مُمْتاز	four-star petrol	خِرْقة	cloth
بُوق pl. أَبْواق, ـات	horn	خُرْم العَجَلة	puncture
تأمين السَّيَّارات	car insurance	خَفَّضَ السُّرْعة	to decrease speed
تَدْفِئة	heating	دَبْرِياج	coupling
		دِهان	paintwork

دَوَّاسة البَنْزين	throttle	صَدَأ	rust
دَوَّاسة الدِّبْرِياج	clutch	صَدِئ	rusty, rust-covered
دَوَّاسة الفَرْمَلة	brake pedal	صَفيحة تَسْجيل	licence plate
دولاب pl. دواليب	tyre	صَمَّام	valve
ديزِل	diesel	صِناعة السَّيَّارات	car industry
دينامو
dynamo	صُنْدوق الإسْعاف	First Aid kit
رَفْرَف pl. رَفارِف	wing	صُنْدوق التُّروس	gearbox
زادَ السُّرْعة	to increase speed	صُنْدوق العُدَد	toolbox
زِنْبَرَك، زُنْبُرُك	spring	ضَغْط الهَواء	pressure (tyres)
زَيَّتَ	to oil, lubricate	ضَوْء pl. أَضْواءٌ	light
زَيْت التُّروس	gear oil	ضَوْء عالٍ	headlight
زَيْت الفَرْمَلة	brake oil	ضَوء فَحْص	warning light
زَيْت المُحَرِّك	engine oil	ضَوْء الوُقوف	parking light
زِينة عَجَلة	hubcap	ضَوء وَمَّاض	blinkers (warning)
زُيُوت التَّشْحيم	lubricants	طارة الفَرْمَلة	brake drum
سَخُنَ (u)	to overheat	طَفَّاية (النَار)	fire extinguisher
سَقْف	roof	طُلُمْبة البَنْزين	petrol pump
سِلْك الأَشْعال	ignition cable	عامِل مَحَطّة بنزين	petrol station attendant
سِلِنْدَر pl. ـات	cylinder	عامُود الكَرَنْك	crankshaft
سِنّ pl. أَسْنان	cog	عَجَلة	wheel
سَيَّارة	car	عَجَلة احْتِياطِيَّة	spare wheel
شَحْم	grease	عَجَلة أمامِيَّة	front wheel
شَرارة	spark	عَجَلة خَلَفِيَّة	rear wheel
شَمْعة الشَّرارة	spark plug	عَجَلة القِيادة	steering wheel
		عدَّة pl. عدَد	tool

عَشَّقَ التِّرْس	to engage gear	مُحَرِّك ـات .pl	engine
عَوادِم	exhaust fumes	محرك ثُنائيّ المِشْوار	two-stroke engine
غِطاء المُحَرِّك	bonnet	محرك خَلَفِيّ	rear engine
غَيَّرَ التُّرُوس	to change gear	محرك رُباعيّ المِشْوار	four-stroke engine
فِرْقة المَطافىء	fire brigade	مَحَطّة بَنْزين	petrol station
فَرْمَلة فَرامِل .pl	brake	مِحْوَر العَجَلة	axle
فَرْمَلة الرِّجْل	foot brake	مَدْرَسة قِيادة السَّيّارة	driving school
فَرْمَلة قُرْصِيّة	disc brake	مِرآة جانِبِيّة	outside mirror
فَرْمَلة اليَد	hand brake	مِرآة خَلَفِيّة	rear-view mirror
قَبْضة قِباض .pl	handle	مُرَشِّح الهَواء	air filter
قَطْعة غِيارة	spare part	مَرْوَحة	ventilator
قُفْل أقْفال .pl	lock	مَزْيَتة	oil can
قُفْل الأشْعال	ignition lock	مُزَيَّت	oiled
قُمْع	funnel	مُسْتَرْكِب	hitchhiker
قِيادة	steering	مُسْتَوى الزَّيْت	oil level
كَرَنْك	crank	مِشْوار مَشاويرُ .pl	stroke (internal combustion engine)
كُريك	jack	مِصْباح مَصابيحُ .pl	lamp
لَحَّمَ	to weld, to solder		
لَوْحة باب	door panel	مِصْباح كَهْرَبائيّ	electrical lamp, torch
لَوْحة جِنْسِيّة	nationality sticker	مِصْهَر ـات .pl	fuse
ماء مُقَطَّرة	distilled water		
ماسورة البَنْزين	petrol line	مِضَخّة الهَواء	air pump
ماسورة العَوادِم	exhaust pipe	مِفْتاح الشَّرارة	ignition key
مالك السَّيّارة	car owner	مَقْبِض الباب مَقابِضُ .pl	door handle
مُثَلَّث الخَطَر	warning triangle		

مُقَطِّع	circuit breaker	مِيكانِيكِيّ	mechanic
مَقْعَد	seat	هَيْكَل السَّيَّارة	chassis
مِقْياس الزَّيْت	dipstick	واقِيَّة صَدَمات	bumper
مِكْبَس	piston	واقِيَّة مُبَرِّد	radiator grid
pl. مَكابِس			
		واقِيَّة هَواء	windscreen
مِمْسَحة زُجاج	windscreen wiper		
مُؤَشِّر	indicator	وَقُود	fuel
مُوَزِّع كَهْرَبائِيّ	distributor	وَلَّدَ كَهْرَباء	to generate power

The weather

أَبْرَقت الدُّنْيا	there was lightning	بَهيج	pleasant (weather)
إرْصاد جَوِّيّة	meteorological observations	تَجَمَّدَ	to freeze, become icebound
أَشْرَقَ	1. to shine (sun)	تَجَمُّد	frost
	2. to rise (sun)	تَحْتَ الصِّفْر	below zero
إعْصار	hurricane	تَدَفَّأَ (ب)	to warm oneself (with)
أَغْدَقَ السَّماء	it's raining cats and dogs	تَنَبُّؤ جَوِّيّ	weather forecast
إنْجِماد	ice formation	ثَلْج	1. snow
انْهِيار طِينِيّ	mudslide	pl. ثُلُوج	2. ice
بارِد	cold, cool	جافّ	dry
باهِظ	heavy, oppressive	جَفاف	dryness
بَرَدَ (u)	to feel cold	جَوّ	1. air
بَرَد	hail	pl. جِواء, أَجْواء	2. atmosphere
بَرَدة	hailstone	حَرَّ (u, i)	to be hot
بَرْد	cold (n.)	حَرّ	hot
بَرْق	lightning	حَرارة	heat
pl. بُرُوق		خُسُوف	lunar eclipse
		دَرَجة الحَرارة	temperature

دِفْء	warmth	ضَغْط جَوِّيّ	atmospheric pressure
دَفِئَ (a)	to be warm	طَبَقة جَوِّيَّة	air layer
رَخّ (coll.)	shower (rain)	طَقْس pl. طُقُوس	weather
رَذاذ	drizzle	ظاهِر طَبِيعِيّ pl. ظَواهِرُ طَبِيعِيَّة	natural phenomenon
رُطُوبة	humidity		
رَطِيب	humid	ظِلّ pl. أَظْلال, ظُلُول, ظِلال	shade, shadow
رَعَدَ (u)	to thunder		
رَعْد pl. رُعُود	thunder	ظَلام	darkness
رَعَدَت الدُّنْيا	it thundered	عاصِفة pl. عَواصِفُ	storm
رِيح (f.) pl. أَرْياح	wind	عَجاج البَحْر	raging of the sea
سَحاب (coll.) pl. سَحائِبُ, سُحُب	clouds	عَصَفَ (i)	to rage (wind)
		فَوْقَ الصِّفْر	above zero
سُخْن	warm	قَصَفَ (i)	to rumble (thunder)
سَراب	mirage	قَوْس قُزَح	rainbow
سَماء pl. سَمَوات	sky	كُسُوف	solar eclipse
سَمُوم pl. سَمائِمُ	hot desert wind	مُشْمِس	sunny
شَدِيد	strong (e.g. wind)	مَطَر pl. أَمْطار	rain
شَمَسَ (i, u)	to be sunny (day)	مَطَر حَمْضِيّ	acid rain
شَمْسِيَّة	parasol	مَطْرة	downpour
صاحٍ	clear (sky)	مَطَرَت السَّماء	it rained
صاعِقة	thunderbolt	مِظَلَّة pl. مَظالّ, -ات	umbrella
صَحا (u)	to be bright		
صَقْعة	frost, severe cold	مُظْلِم	dark
ضَباب	fog, mist	مُغَيِّم	cloudy
ضِدّ الأَعْصار	anticyclone	مُمْطِر	rainy

مَناخ pl. ‑ات	climate	نَسيم pl. نَسائمُ, نِسام	breeze
مَواسِم مُمْطِرة	rainy seasons	هَبَّ (u)	to blow (wind)
نُدْفة الثَّلْج	snowflake	وابِل	downpour
نَدَى	dew	وَبَلَ (يَبِلُ)	to rain heavily

Language and communication

إبْهام	opaqueness (e.g. meaning)	اسْم عَلَم	proper noun
أجاب	to answer	إشْكال	ambiguity
إخْتَصَرَ	to abbreviate, abridge	إشْكاليّ	ambiguous
أداة التَّعْريف	definite article	اسْم العَيْن	concrete noun
أداة العَطْف	conjunction	اسْم الفاعِل	active participle
أدْخَلَ	to insert	اسْم الفِعْل	infinitive
إدْغام	assimilation (letter, sound)	اسْم مُبْهَم	indefinite pronoun
أدْغَمَ (في)	to assimilate (a letter with another one)	اسْم المُصَغَّر	diminutive
إسْتِثْناء	exception	اسْم المُضاف	first noun in genetive construction
إسْتَجابَ (ل)	to respond (to s.o.)	اسْم المَعْنَى	abstract noun
إسْتِطْراد	digression	اسْم المَوْصُول	relative pronoun
اسْم pl. أسْماء	noun	انْتِحال	plagiarism
اسْم الاسْتِفْهام	interrogative noun	أنَّثَ	to put in the feminine form
اسْم الإشارة	demonstrative pronoun	أنْثَى	feminine
اسْم التَفْضيل	elative	أوَّلَ	to interpret, explain
اسْم الجَمْع	collective noun	بَحْر pl. أبْحُر	metre (poetry)
اسْم العَدَد	numeral	بَلاغة	rhetoric

بَيْت	verse	الجَرّ	genitive
pl. أَبْيات		جَمْع	plural
تَأْتَأَ	to stammer	جمع التَّكْسير	broken (= irregular) plural
تَأْنيث	the feminine form	جمع صَحيح	sound (= regular) plural
تَحَدَّثَ	to speak	جُمْلة	sentence
تَحْريف	mispronunciation	pl. جُمَل	
تَحْويل	transformation	جملة اسْمِيَّة	nominal sentence
تَرْجَمَ	to translate	جملة إخْبارِيَّة	declarative sentence
تَرْجَمة فَوْرِيَّة	interpreting	جملة اسْتِفْهامِيَّة	interrogative sentence
تَرْجَمة آلِيَّة	machine translation	جملة التَّعَجُّب	exclamatory sentence
تَرْقيم	punctuation	جُمْلة حال	circumstantial clause
تَصَرَّفَ	to be inflected (verb)	جملة فِعْلِيَّة	verbal sentence
تَصْغير	diminutive	جَواب	answer
تَضْعيف	doubling	pl. أَجْوِبة	
تَعدُّدِيّة المَعانى	polysemy	جُمْلة حال	see جملة حال
تلاوة	recitation (Qur.)	(i) حَذَفَ	to elide
تَفْعيل	foot (verse)	حَرْف	letter
pl. تَفاعيل		pl. حُرُوف	
تَقدَّمَ على	to precede	بالحَرْف	literally
تَكَلَّمَ	see تحدث	حرف الاسْتِفْهام	interrogative particle
تَلْخيص	abridgement, summary	حرف صامِت	consonant
تَمْييز	specification	حَرْف النِّداء	interjection
تَنْغيم	intonation	حَرَكة	vowel
تَنْكير	indefiniteness	حَظُّورة	riddle, puzzle
تَنْميق	ornamentation (style)	(i) حَكَى	to tell a story, give an account of
تَوْكيد	pleonasm	حَيْز	scope, realm
ثَرْثَرَ	to prattle, chatter	pl. أَحْياز	
		خَبَر	predicate (nominal clause)

خَطّ	1. handwriting 2. script	صَوْتَم صَواتِم .pl	phoneme
الخَطّ اللاتِنيّ	Latin script	ضَعَّفَ	to double (letter)
الخَطّ المِسْماريّ	cuneiform	ضَمير ضَمائِرُ .pl	personal pronoun
خَطّيّ	handwritten	ضَمير عائِد	resumptive pronoun
دَرَجات المُقارَنة	degrees of comparison	ضَمير الغائِب	third-person personal pronoun
دَرْدَشة	prattle	ضَمير المُتَكَلِّم	first-person personal pronoun
الرَفْع	nominative		
رُقْعة	common cursive writing style	ضَمير المُخاطَب	second-person personal pronoun
رَقَمَ (u)	to add diacritic points to a text	ضَمير المَفْعُول	object suffix
زَعَقَ (a)	to shout, scream	طَلَبَ (u)	to demand, request
زَلّة اللِسان	slip of the tongue	طَلَب ـات .pl	demand
سَألَ (a)	to ask		
سُؤال أسئلة .pl	question	ظَرْف ظُرُوف .pl	1. adverb 2. particle
سَماعيّ	acoustic	ظرف المَكان	place adverbial
سَماعيّات	acoustics	ظرف الوقت	time adverbial
شادَ (u)	to chant	العامِّيّة	colloquial language
شَتَمَ (i)	to insult	عِبارة	expression
شَتيمة شَتائِمُ .pl	insult	عَدّا	to make transitive
		عَدَد أصْليّ	cardinal number
شَدْو	chant, song	عَدَد تَرْتيبيّ	ordinal number
صَرْخة	scream, outcry	عَرَّفَ	to make definite (noun)
صَرَفَ (i)	to inflect (a word)	عَلامة الاسْتِفْهام	question mark
صَرْف	morphology	عَلامة التَعَجُّب	exclamation mark
صِفة	adjective	عَلامة الاقْتِباس	quotation mark
صِلة	relative clause	عِلْم الأصْوات	phonetics

فاصِلة	comma	قَوْسان (dual)	(round) brackets
فاصِلة مَنْقُوطة	semi-colon	قَوْسان أَخْبار	angular brackets
فاعِل	active subject in verbal clause	قَوْسان كَبيران	square brackets
فَصاحة	eloquence	كَتَبَ (u)	to write
فَصيح	eloquent	كِناية	metonymy
فِعْل	verb	لَخَّصَ	to abridge, summarize
pl. أَفْعال		لُغة	language
فِعل أَجْوَف	hollow verb (و/ي as second radical)	لُغة الإشارة	sign language
فِعل ثُلاثِيّ	triliteral verb	لَفْظ	term
		pl. أَلْفاظ	
فِعل رُباعِيّ	quadriliteral verb	لَهْجة	dialect, language variety
فِعل سالِم	sound verb	لهجة دارِجة	see العامية
فِعل الشُّرُوع	inchoative verb		
فِعل مُضاعَف	geminated verb	الماضي	past tense
فِعل مُعْتَلّ	weak verb	مُؤَنَّث	feminine
فِعل مَهْمُوز الفاء	verb with hamza as first radical	مُبالَغة	exaggeration
		مُبْتَدَأ	subject (nominal clause)
فِعل مَهْمُوز العَيْن	verb with hamza as second radical	مُبْهَم	opaque, obscure
		مُتَصَرَّف	inflected
فِعل مَهْمُوز اللام	verb with hamza as third radical	مُتَعَثِّر	broken (speech in foreign language)
فِعل ناقِص	defective verb (و/ي as third radical)	مُتَلازِم لَفْظِيّ	collocation
		pl. مُتَلازِمات لَفْظِيّة	
قافِية	rhyme	مَثَل	saying, proverb
pl. قَواف		pl. أَمْثال	
قالَ (u)	to say	المُثَنَّى	dual
قامُوس	dictionary	مَخْبَر	intrinsic meaning
pl. قَوامِيسُ			
قامُوسِيَّة	lexicography	المُذَكَّر	masculine
قَفَّى	to put into rhyme, to rhyme	مُرادِف	synonym

مَرْفوع	word in the nominative/ indicative	مُفْرَد	singular
مَرَكَّب	compound	مُفْرَدات	vocabulary
المُسْتَقْبِل	future (tense)	المَفْعُول المُطْلَق	absolute object
مَسْرَد pl. مَسارِد	glossary	مُقارَنة	comparison
مُسْنَد	predicate	مَقْطَع pl. مقاطِعُ	syllable
المُسْنَد اليه	subject	مُلَخَّص pl. ـات	1. abridged, summarized 2. extract, essence
مَصْدَر	verbal noun	مِمْلاة	dictaphone
مِصْرَع pl. مَصارِعُ	hemistich	مُنْتَحِل	plagiarist
المُضارِع المَجْزُوم	jussive	مَنْصُوب pl. ـات	in the accusative (word)
المُضارِع المَرْفُوع	imperfect	مُنَكَّر	indefinite (noun)
المُضارِع المَنْصُوب	subjunctive	مُنَمَّق	flowery (style)
المُضاف إلَيْه	second noun in a genitive construction	مُهْمَل	without diacritical points
مُطابَقة	agreement, concord	نادى	to call
مَطْلَع pl. مَطالِعُ	opening verse	نَبْر	stress (word)
مُعْجَم pl. مَعاجِمُ	see قاموس	نَحْو	1. grammar 2. syntax
مُعْجَماتِيّة	lexicology	النحو التَّحْويلِيّ التَّوليدِيّ	transformational generative grammar
مَعْدُود	countable	نَعْت pl. نُعُوت	attribute
مُعْرَب	declinable	نَفا (i)	to negate (a sentence)
المَعْلُوم	active voice	نَفْي	negation
مَعْنى pl. مَعانٍ	meaning	نَقْص	blank, omission
مَعْنُوت	referent	نُقْطة pl. نُقَط	1. diacritical point 2. full stop
مُعَيَّن	specified	النُّقْطَتان	colon

نُقَط اِسْتِرْسال	suspension points	هَمَسَ (i)	to whisper, mumble
نَكِرة	indefinite noun	هِيرُوغْليفِيّ	hieroglyphic
نَمَّقَ	to write in a highly ornate style	وَجَزَ (يَجِزُ)	to be brief
		وَجْز	brief, succinct

Religion

General

إحْسان	charity	تَدَيَّنَ بِ	to profess (a religion)
أُصُولِيّ	fundamentalist	تَشاؤُم	superstition
أُصُولِيّة	fundamentalism	تَصْديق	belief
إلاه	God, divinity	تَعَصُّب	fanaticism
pl. آلِهة		تَقْوَى	devoutness, piety
إلاهِيّ	divine	تَقِى	devout, pious
اللَّه	God	pl. أَتْقِياء	
إلْحاد	apostasy, heresy	تَهَوَّدَ	to become a Jew
أُلُوهِية	divine power	خارِق الطَّبيعة	the supernatural
أمانَ بِ	to believe in	خُرافة	fable, fairytale
اِنْتِهاك	desecration	خُرافِيّ	mythical
اِنْتِهاك الحُرْمة	sacrilege	دين	religion
اِنْتَهَكَ	to defile, desecrate	pl. أَدْيان	
اِنْقاذ	salvation	دينِيّ	religious
بروتِسْتاتِيّ	Protestant	رُوح	soul
بروتِستانتِيّة	Protestantism	pl. أَرْواح	
بُوذا	Buddha	شَبَح	ghost
		pl. شُبُوح, أَشْباح	
بُوذِيّ	Buddhist	شَرّ	evil
بُوذِيّة	Buddhism	pl. شُرُور	

صَهْيُونيّ	Zionist	مَعْبَد	temple
صَهْيُونيَّة	Zionism	pl. مَعابِدُ	
عَقيدة	doctrine, dogma	مُلْحِد	apostate, heretic
pl. عَقائِدُ		pl. مَلاحِدة	
غُفْران	forgiveness	مُؤْمِن	faithful, believing
قَدَر	fate	وَثَن	graven image, idol
pl. أَقْدار		pl. أَوْثان, وُثُن	
كائِن	being (noun)	وَثَنِي	pagan
pl. كَوائِنُ			
كائنات حَيَّة	living beings	وَثَنيَّة	paganism
مُتَعَصِّب	fanatic, bigot	يَهُودِيّ	Jew
		pl. يَهُود	
مَزار	shrine	اليَهُوديَّة	Judaism
pl. ـات			

Islam

إحْرام	state of ritual purity (حجّ)	إمام	imam
		pl. أَئِمَّة	
الآخِرة	the hereafter	إمامة	imamate
اخْتَتَنَ	to be circumcised	آية	1. see معجزة
أَخْلاق	morals		2. Qur. verse
أَخْلاقِيّ	moral (adj.)	إيمان	faith
اسْتَجابَ ل	to answer a prayer	بارَكَ	to bless
اسْتِشْهاد	martyrdom	بَرَكة	blessing
أُسْتُشْهِدَ (pass.)	to die as a martyr, to be martyred	بَسْمَلَ	saying بِسْمِ الله الرحمن الرحيم
اسْتَغْفَرَ	to ask for forgiveness	تَجْديف	blasphemy
أَسْلَمَ	to become a Muslim	pl. تَجاديفُ	
أُصول الدّين	pillars of the faith	تَحْميد	exclamation of الحَمْد لله
إفْطار	meal after fast (Ramadan)	تَسْبيح	exclamation of سُبْحانَ الله
أَفْطَرَ	to break the fast	تَكْبير	the invocation الله أَكْبَر

التَّصَوُّف	sufism	خَلْق	mankind
تَمَذْهَبَ	to follow a religious school	دُعاء	invocation of God
تَوْبة	repentance	.pl أَدْعِية	
تَوْحيدِيّ	monotheistic	دُنْيا	world
جامِع	mosque	دُنْيَوِيّ	worldly
.pl جَوامِع		ذَنْب	sin, guilt
الجاهِلِيّة	pre-Islamic era	.pl ذُنُوب	
جَدَّفَ على	to blaspheme (God)	رَبّ	Lord
جِنّ (coll.)	jinns, demons	.pl أَرْباب	
جَنّة	paradise	رَحِمَ (a)	to have mercy on
جِهاد	holy war, jihad	رُكُوع	bending during prayer
جَهَنَّم	hell	زاهِد	ascetic
حاجّ	pilgrim	.pl زِهاد	
.pl حُجّاج		زاوِية	Sufi lodge
حافِظ	one who knows the Qur'an by	.pl زَوايا	
.pl حُفّاظ	heart	زَكاة	alms
حَجّ (u)	to perform the pilgrimage	زَنْدَقة	atheism
حَجّ	pilgrimage	زِنْديق	atheist
		.pl زَنادقة	
حَرام	unlawful, sacred	زُهْد	1. abstinence
حَلال	lawful		2. asceticism
خِتان	circumcision	سُبْحة	prayer beads
خَطَبَ (u)	to preach	.pl سُبَح ,سُبُحات	
خُطْبة	Friday sermon	سَجّادة	prayer carpet
.pl خُطَب		.pl سَجاجِد, ـات	
خَطِئَ (a)	to sin	سَجَدَ (u)	to bend one's body (in worship)
خَطيئة	sin	سَجْدة	prostration in prayer
خَطيب	preacher	.pl سَجَدات	
خَلَدَ (u)	to be immortal	سُورة	Qur'an chapter
خَلَقَ (u)	to create (God)	شِرْك	idolatry
		شَهادة	Islamic doctrinal formula

شَهِيد	martyr	عالِم	scholar
pl. شُهَداءُ		pl. عُلَماءُ	
شَيْطان	devil	عِشاء (f.)	evening prayer
pl. شَياطِينُ		عَصْر (f.)	afternoon prayer
صامَ (u)	to fast	عِفْرِيت	imp
صائِم	one who fasts	pl. عَفارِيت	
pl. صُوّام		عُمْرة	minor pilgrimage to Mecca
الصَّحابة	the companions of the Prophet	عِيد الأضْحَى (10 الحجة)	sacrificial festival (10 الحجة)
صَلَّى	to pray	عِيد الفِطْر (1 شوّال)	end of Ramadan (1 شوّال)
صلاة	prayer	غُسْل	ritual ablution (of the whole body)
pl. صَلَوات		pl. أغْسال	
صِراط المُسْتَقِيم	the Straight Path (Islam)	فَتْوَى	fatwa
		pl. فَتاوٍ	
صَنَم	idol	فَجْر (f.)	morning prayer
pl. أصْنام			
صُوفِي	Sufi	فِداء	redemption
صَوْم	fast	فَرِيضة	religious duty
		pl. فَرائِضُ	
ضَحَّى بِ	to sacrifice	فَقِيه	faqih, legal scholar
ضَمِير	conscience	pl. فُقَهاءُ	
pl. ضَمائِرُ		قُبّة	dome
ضَحِيّة	sacrifice (noun)	pl. قُبَب	
pl. ضَحايا		قِبْلة	qibla (direction of Mekka)
طاهِر	pure	قَدَر	destiny
طَرِيقة	sect	القُرآن الكَرِيم	the Holy Qur'an
pl. طَرائِقُ			
طَقْس	ritual	كافِر	unbeliever
pl. طُقُوس		pl. كُفّار	
		كُتّاب	Qur'anic school
طَهارة	ritual purity	pl. كَتاتِيبُ	
طَوّاف	circumambulation of the Kaaba	الكَعَبة	the Kaaba
		مَأَذَنة	minaret
ظُهْر (f.)	midday prayer	pl. مآذِن	

مُبارَك	blessed	مُؤَذِّن	muezzin
مُتَدايِن	devout	مَوْسِم pl. مَواسِم	(religious) feast
مِحْراب pl. مَحاريب	prayer niche in mosque	مَوْكِب pl. مَواكِبُ	procession
مَخْلُوق pl. ـات	creature	مُؤْمِن	believer (Muslim)
مَذْهَب pl. مَذاهِبُ	religious school (jurisprudence)	نُبُوَّة	prophecy
		نَبَوِيّ	prophetic
مَسْجِد pl. مَساجِدُ	Friday mosque	نَبِي pl. أَنْبِياءُ	prophet
مُسْلِم	Muslim	نَجاسة	impurity
مُشْرِك	idolater	هُدًى	good guidance
مُعْجِزة	miracle	واعِظ pl. وُعَّاظ	preacher
مَغْرِب (f.)	prayer at sunset	وَحْى	revelation
مَنْسِك pl. مَناسِكُ	ceremony, ritual (esp. during حج)	وُضُوء	ablution (prior to prayer)
		وَعْظة	sermon
المَوْلِد النَّبَوِي	the Prophet's birthday (12 ربيع الأوّل)	يَوْم القيامة	Judgement Day

Christianity

ابْتِهال	supplication, prayer	اضطهاد	persecution
ابْتَهَلَ	to supplicate (God)	اضْطَهَدَ	to persecute
أَبُو الاعْتِراف	father confessor	اعْتِراف	confession
أَحَد الشَّعانين	Palm Sunday	اعْتَرَفَ	to confess
أُسْبُوع الآلام	Passion Week	إفْشين pl. أَفاشينُ	litany
أُسْقُف pl. أَساقِفُ، أَساقِفة	bishop		
		أَفْصَحَ	to celebrate Easter
أُسْقُفِّيَّة	bishopric	أُقْنُوم pl. أَقانيمُ	hypostasis
أَصْحاح	Bible chapter		

أمّ النُّور	the Virgin Mary	جِنّاز pl. جنانِيزُ	funeral procession
إنْجِيل pl. أناجِيلُ	Gospel	حَرَم (a)	to excommunicate
إيقُونة	icon	حُرُوم	excommunication
البابا	the Pope	حِلّة	absolution
بَطْرَك، بَطْرِيرك pl. بَطاركة	patriarch	حَوارِي	apostle
بَطْرَكِيَّة	patriarchate	الحَياة الأَبَدِيَّة	eternal life
تاب (u)	to repent	خاطِئ	sinner
تَأَنُّس	incarnation	خَدَمَ القُدّاس	to celebrate mass
تَبْشِير	preaching of the Gospel	خَطِية ، خَطِيئة	sin
تَبْشِيرِيّ	missionary (adj.)	خَلاص	redemption
تَجْرِبة pl. تَجارِبُ	temptation	دَيْر pl. أدْيار, أدْيِرة	monastery
تَرَهَّب	to become a monk	ذَخِيرة pl. ذَخائِرُ	relic
تَرَهُّب	monasticism	راهِب pl. رُهْبان	monk
تَسْبِيحة	hymn, song of praise	راهِبة	nun
تَعَالَى	to be exalted (God)	رِسالة pl. رَسائِلُ	calling (e.g. of a priest)
تَعَمَّد	to be baptized	رِسامة قُسُوسِيَة	ordination
تَعْمِيد	baptism	رَعِية	parish (believers)
تَقْدِيس	consecration	الرُّوح القُدْس	the Holy Ghost
تِلْمِيذ pl. تَلامِذة	disciple	سادِن pl. سَدَنة	sexton
تَنَاوَلَ القُرْبان	to receive Communion	سَبْت النُّور	Easter Saturday
تَنَصَّر	to become a Christian	السُّدَّة الرَّسُولِيَّة	the Holy See
تَوْبة	penance	سِرّ pl. أسْرار	sacrament
جَحِيم (f./m.)	hell(fire)	سِفْر التَّكْوِين	genesis
الجُمْعة الحَزِينة	Good Friday		

سِفْر الرُّؤْيا	the Apocalypse	عيد البشارة	Annunciation
سُلَّاق	ascension of Christ	عيد حُلُول الرُّوح القُدْس	Whitsuntide
شِرْكة	communion	عيد الصُّعُود	Ascension Day
شَمَّاس pl. شَمامسة	deacon	عيد الغِطاس	Epiphany
صُعُود الرَّبّ	Ascension	عيد القُرْبان	Corpus Christi
الصَّلاة الرَّبّانيّة	the Lord's Prayer	عيد كُلّ القِدِّيسين	All Saints Day
صلَب (i)	to crucify	عيد المِيلاد	Christmas
صَليب pl. صُلْبان	cross	غُفْران	forgiveness
الصَّوْم الكَبِير	Lent	فِصْح pl. فُصُوح	Easter
صَوْمَعة pl. صَوامِعُ	monk's cell	قُبَّة	dome
طَقْس pl. طُقُوس	rite, liturgy	قِبْط pl. أَقْباط	Copt
العَذْراء	the Holy Virgin	قِبْطِيّ	Coptic
عَرَّاب	godfather	قُدَّاس pl. قَدَاديسُ	mass
عَرَّابة	godmother	قَدَّسَ	to canonize
العَشاء السِّرّيّ	the Last Supper	قدَّم القُرْبان على	to read mass for someone
عَلْمانيّ	layman	القَدُّوس	the Most Holy (= God)
عَمَّدَ	to baptize	قِدِّيس	saint
العُنْصُرة	Pentecost	قَرَّبَ	to administer Communion
العَهْد الجَدِيد	the New Testament	قُرْبان	Eucharist
العَهْد القَدِيم	the Old Testament	قُرْبانة	Holy Communion
العَوامّ	the laity	قُسُوسة	priesthood
عَيَّدَ	to celebrate a feast	قِسِّيس pl. قُسَّاء, أَقِسَّة, قُسَّان, قَسَاوسة, -ون	priest, minister
عيد pl. أَعْياد	feast	قِيامة	resurrection

كاثِدْرائِيّة	cathedral	المَسِيح	the Anointed
كاثُولِيكِيّ	Catholic	مَسِيحِيّ	Christian
كاثُولِيكِيّ مُمارِس	practising Catholic	مَسِيحِيّة	Christianity
كارِز	preacher	مَطْهَر	purgatory
كاهِن pl. كُهّان, كَهَنة	diviner, soothsayer	مَعْمُودِيّة	baptism, baptismal feast
الكِتاب المُقَدَّس	Holy Bible	مَلاك pl. مَلائِكة, مَلائِك	angel
كَنِيسة pl. كَنائِسُ	church	ملاك حارِس	guardian angle
كَنِيسة رَعَوِيّة	parish church	مَلَكُوت السَّمَوات	the Kingdom of Heaven
مِبْخَرة pl. مَباخِرُ, -ات	censer, thurible	مَلَكُوتِيّ	heavenly, divine
مُبَشِّر	evangelist, missionary	مِنْبَر pl. مَنابِرُ	pulpit
مَجَّد	to glorify	المِيلاد	Nativity
مُخَلِّص	redeemer	نَصَّر	to convert to Christianity (*trans.*)
مَزْمُور pl. مَزامِيرُ	psalm	الوَصايا العَشْر	the Ten Commandments
مِسْبَحة pl. مَسَابِحُ	rosary	يَسُوع	Jesus
		يَوْم الدِّين	Judgement Day

Colours

أَبْيَض f. بِيض, pl. بَيْضاء	white	أَخْضَر f. خُضْر, pl. خَضْراء	green
أَحْمَر f. حُمْر, pl. حَمْراء	red	أَرْجُوان	purple
		أَزْرَق f. زُرْق, pl. زَرْقاء	blue
أَحْمَر فاتِح	scarlet	أَسْفَع f. سُفْع, pl. سَفْعاء	dark brown
أَحْمَر قِرْمِزِيّ	crimson		

أَسْمَر	brown	خَمْرِيّ	reddish brown, wine-coloured
سُمْر .pl ,سَمْراء .f		داكِن	dark(-coloured)
أَسْوَد	black	دَلْهَم	deep black
سُود .pl ,سَوْداء .f		ذَهَبِيّ	gold
أَشْقَر	1. blond	رُمادِيّ	grey
شُقْر .pl ,شَقْراء .f	2. chestnut	سَمَنْجُونى	azure
أَسْوَد قاتِم	pitch black	شَفَّاف	transparent
أَصْفَر	yellow	غامِق	dark
صُفُر .pl ,صَفْراء .f		فاتِح	light
أَصْفَر باهِت	cream	فاقِع	bright
أَكْحَل	black (eye)	فِضِّيّ	silver
كُحْل .pl ,كَحْلاء .f		قِرْمِزِي	scarlet
باهِت	pale, faded	كُحْلِيّ	dark blue, navy
بُرْتُقالي	orange	كَسْتَنائِيّ	maroon
بَنَفْسَجي	1. lilac	لَوْن البَشْرة	skin-coloured
	2. purple, violet	مُلَوَّن	multi-coloured
بُنِّي	coffee-coloured, brown		
بَيج	beige	وَرْدِيّ	pink

The zodiac

الأَسَد	Leo	الجَوْزاء	Gemini
بُرْج	sign (of the zodiac)	الحُوت	Pisces
بُروج .pl		الحَمَل	Aries
تَنْجيم	astrology	خَريطة البُرُوج	horoscope
الثَوْر	Taurus	الدَّلْو	Aquarius
الجَدْي	Capricorn	الرّامي	Sagittarius

زُحَل	Saturn	الكَوْن	the Universe
الزُّهْرة	Venus	مَجَرَّة	galaxy, Milky Way
السَّرَطان	Cancer	مِرِّيخ	Mars
العَذْراء	Virgo	مُشْتَرى	Jupiter
العَقْرَب	Scorpio	مُنَجِّم	astrologer
فَضاء	cosmic space	مِنْطَقة البُروج	zodiac
كَوْكَب	planet	الميزان	Libra
pl. كَواكِبُ		هِلال	new moon

Weights and measures

أوقية	ounce	رَطْل	rotl (variable Levantine
بَرْميل	barrel	pl. أرْطال	measure)
pl. بَراميلُ		سُبْع	seventh
بُوصة	inch	pl. أسْباع	
تُسْع	ninth	سُدْس	sixth
pl. أتْساع		pl. أسْداس	
ثَقيل	heavy	سنتيمتر	centimetre
pl. ثُقَلاء, ثِقال		شِبْر	span of the hand
ثُمْن	eighth	pl. أشْبار	
pl. أثْمان		طُنّ	ton
خَفيف	light	pl. أطْنان	
pl. أخْفاء, أخْفاف, خِفاف		طُنّ مُسَجَّل	register ton
خُمْس	fifth	عُشْر	tenth
pl. أخْماس		pl. أعْشار	
ذِراع (f./m.)	cubit	عَظيم	great
pl. ذُرْعان, أذْرُع		pl. عِظام, عُظَماءُ	
رُبْع	quarter	غرام	gram
pl. أرْباع			

(i) قاسَ	to measure	لِتْر	litre
قامة	fathom (6 feet)	pl. ـات	
قَدَم	foot	مِتْر	metre
pl. أَقْدام		pl. أَمْتار	
قَصير	short	مُسْتَدير	round
pl. قِصار		مُسْتَقيم	straight
قَليل	little, few	مليمتر	millimetre
pl. قِلال, قلائِلُ, أَقلاءُ		مَحْنى	crooked, bent
قِياسيّ	comparable	ميل	mile
قيراط	carat	pl. أَمْيال	
كَبير	big	ميل بَحْريّ	nautical mile
pl. كُبَراءُ, كِبار		نُصْف	half
كَثير	many, much	pl. أَنْصاف	
pl. كِثار, ـون		وَزْن	weight
كيلوغرام	kilogram	pl. أَوْزان	
كيلومتر	kilometre	وَزَنَ (يَزِنُ)	to weigh

Appendix I

Arab regions, countries and capitals

الأُرْدُنّ	Jordan	أَلشَّرْق الأَوْسَط	the Middle East
عَمَان	Amman	العِراق	Iraq
آسِيا	Asia	بَغْداد	Baghdad
إفريقيا	Africa	فَلَسْطين	Palestine
إفريقيا الشَّمالِيّة	North Africa	رام الله	Ramalla
الامارات العَرَبِيَّة المُتَّحدة	The United Arab Emirates	قَطَر	Qatar
أبوُظَبِي	Abu Dhabi	الدَّوْحة	Doha
السُّودان	Sudan	الكُوَيت	Kuwait
الخَرْطُوم	Khartoum	مَدينة كويت	Kuwait City
تُونِس	Tunisia	لُبْنان	Lebanon
تُونِس	Tunis	بَيْرُوت	Beirut
الجزائر	Algeria	لِيبِيا	Libya
الجَزَائر	Algiers	طَرَابُلُس (الغَرْب)	Tripoli (of the West)
سُوريا	Syria	مِصْر	Egypt
دمَشْق	Damascus	القاهِرة	Cairo
البَحرَيْن	Bahrain	المَغْرِب	Morocco
المَنامة	Manama	الرِّباط	Rabat
عُمان	Oman	المَمْلَكة السَّعُودِيّة	the Kingdom of Saudi Arabia
مَسْقَط	Muscat	الرِّياض	Riyadh
أَلشَّرْق الأَدْنَى	the Near East	اليَمَن	The Yemen
		صنْعاء	Sanaa

Appendix II

Selected non-Arab regions, countries and capitals

إسْبانِيا	Spain	الدانمارك	Denmark
مدريد	Madrid	كوبوهاغن	Copenhagen
أستراليا	Australia	رُوسيا	Russia
سيدنى	Sydney	مُوسْكُو	Moscow
الارجنتين	Argentina	السُّوِيد	Sweden
بوينس أيرس	Buenos Aires	إسْتُكهُولم	Stockholm
ألْمانِيا	Germany	الصِّين	China
بَرْلِين	Berlin	بيكين	Beijing
أمريكا الجَنُوبِيَّة	South America	فَرَنْسا	France
أمريكا الشَّمالِيَّة	North America	باريس	Paris
أمريكا الوُسْطَى	Central America	فِنْلَنْدا	Finland
انكلترًّا	England	هَلْسِنْكي	Helsinki
أوروبا	Europe	النُّرْوِيج	Norway
إيرلندا	Ireland	أُوسْلُو	Oslo
دبلن	Dublin	نِمْسا	Austria
إيطاليا	Italy	فينا	Vienna
ميلانو	Milan	هولَنْدا	The Netherlands
بريطانيا العُظْمَى	Great Britain	أمستردام	Amsterdam
لَنْدَن	London	لاهاي	The Hague
بُرْتُغال	Portugal	ألوِلايات المُتَّحِدة الأمريكِيَّة	United States of America
لِشْبونة	Lisbon	وشنطن	Washington
بلجِيكا	Belgium	اليابان	Japan
برُكْسِيل	Brussels	طوكيو	Tokyo
تُرْكِيا	Turkey	اليُونان	Greece
أنْقَرة	Ankara	أثِينا	Athens
جنُوب إفريقيا	South Africa		
بريتوريا	Pretoria		

Appendix III

International organizations

الاتّحاد الأُورُبِّيّ	the European Union (EU)
الاتحاد الإفْرِيقِيّ	the African Union
بَرْنامَج الأُمَم المُتَّحِدة الأنْمائِيّ	the United Nations Development Programme (UNDP)
البَنْك الدُّوَلِيّ	the World Bank
البَنْك المَرْكَزِيّ الأُورُبِّيّ	the European Central Bank
البَنْك الدُّوَلِيّ للأنْشاء و المَّتعْمير	the International Bank for Reconstruction and Development (IBRD)
جامعة الدُّوَل العَرَبِيّة	the Arab League
جَماعة الإخْوان المُسْلِمين	the Muslim Brotherhood
جَماعة السَّلام الأخْضَر	Greenpeace
الجَمْعِية العامَّة	the General Assembly (UN)
الدُّوَل المُنْتِجة للنَّفْط غَيْر الأعْضاء في أُوبك	non-OPEC countries
الرَّابطة الإسْلامِيّة	The Muslim League
رابطة دُوَل جَنُوب شَرْق آسِيا	the Association of Southeast Asian Nations
صُنْدُوق النَّقْد الدُّوَلِيّ	the International Monetary Fund (IMF)
اللجنة الأُولِمْبِيّة العالَمِيّة	the International Olympic Committee (IOC)
مجلس الأمْن	the Security Council (UN)
مَجْلِس التَّعاوُن الخَلِيجِيّ	the Gulf Cooperation Council (GCC)
مَجْمُوعة الثَّماني	the G8
المَحْكَمة الجِنائِيّة الدُّوَلِيّة	the International Criminal Court (ICC)
مَحكَمة العَدْل الدُّوَلِيّة	the International Court of Justice
المُفَوَّضِيّة الأُوروبِيّة	the European Commission
مُفَوَّضِيّة سامِيّة لشُؤُون اللاجِئين	the High Commission for Refugees
مُنَظَّمة الأغْذِيّة و الزِّراعة	the Food and Agriculture Organization (FAO)
و الثَّقافة	(ISESCO)

مُنَظَّمة الأَقْطار العَرَبِيَّة المُصَدِّرة للنَّفْط	the Organization of Arab Petroleum Exporting Countries (OAPEC)
مُنَظَّمة الأُمَم المُتَّحِدة	the United Nations (UN)
مُؤْتَمَر الأُمَم المُتَّحِدة للتِّجارة و التَّنْمِيَّة	the United Nations Conference on Trade and Development (UNCTAD)
مُنَظَّمة الأُمَم المُتَّحِدة للتَّرْبِيَّة والعِلْم و الثَّقافة (اليُونِسْكُو)	the United Nations Educational, Scientific and Culture Organization (UNESCO)
مُنَظَّمة الأُمَم المُتَّحِدة للتَّنْمِيَّة الصِّناعِيَّة	the United Nations Industrial Development Organization (UNIDO)
المُنَظَّمة البَحْرِيَّة الدُّوَلِيَّة	the International Maritime Organization (IMO)
مُنَظَّمة التِّجارة العالَمِيَّة	the World Trade Organization (WTO)
مُنَظَّمة التَّحْرير الفَلَسْطِينِيّة	the Palestinian Liberation Organization (PLO)
مُنَظَّمة التَّعاوُن الاقْتِصادِيّ والتَّنْمِيَّة	the Organization for Economic Co-operation and Development (OECD)
مُنَظَّمة حِلْف شِمال الأَطْلَسِيّ (ناتو)	the North Atlantic Treaty Organization (NATO)
مُنَظَّمة الدُّوَل الأَمْرِيكِيّة	the Organization of American States (OAS)
مُنَظَّمة الدُّوَل المُصَدِّرة للنَّفْط	the Organization of the Petroleum Exporting Countries (OPEC)
مُنَظَّمة الصِّحَّة العالَمِيَّة	the World Health Organization (WHO)
مُنَظَّمة الطَّيَران المَدَنيِّ والدُّوَليّ	the International Civil Aviation Organization (ICAO)
مُنَظَّمة العَمَل الدُّوَليّ	the International Labour Organization (ILO)
المُنَظَّمة العالَمِيَّة للإرْصاد الجَوِّيَّة	the World Meteorological Organization (WMO)
مُنَظَّمة العَفْو الدُّوَليّ	Amnesty International
مُنَظَّمة المُؤْتَمَر الإسْلامِيْ	the Organization of the Islamic Conference (OIC)
مُنَظَّمة الوَحْدة الإفْرِيقِيّة	the Organization of African Unity (OAU)
المُؤْتَمَر اليُهُودِيّ العالَميّ	the World Jewish Congress (WJC)
الهِلال الأَحْمَر	the Red Crescent
هَيْئة الصَّلِيب الأَحْمَر	the Red Cross
الوِكالة الدُّولِيّة للطَّاقة الذَّرِّيَّة	the International Atomic Energy Agency (IAEA)

Related titles from Routledge

Colloquial Arabic of Egypt
2nd Edition
Jane Wightwick and Mahmoud Gafaar

The second edition of this course in Arabic of Egypt for beginners has been completely revised and updated to make learning Arabic of Egypt easier and more enjoyable than ever before.

Specially written by experienced teachers for self-study and class use, the course offers you a step-by-step approach to written and spoken Arabic of Egypt. No prior knowledge of the language is required.

What makes *Colloquial Arabic of Egypt* your best choice in personal language learning?

- the Arabic presented in this course is given in romanised form throughout
- the Arabic script is introduced progressively to aid familiarity with the standard written language
- emphasis on modern conversational language with clear pronunciation guidance
- grammar section for easy reference
- stimulating exercises with lively illustrations

By the end of this rewarding course you will be able to communicate confidently and effectively in Arabic of Egypt in a broad range of everyday situations. This title is available to purchase as a paperback with accompanying CDs to be bought separately, or alternatively as a great value pack containing both book and audio.

ISBN13: 978–0–415–276894 (pbk)
ISBN13: 978–0415286947 (cds)
ISBN13: 978–0–415–276917 (book and cds pack)

Available at all good bookshops
For ordering and further information please visit:
www.routledge.com

Related titles from Routledge

Colloquial Arabic (Levantine)
Leslie McLoughlin

Colloquial Arabic (Levantine) is specially written by an experienced teacher for self-study or class use. The course offers you a step-by-step approach to spoken Arabic (Levantine). No previous knowledge of the language is required.

What makes *Colloquial Arabic* your best choice in personal language learning?

- interactive – lots of dialogues and exercises for regular practice
- clear – concise grammar notes
- practical – useful vocabulary and pronunciation guide
- complete – including answer key and special reference section

By the end of this rewarding course you will be able to communicate confidently and effectively in a broad range of situations.

ISBN13: 978–0–415–05107–1 (pbk)
ISBN13: 978–0–415–45007–2 (cds)
ISBN13: 978–0–415–45006–5 (book and cds pack)

NEW EDITION FORTHCOMING (2008)

Available at all good bookshops
For ordering and further information please visit:
www.routledge.com

Related titles from Routledge

Colloquial Arabic of the Gulf and Saudi Arabia
Clive Holes

Specially written by an experienced teacher for self-study or class use, this course offers you a step-by-step approach to spoken Arabic of the Gulf and Saudi Arabia. No prior knowledge of the language is required.

What makes *Colloquial Arabic of the Gulf and Saudi Arabia* your best choice in personal language learning?

- interactive – lots of dialogues and exercises for regular practice

- clear – concise grammar notes

- practical – useful vocabulary and pronunciation guide

- complete – including answer key and special reference section

Cassettes accompany the course to help you with listening and pronunciation skills. By the end of this rewarding course you will be able to communicate confidently and effectively in a broad range of situations.

ISBN13: 978–0–415–08027–9 (pbk)
ISBN13: 978–0–415–04554–4 (cassettes)
ISBN13: 978–0–415–00074–1 (book and cassettes pack)

NEW EDITION FORTHCOMING (2008)

Available at all good bookshops
For ordering and further information please visit:
www.routledge.com